The Classroom X-Factor: The Power of Body Language and Nonverbal Communication in Teaching

Why is it that some teachers have a kind of magical charisma and charm which sets them apart from their peers? This book gives us a fresh and exciting answer – they have the classroom X-Factor! White and Gardner's gripping text, *The Classroom X-Factor*, examines the notion of having what the public has come to call the 'X-Factor' from the perspective of the teacher, offering fascinating insights into the use of nonverbal communication in the classroom.

Using classroom and curricular examples, this book sets out to show how both trainee and practising teachers can identify their own 'X-Factor' in order to help transform their perspectives and perceptions of themselves during the 'live act' of teaching. The book demonstrates how teachers can transform the way in which they connect with their students, whilst also creating meaningful and potent learning experiences for them. White and Gardner show that by following simple methods borrowed from psychology and cognitive science, teachers can develop their own 'X-Factor' and in so doing increase their enjoyment and efficacy as professionals. The techniques described include some of the following:

- facial and vocal expression;
- gesture and body language;
- eye contact and smiling;
- teacher attire, colour and the use of space;
- nonverbal communication and pedagogical approaches.

In addition, the book provides a section containing fictional stories that aim to contextualise the findings detailed throughout the text. The inclusion of chapter summaries, questions aimed at identifying the readers' own 'X-Factor', lesson exemplars and a user-friendly self-evaluation framework all work together to make the book a stimulating and easy read where reflective learning and the practical application of classroom techniques are the order of the day.

This comprehensive guide to developing the classroom X-Factor within you will be of value to teaching and learning and is of immense use to both practising and student teachers and to schools seeking to develop models of reflective practice. It will also be of interest to curriculum and assessment agencies, policy makers, academics and others whose roles involve the design, provision, support and evaluation of teachers' efficacy in the classroom.

John White (Ed. D) is a primary school inspector for the Department of Education and Skills in Ireland. Prior to this, he worked as a primary teacher, head teacher and lecturer. He has also been involved in research on school leadership, classroom nonverbal communication and teaching skills.

John Gardner is a Professor of Education in the School of Education at Queen's University, Belfast. He is President of the British Educational Research Association, and was a founding member of the Universities' Council for the Education of Teachers – Northern Ireland (UCET-NI).

The Classroom X-Factor: The Power of Body Language and Nonverbal Communication in Teaching

John White and John Gardner

Routledge
Taylor & Francis Group

LONDON AND NEW YORK

First published 2012
by Routledge
2 Park Square, Milton Park, Abingdon, Oxon OX14 4RN

Simultaneously published in the USA and Canada
by Routledge
711 Third Avenue, New York, NY 10017

Routledge is an imprint of the Taylor & Francis Group, an informa business

British Library Cataloguing in Publication Data
A catalogue record for this book is available from the British Library

Library of Congress Cataloging in Publication Data
White, John, 1934 Nov. 7–
   The classroom x-factor: the power of body language and nonverbal communication in teaching/John White, John Gardner.
   p. cm.
   Includes bibliographical references and index.
   1. Nonverbal communication in education. 2. Body language. I. Gardner, John, 1953–
   II. Title.
   LB1033.5.W5 2011
   371.102′2–dc22

                                                                    2011005342

ISBN: 978-0-415-59314-4 (hbk)
ISBN: 978-0-415-59315-1 (pbk)
ISBN: 978-0-203-81870-1 (ebk)

Typeset in Bembo
by Wearset Ltd, Boldon, Tyne and Wear

Table 11.1 taken from: David W. Addington, *The relationship of selected vocal characteristics to personality perception*, Communication Monographs, Vol. 35, 4, copyright © National Communication Association (1968) reprinted by permission of Taylor & Francis Ltd (http://www.tandf.co.uk/journals) on behalf of National Communication Association.

Table 16.1 taken from: J.K. Burgoon and T. Saine, *The Unspoken Dialogue* (Boston: Houghton-Mifflin, 1974), with permission of the author.

p. 93, The relationship of selected vocal characteristics to personality perception, David W. Addington, Communication Monographs, Vol. 35, Issue 4, 1968, copyright © National Communication Association reprinted by permission of (Taylor & Francis Ltd, http://www.tandf.co.uk/journals) on behalf of National Communication Association.

MIX
Paper from responsible sources
FSC   www.fsc.org   FSC® C004839

Printed and bound in Great Britain by
TJ International Ltd, Padstow, Cornwall

Contents

List of Figures and Tables

Figures

Tables

Acknowledgements

We wish to acknowledge the support and commitment of the teachers who participated in our research work. Of course the support, smiles, nods, gestures and sometimes even 'flashbulb eyes' of our respective families and friends were, as always, uplifting and inspiring. The very creative and careful work of our illustrator, Anne Marie Carroll was of immense value. Finally we wish to thank the team at Taylor & Francis for their encouragement and unerring professional support.

Part I

The X-Factor and You the Teacher

General Introduction

Their teacher, Tony Nolan never entered a room. He arrived. Students never needed to scatter rose petals in his path. He always entered with the poise and purposeful march of a leader. Before he even got to his desk, students would be watching him. It wasn't just the erect manner in which he held his head, nor the imposing stance he took at the window, it was those alert eyes, taking in everything and flashing confidently from his calm and relaxed face. His hands were on his hips and ready for business.

'Hi guys. Welcome to woodwork class for this semester. My name is Tony Nolan, your woodwork teacher. Today is your big day. I know many of you are inexperienced, but I am going to make sure no-one gets knotted up. This is a joint endeavour.'

The puns were largely wasted on the class, but his chirpy, enthusiastic voice, his lively movements and eye contact with all of them caught their attention.

This is an excerpt from one of the stories we use later in this book to illustrate some of its key messages. Everything about Tony Nolan's manner, his eye contact, facial expressions, poise, chirpy voice, hands and lively movements spark interest and intrigue. As Shakespeare would put it: 'for now sits expectation in the air' (*Henry V*, Act 2). So, how does he do it? Tony has the classroom X-Factor. And the good news is, so do you! This book is going to help you develop your own X-Factor.

Of course, we can all think of teachers like Tony Nolan. Think about your own days in school. They took place in the heyday of our lives, when we were young, energetic and filled with dreams. At get-togethers, we talk of funny incidents, football matches, school plays and so on. But inevitably, we also talk about our favourite teachers. If you think for a moment, you can probably recollect a teacher whose lessons you particularly enjoyed. It may not have been your best subject, but this teacher probably managed to capture your attention and spark your enthusiasm. Remember the English teacher who never seemed to have problems getting your attention or captivating your interests. You would look forward to her class, hang on her every word, watch her every move. She didn't have wheelbarrows of props, gimmicks or resources. How did she do it? Of course, we can also remember other teachers who didn't connect with us. Teachers who seemed remote and lacked that ability to walk into a room and spark enthusiasm and interest. How did they do it?

Ask yourself, why did some teachers have a magical connection? An ability to engage and enthuse you. What special qualities did they have? As you think about it, you will probably remember faces, voices, classrooms and so on. When we first did this, we found ourselves in a cul-de-sac. We couldn't specifically pinpoint what piece of magic one teacher had over another. Was it the subject? Was it the activities? Was it their teaching methods? Obviously all of these are interwoven, but the more we thought about it, the more we realised there was something else which set them apart. If we think about it in modern parlance, we could call it the X-Factor. Every teacher has their own magic, be it good or bad, and manage to radiate it in a very potent way. So potent, that it sticks with us for decades later, allowing us to remember them with fondness or disillusionment, excitement or apathy, and ultimately in some way or other as having played a part in landing us where we are now as learners. Indeed, some would say they played a part in the fulfilment of the heady dreams of our youth. So what is this X-Factor?

FIGURE 1.1 Singer on *The X-Factor* TV show.

You may or may not be familiar with the term X-Factor. The term is defined by the *Cambridge Advanced Learner's Dictionary* as 'a quality that you cannot describe which makes someone very special'. This book seeks to unravel this indescribable quality which can make teachers 'very special'. Of course, you may be more familiar with the term as it relates to the TV show entitled *The X-Factor* which has enjoyed remarkable success in the ratings charts. It is a UK musical talent contest which auditions thousands of contestants and ultimately whittles them down through successive performances and public voting to one single individual who has the 'X-Factor'. This contestant has musical talent but also that X-Factor which judges and the general public believe will catapult them to success in the commercial world of music.

It is fascinating to watch, as week after week, contestants perform and are either forwarded to the next round or are dismissed as 'lacking the X-Factor'. Most interestingly, it is not always the best singing ability that guarantees success. There are other factors at play which capture the votes. It is the nebulous nature of these factors which seem to trap and win the hearts and minds of the public voters and judges alike. The manner in which contestants can connect with the audience in this magical way served as the impetus for this book. Just like our favourite teachers, there is something at play in human communication which allows one individual to relate more effectively and deeply than another. The time to consider the classroom X-Factor has arrived!

And just as talent is not the exclusive requirement of the X-Factor entertainer, subject knowledge and teaching ability are not the exclusive requirements of the classroom X-Factor. There is something more – and we are convinced that this something is quite fundamental. Clearly, how we speak, the attractiveness of our voice, our accent have a major bearing, but, in our experience, the really inspiring teacher has much more than subject knowledge; teaching ability and an attractive or clear voice. Their magnetic quality comes in many subtle ways of which we are often unaware: the way we 'carry ourselves' in the classroom, our body language, whether we smile or grimace, how we dress, how we gesture and in many other ways. Academically, this collection of X-Factor attributes is known as 'nonverbal communication'. It is our intention in this book to help you to become aware of these nonverbal communication X-Factors, to recognise their importance in the classroom and to help you develop your own X-Factor!

When we consider the classroom X-Factor then, the key thing to remember is that the X-Factor is about the entirety of our communication. To illustrate this, think of a text message you receive from a friend: 'Ok ... that's fine.' Now this text could have two meanings. It could mean: 'everything is okay and I support you in what you're doing'. Or it could mean: 'you are obviously going to do your own thing so that's fine, I will do mine'. The message can be interpreted emotionally in two ways – either as a text of support or as a text of rebuke. The critical point here is that we quickly imagine the tone of the text and most likely imagine the facial expression of the sender. Is it happy, sad, angry, etc.? Of course, hopefully, we then make the correct interpretation.

FIGURE 1.2 Support or rebuke?

The same thing happens the world over in the classroom. Teachers say 'very good' which can be interpreted by the student as 'wow, I have done really well!' or 'It looks like I have done nothing wrong!' Teacher use of nonverbal components such as vocal intonation, facial expressions, gestures and body language can infuse the message with either clear praise or passing and flippant acknowledgement. The most important point here is that while the teacher may think they have praised very effectively, using the 'correct words', the pupil will have read the 'real message' nonverbally and made the correct inferences.

This example is just one of the many millions of situations where teachers and students interact and exchange vital information nonverbally. The classroom is probably one of the few humanly constructed contexts where one adult aims to communicate with a large number of students for extended periods of time and in ways which continuously engage all of them. No small challenge! Add to this the hustle and bustle of classroom life, the varying needs of a class of students, the demands of modern curricula and society, and the famous words of a New York teacher almost become true:

> The teacher like the doctor in the midst of an epidemic is so busy with the daily doings that she finds it hard to get some distance between herself and her functions, to see what is happening. As a result, she is vulnerable to each day's experience in a special transient way.

> (Brophy and Good, 1984, 22)

While this quote may seem a little exaggerated, it does bear some truth in relation to the stress and demands on teachers. Cohen *et al.* (2004, 4) describe schools in the UK as being in a state of 'permanent flux' with teachers needing to be able to cope with innovations, pressures to raise standards, the need to energise learning and the necessity to meet the diverse needs of learners. In 2001, a survey in the UK by Smithers and Robinson uncovered 'sad statistics' which represented a disillusioned workforce who had come into teaching with high hopes, commitment and ideals, who had made a positive and deliberate choice to teach and were now disillusioned by the world of education. This research also uncovered the startling statistic that 18 per cent of those who started teaching left within three years. This raises the very important question – why?

Smithers and Robinson's (2001) work identified a range of factors associated with this disillusionment, but, in particular, the issue of pupil behaviour and coping with government initiatives emerged frequently. Once again, one is reminded of our New York teacher in the midst of an epidemic (or perhaps it should be academic!). Could it be that teachers are not coping as effectively as they used to? Dealing with new initiatives and managing pupil behaviour to name but a few, demand much from the individual. For teachers to respond to such necessities they must be self-efficient. Like well-toned athletes, they must be ready and equipped for the 'classroom event'. They must be able to roll with the jolts of change, tango with the petulance and energy of youth and tap their own creativity in order to deliver lessons that inspire and enthuse. Akin to some of the great soccer players we see on our televisions or the magnificent singers we see and hear on *The X-Factor*, they must be fit and aware of themselves as key players in the tango of classroom communication. Such match fitness means being aware of the rapid and nuanced ways in which they give messages. It also means being aware of the most effective ways of capitalising on one's abilities to communicate nonverbally. In short, like the comment in the film *Austin Powers, International Man of Mystery*, it means finding and utilising one's mojo – knowing your X-Factor.

As mentioned earlier, it is surprising that given the potency of nonverbal communication and its value to our daily forms of communication, it is given scant attention by the education world. Like the lost cousin of the educational family, it is acknowledged but rarely asked to come for dinner. Why is this? The literature on the topic identifies a number of reasons which include the cumbersome and costly nature of undertaking research on nonverbal communication (e.g. videotaping, etc.), the fact that it is still envisaged as what Edwards *et al.* (1998, 7) call a 'newcomer to the educational field' and finally its reliance on other disciplines (e.g. neuroscience, psychology).

Perhaps some of the reasons for its lowly status also lie in its very nature. As nonverbal communication is unique to each individual and as it is often picked up within seconds with no 'text' record and usually no video record, we have little tangible record of its use. Its impact may be clear and sometimes individuals will remember 'the way he glared at me', or 'wagged his finger', but because it is often spontaneous, subtle and fleeting, it leaves little tangible evidence. There is no paper trail. For example, when questioning a pupil, teachers watch the eyes closely, if the pupil looks down or away, it may be an indication they are either recollecting or are uncomfortable with giving an answer. Whatever the case, it usually is a signal to the teacher that the pupil is not ready to give an answer and prompts the teacher to move on. The point here is that we are finely attuned to reading nonverbal communication and do so on a continuous basis. Yet as teachers we give little deliberate attention to such practices.

This book sets out to redress this imbalance. Calling it the X-Factor, reminds us that there are 'forces' at play in our classroom practice and communication which are intangible to us. One could say they are mysterious and even magical. This book seeks to unravel these mysterious 'forces'. To do this, we have written the book in three main parts. First, we provide you with a broad overview of nonverbal communication. We look at relevant theories and examine classroom nonverbal communication in general. Second, we will help you to understand the specific 'mechanics' of the various types of nonverbal communication (e.g. eye contact/body language, etc.). Think of this a bit like looking at the instruments of an orchestra. Smiling complements eye contact, in the same way as the cello complements the violin and so on. Hence, this part will examine each of the instruments of the nonverbal orchestra individually with some focus on symphonic interplay.

As teachers, academics and writers we are also acutely aware of what we would call 'theory exposure'! Often, when reading academic books, we read a chunk of pages and then stop and wonder – 'What have I learned so far?' 'What are the key points discussed so far in the chapter?' Or sometimes we read half a chapter and then return to it a week later, asking similar questions – 'Where did I leave off in this chapter?' So to address this 'syndrome', we have decided to give you mini-summaries throughout the big chapters and at the end of shorter ones. A bit like a good teacher would ask – 'Now what have we learned so far in this lesson?' 'What did we learn yesterday?' (We are presuming you will not read the book in one sitting!). So too, we have included mini-summaries entitled: 'What have we covered so far…'. Throughout the first and second parts of the book we will also give you mini-exemplars of how the X-Factor can operate in a classroom and will also present you with questions to help you develop your own X-Factor.

The third part of the book will show you how the various instruments of the nonverbal orchestra synchronise together to produce symphonies – sometimes they are in tune and sometimes not! This has to do with the examination of 'clusters' of nonverbal signs and signals as often the examination of just one nonverbal behaviour may not be sufficient to offer insights into the communication at play. We have worked in a variety of primary, secondary and tertiary classrooms, and are keenly aware of the importance of making theory amenable to everyday practice. So for this third part, we have written stories based on classroom contexts to illustrate the various points in the book and also to refer to some of our own research on classroom nonverbal communication. So without further ado, let us now look at each of the three parts more closely.

Part I looks at the X-Factor in the context of the classroom. You will be asked to think about your nonverbal communication in the following areas: smiling, voice intonation, occupancy of space, facial expressions, eye contact, looking at students, body language, gesturing, walking, movement and finally your appearance. A personal audit which will serve as a useful reference base for you as you learn about your own unique classroom X-Factor. This part also considers the relevance of nonverbal communication to our lives in general. In so doing, it reaches right back to our ancestors and begins with the question: did early humans have an X-Factor? Obviously, our abilities to access the archives on the communication styles of early humans are limited! However, from the fields of archaeology and neuroscience, we learn that nonverbal communication was probably a relevant and often vital form of communication for our ancestors. No doubt a few hand signals were important

FIGURE 1.3 Silent signals: there's a tiger in the bushes.

when tigers lurked in the undergrowth! The interesting points to glean from the study of early human communication, is that for millennia, man has used nonverbal communication to survive. Hence, for the teacher in the classroom, their abilities to source this fount of learning is neither new nor difficult. It is part of what we are. Moving to the twenty-first century, the first part then considers communication in the modern classroom. It examines how classroom communication has evolved in the past two decades and in particular considers what Edwards and Westgate term 'primacy of speech' (1994, 4). Modern curricula place a strong emphasis on 'oracy' as a medium of learning in all subjects and accordingly, this part examines whether the 'speech act' as we know it places enough emphasis on nonverbal communication. As Burman (2004, 54) observes: 'meaning is not uniquely linguistic but arises from action'.

In an endeavour to construct an understanding of communication in the modern classroom, we also consider how attention to nonverbal communication can fill the void which now appears to be emerging in communication at a social level. It looks at what Goleman (2006, 8) calls 'social autism' and the 'continuing invasion of technology into our daily lives' creating scenarios where 'people are absorbed in a virtual reality' and are 'deadened to those around them'. For example, think of the iPod wearer or a child playing Nintendo. To what degree are they developing their communication skills with those around them? To what degree can teachers spark and maintain their interest? In answering these questions, we then examine the relevance of nonverbal communication to learning itself. What does the research tell us about the educational value of nonverbal communication? This discussion leads us to examine the strong connections between nonverbal communication and emotional expression. In particular, this part discusses the role of emotion in the governance and creation of knowledge. If we think of our X-Factor singers, or our favourite teachers, we can all agree that they made us feel something. How did they do this? How do we absorb such feelings? To help us answer these questions, we will look at the theory of emotional contagion which asserts that our emotions are contagious with nonverbal communication playing a critical role in transmitting our feelings to others. Often termed 'messy' and once demoted to the lower divisions in the hierarchy of educational importance, the value and significance of emotion in learning is now firmly at the top of the educational league.

Hopefully, you will discover that through your use of nonverbal communication, moods can be created and specifically learning 'moods' which in turn have positive learning outcomes. Of course, the question for teachers is whether they are aware of the necessity and value of imbuing their teaching with emotional meaning. If they are aware, then the next obvious question is: can they do it? This question leads us naturally to the next part of the book which looks at 'how we do it'. How do we develop our own X-Factors? What instruments do we need to learn to play?

Part II of this book looks at the various components of nonverbal communication and works with you the reader to develop your own X-Factor.

Chapter by chapter, each type of nonverbal communication is examined through a dual lens showing you some of the relevant theories and findings and then giving you concrete examples of how they operate in the classroom. For example, let's take body language. This chapter looks at the various forms of body languages such as open and closed body language. The study of open and closed body language involves looking at how we use the hands, the arms, the trunk, and the head. For example, if someone sits down and promptly folds their arms and crosses their legs, we can describe this as closed body language. On the other hand, open body language is communicated when your body is exposed. There is a distinct lack of barriers of any sort.

So, what messages do these actions give? When are we likely to have closed or open body language? Is this beneficial to our teaching? For example, when reprimanding a pupil, is your body language open or closed? Which style do you think is better? Well, the fact is that as a teacher, open body language conveys a message of confidence and assuredness, indicating that you are clear and confident about your message, while also being inclusive to hearing the pupils' response and establishing a positive outcome. Open body language always has the upper hand. With a firm understanding of how nonverbal communication operates in the world of human communication, and armed with a selection of examples of how to apply this to the world of the classroom, we then move to the last part of the book.

We debated at length how we could best do this. By the time you get to Part III, you will have read over 50,000 words! We were conscious therefore that you the reader might be suffering from 'over-exposure' to nonverbal communication and also that at that stage of the book, you would want to know 'how does all this work in harmony in the classroom?' So, as we cannot include a video with this book, we decided to paint pictures of nonverbal communication in action in the classroom. To this end, we have created fictional stories which are all classroom based. According to some of our colleagues, these stories are lively and interesting (well, that's what they told us!) and so should make the last part of the book an exciting and stimulating read.

In constructing these stories we grounded them in the classroom X-Factor insights from the previous parts but also included some of our own research on classroom nonverbal communication. So this final part of the book looks at the various instruments of the classroom X-Factor orchestra (e.g. eye contact, gesturing, etc.) and illustrates the manner in which they play in harmony. You are probably saying to yourself at this point: 'Will I know how to analyse these stories?' Don't worry! Throughout each story we give you little pointers showing how the teacher's X-Factor is at play and at the end of each story there is an analysis showing you the key themes and points in the story.

For example, let's take the first story called 'The Yellow Teddy Lunchbox'. This story looks at a 'live' classroom scenario and shows how gesture and eye contact, etc., weave their way into the 'live teaching event'. On another level, it looks at differentiated teaching. While differentiated teaching has always prevailed to some degree or other, it has gained increased recognition in recent times. It is interesting to note that amidst the wide array of literature on differentiation, there is little on the manner in which nonverbal communication contributes to this aspect of teaching. In our analysis of this story we discuss how classroom nonverbal communication can be differentiated.

The last part of the book is very short and aims to give you some ideas about how to further develop your own X-Factor. It also contains some final words of advice.

2

Your X-Factor and Classroom Communication

Introduction

Have you listened to the radio recently? A recent song by Lady Gaga makes reference to poker faces and how we try to read them. Now we doubt that Lady Gaga was singing about classroom nonverbal communication, although no doubt all of us have at some time or other pulled a classroom poker face, but the lines of this song remind us of the prevalence and pertinence of nonverbal communication in the youth cultures of today. Almost all pop songs make some reference to nonverbal communication, be it 'body talk' (an eighties classic!) or 'lying eyes', 'smiling eyes' and even 'hungry eyes'.

It is important for us as teachers to remember that our students are immersed in a culture which makes widespread use of nonverbal communication. Of course, this also applies to the adult world, where salesmen talk of firm handshakes, lovers talk of holding hands and so on. Nonverbal communication is part and parcel of our daily interactions, it has stood the test of time and, more importantly, we pay considerable attention to its manifestations in all human communication. So developing your X-Factor is relevant to your life both in and out of the classroom. To bring this home a little more we want you to have a look at a list of the characteristics of people who do well on tests which measure their abilities to read nonverbal communication as compared to those who don't perform well on those tests. We want you to look at these characteristics and take a mental note of the ones you would like to have: well adjusted; less hostile; less manipulating; interpersonally democratic; interpersonally encouraging; extraverted; less shy; less socially anxious; warmer; more empathic; more popular; seen by others as interpersonally sensitive; able to judge others' interpersonal sensitivity; having warmer and more satisfying relationships.

We bet you have taken note of most of this list! It's impressive is it not? It relates to work undertaken by a range of researchers (Carney and Harrigan, 2003; Funder and Harris, 1986; Rosenthal *et al.*, 1979) which found that developing nonverbal skills resulted in this range of empathetic characteristics. If you had all of these characteristics you would have a very x-citing X-Factor (apologies about this lame alliteration!).

Interpersonally engaging, warm, empathic, interpersonally democratic, interpersonally sensitive, to mention but a few, are fine traits for any teacher and indeed any human being to have. So, we should now have your attention for the rest of the book!

The X-Factor and communication

Look around you for a moment. You probably have a TV, camera, radio, newspaper and mobile phone close to hand. What have they in common? They are all tools of communication. This book is primarily about communication. We want to develop your X-Factor and, in so doing, make you a better communicator in the classroom and perhaps beyond. Thankfully, the topic is all around us, and you may be more aware of it than you think. As humans we talk to each other, to animals, often to inanimate objects (think of the last time you got a flat tyre!) and to ourselves. Children often come out with the refrain 'But you didn't say that'. Adults talk of the 'tone of your voice', 'wagging fingers' and of course Oliver Goldsmith ('The Village Schoolmaster', 1770) gave us the great phrase 'the day's disaster in his morning face'. Humans like to communicate.

The word communication comes from the Latin word 'communicare', which means to share, impart or make common. This definition is ideally suited to this book. We want to develop your abilities to share, impart or make common. Now in developing your X-Factor, we have made clear that this book is not going to concern itself with the words you use. Rather, it looks at 'communication effected by means other than words' (Knapp and Hall, 2002, 5). It is concerned with nonverbal communication.

Some researchers have difficulty with this, arguing that it is difficult to separate words from their expression. Indeed, Birdwhistle (1970) has argued that studying nonverbal communication without words was akin to studying non-cardiac physiology! Nonetheless, there is evidence that there are differences in the ways we perceive verbal and nonverbal signals (Ekman and Friesen, 1969a). For example, waving goodbye does not have a verbal component, yet imparts information. On the other hand, the use of nonverbal communication can either support or contradict the actual meaning of the word (Woolfolk, 2001). Think of the concussed football player who declares he is still fit to play, while staggering to his feet. One famous example of the difference between verbal and nonverbal messages concerned the presidential debate between Richard Nixon and John F. Kennedy in 1960. Radio listeners judged the debate a draw, while television viewers, who saw the full picture, judged Kennedy the winner (Knapp and Hall, 2002).

This chapter and the chapters that follow will talk about your X-Factor in a variety of ways. We will talk about gestures, body language, eye contact, smiles and so on. To prepare you for these kinds of terms and to get the terminology of nonverbal communication 'swirling in your head' we ask you to think about the following questions:

How often do you *smile* in the classroom? Why?
What kinds of *voice intonation* do you use in the classroom?
How do you *occupy space* in the classroom – do you always stand at the front?
What kinds of *emotions* do students read *on your face*?
Would you say you use your face to hide or to reveal emotions?
What kind of *eye contact* do you maintain with students?

How much do you actually '*look*' at your students as you teach?

Would you say your *body language* is typically *open* or *closed* in the classroom?

To what degree do you use *gestures* as you teach?

How do you move in the classroom?

What kind of *walk* do you have? Does it project confidence?

Would you say your *appearance* could be classed as attractive?

These questions will start you thinking about your X-Factor and will serve as a personal reference base to much of the topics we discuss in this and later chapters.

The X-Factor and classroom communication

We all know that communication is important in the classroom (Barnes, 1975). But our concern is that much of the literature on classroom communication has focused on 'talk' and in particular on teacher talk. There is an endearing and famous quote which gives us a good picture of this:

> Any child playing teacher will produce most of the behaviours used by most teachers ... standing in front of a group of relatively passive onlookers, doing most of the talking, asking questions to which they already know the answers, and evaluating by passing judgements.
>
> (Simon and Boyer, 1970, 29)

FIGURE 2.1 Is the teacher talking too much?

Although somewhat dated, this comment does highlight the manner in which we think of classroom communication. Do you think you talk much in the classroom? Well, the reality is that teachers tend to do a lot of the classroom talking. You have probably heard of the 'two-thirds rule'. Two-thirds of a lesson is talk, two-thirds of this talk is teacher talk and two-thirds of this teacher talk is concerned with discipline and procedural matters rather than lesson content itself (Cohen *et al.*, 2004).

In doing all this talking, there is obviously a nonverbal channel of communication in action also. As teachers we tend to talk a lot and therefore communicate a lot nonverbally. It is very interesting to consider how we orchestrate this talk. We like to be 'centre stage', like a clairvoyant, acting as a medium for all the communication happening in the classroom. The classic example of this is the tendency to repeat pupils' answers. We channel all communication through ourselves, and, in so doing, make a point nonverbally. We are 'centre stage' – the star attraction. Needless to say, this jars with the modern emphasis on 'child-centred' education.

To take this issue a little further, can you think of the last time you entered another teacher's classroom? Where was the teacher? The odds are that the teacher was at the front of the classroom, standing up, with students seated 'beneath' him/her in what Edwards and Furlong (1978) call 'dominant performance'. As teachers we adopt class-room positions and formulate seating arrangements which make us the 'key medium' for communication. The X in your X-Factor may be a mark on the floor at the top of the classroom! Think of a student teacher in a junior infant class. As part of the introduction to a mathematics class, he takes a position at the top of the class-room and poses the 'big question': 'Does anyone know what colour my jumper is?' One pupil answers 'green' which is the cor-rect answer, but then asks in a concerned and somewhat confused tone: 'Do you not know what colour it is?' In asking his ques-

FIGURE 2.2 Teacher at the front of the classroom.

tion, the young teacher centred himself as the key point of reference rather than the pupils. This was a nonverbal message – he was centre stage! Of course, this also has to do with occupancy of space, a topic to be discussed in Chapter 13.

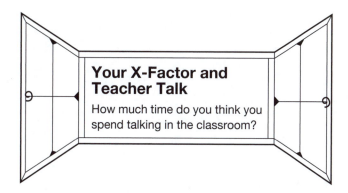

Your X-Factor and Teacher Talk

How much time do you think you spend talking in the classroom?

As mentioned earlier, this book does not address the words and language we use as teachers. However, developing your X-Factor helps you with the delivery of these words. For example, the length of your sentences can have an impact on some students' understanding. Studies have shown that children from disadvantaged backgrounds rely on shorter sentences (e.g. De Cecco, 1970, 118). Obviously this has relevance for the timing and the length of the sentences we use.

No doubt, at some point or another you have found yourself searching for a word. It is on 'the tip of your tongue'. Take, for example, the scenario where you are explain-ing to the students about the measurement of angles, and you ask them to take out their ... their ... oh dear ... you cannot locate the word you need. What do you do? You probably make the shape of an arc and refer to a semicircle. By the way, the miss-ing word is 'protractor'! Butterworth and Hadar's work (1989) points to the value of using gestures to create a visual image in the brain, which raises the overall activation in the system through the production of a motor movement (how you move your limbs). This work, and that of others such as Beattie (2004), indicates the significant relationships between nonverbal communication and language usage.

It also highlights the intricate manner in which the brain is hard-wired to communicate. Such hardwiring is as old as the human race itself. Stone Age man had the X-Factor too!

So far we have covered...

The nonverbal signs and signals we make are important to how we are perceived by others and are often intertwined with your use of language. Remember research shows us that as teachers we like to talk. So how much talking do you do? How is it mirrored in your nonverbal signals?

3

The X-Factor within You

Early man and the X-Factor

When early humans spotted a tiger lurking in the undergrowth near their family, it would have been in their own best interests to use some form of silent signal to warn them of imminent danger! Nonverbal communication dates back to the earliest forms of intelligible communication. Take for example the expressions 'yuk' or 'eeeurr'. No doubt at some point or other you have uttered one or both of these expressions and perhaps even in a classroom – think of the decaying lunch you found in an old school-bag! Mithen (2006) observes that these expressions are found in all modern human cultures and are typically accompanied with facial expression of wrinkling the nose and pulling down the corners of the mouth – in short a look of disgust. We use these expressions when confronted with such things as vomit, faeces, spilled blood, maggots and rotting food! We promise this chapter will get better!

Curtis and Biran (2001) argue that the expression of disgust is an evolved human mechanism for defence against infectious disease. According to Mithen (2006) for example, thousands of years ago, as a caring mother minded her young baby on the savannah lands of Africa, it is probable that she used an expression like 'yuk' to warn her young offspring from crawling into the carcass of a butchered and rotting animal. As teachers, we often 'wrinkle our noses' when giving explanations of disgusting things. And let's face it, children love stories which have a disgusting element.

You may be surprised to note that there are often features of our classroom work which have antecedents in the human behaviour of millennia ago! In his book, *Origins of the Modern Mind*, the neuroscientist, Merlin Donald (1991) argues that early humans may have used a form of communication called mimesis. This involved mimicking or imitation, but also extended to another level where the human used nonverbal communication to make a representation. For example, holding one's hand to one's heart to express grief or covering one's face to express regret. As teachers we have, no doubt, used these forms of representation at some point or other. Think of the time you held your hand to your head when you heard that Mark and Paul were once again fighting in the yard at break time.

So what is mimesis? Donald (1991, 68) defines mimesis as 'the ability to produce conscious, self-initiated, representational acts that are intentional but not linguistic'. It involves your tone of voice, facial expressions, eye movements, gestures, posture and whole body movements. Donald points out that throughout history we have been engaged in mimesis. For example, early Chinese and Indian dances used mimesis, the ancient Greeks and

FIGURE 3.1 Mimesis: let me show you how I made this mallet.

Romans loved mime and if we go to the Australian aborigines, we find it in their dance celebrations also. For the early human, the use of mimesis could involve signals on how to create a new tool, or signs that a big fat deer was nearby.

Now you may wonder what early humans and the modern classroom have in common. Well clearly it demonstrates that non-verbal communication is a natural and innate skill. For us to tap into it and usurp its potential is as natural as it was for a prehistoric mother to warn her young of a rotting carcass. Furthermore, if we can make greater use of features of nonverbal communication such as representational gestures, mimicry and imitation, we are not inventing a new form of human communication. We are employing one which is natural to us and which has strong communicative power. It is innate.

We are built for the X-Factor

People are hard-wired to use nonverbal communication; their X-Factor. Research from the field of neuroscience clearly highlights the power of nonverbal communication, and in particular the speed at which it operates. Closely connected with these speedy reactions is a recently discovered class of neuron known as the 'spindle cell'. Neuroscientists now suspect that spindle cells hold some of the secrets to social intuition and in particular the speed at which social intuition operates. As Daniel Goleman (2006, 66) puts it: 'they put the snap in snap judgements'. Incidentally, it is argued that because the human has about 1000 times more spindle cells than its closest primate cousins, it is these spindle cells which set us apart from all other mammalian brains. This spindle cell relies heavily on nonverbal messages such as facial expression.

You may or may not be familiar with the Harry Potter books. There is a scene in the book *Harry Potter and the Order of the Phoenix* where Harry (an apprentice wizard) is learning how to stop Lord Voldemort, an evil wizard, from invading his mind to gain information. His teacher, Professor Snape advises Harry as follows:

> 'The Dark Lord is highly skilled at … extracting feelings and memories from another person's mind.' Harry is surprised by this statement and replies excitedly:
> 'He can read minds?'
> Professor Snape replies: 'You have no subtlety, Potter … Only Muggles talk of mind reading. The mind is not a book.'
>
> (Iacoboni, 2008, 78)

As Marco Iacoboni, a neurologist and neuroscientist from UCLA, observes in relation to the extract above, humans do not actually possess the ability to 'read minds' as Harry

Potter envisaged; however, we do have the ability to get inside another person's head. Our abilities to empathise and to know what someone else is thinking and feeling, is at the heart of what it means to be human. Iacoboni (2008, 7) observes that our brains are capable of 'mirroring the deepest aspects of the minds of others'. But how do we do this? Recent groundbreaking research in the field of neuroscience provides us with many valuable answers in the form of special cells in our brains called mirror neurons. Iacoboni argues that these 'tiny miracles' are 'at the heart of how we navigate through our lives'. They are also present in other mammals such as monkeys, but we have a lot of them – in fact the human brain contains about 100 billion neurons! These mirror neurons enable us to imitate the actions and intentions of others. They sense the feelings and moves another person is about to make and then 'fire' in the brain, instantly preparing us to imitate these moves or feelings.

So what have these mirror neurons got to do with your X-Factor? Iacoboni (2008, 79) asks the question: 'Do you see what I am saying?' The mirror neuron system is strongly dependent on observation and on examining gestures and facial expressions. As you shall discover in later chapters, these are all features of your X-Factor. As Pfeifer and Dapretto (2009, 187) put it: 'When I see your angry facial expression, that activates some of the neural circuitry as when I myself am angry, allowing me to connect your action with the mental representation of anger.' In short, mirror neurons have a strong nonverbal component. What is fascinating about the brain circuitry of mirror neurons is the speed at which they act. We observe and process the actions of others in milliseconds.

Goleman (2006, 16) describes this rapid analysis of nonverbal messages as a type of 'low road' we navigate when communicating with others. This 'low road' operates 'beneath our awareness' in an automatic and effortless manner. For example, when we are captivated by an attractive voice or sense the sarcasm in a remark, we are travelling on the low road. On this road, we extract meaning from nonverbal messages in milliseconds, even before we know what we are looking at. We respond to someone else's X-Factor almost instantaneously. When we are having a chat with someone our senses are collecting all kinds of information. A sudden change in their posture, or a shift in their tone of voice sends information rushing to a part of the brain known as the 'amygdala'. This extracts emotional meaning from these nonverbal signals and primes us to respond. We may mimic that emotion in our own bodies or react to it, e.g. becoming fearful if the low road extracts a feeling of anger from the nonverbal messages. On this low road we respond in a reflexive and unconscious manner. We do not relay information through the speech centre of our brain. Instead, we react almost instantaneously. Goleman (2006, 16) points out that 'most of what we do seems to be piloted by massive neural networks operating via the low road – particularly in our emotional life'. This reminds us of a comment made by one of the teachers in our own research: 'We have a firewall for verbal communication ... but there's none for nonverbal communication ... it's extremely important because it can be involuntary and expresses emotions you're not ready to let go' (White, 2008, 122).

On the other hand, we also navigate a 'high road'. This road operates through neural systems which are much more methodical. We are aware of being on the high road. It gives us the time to think about what we feel. So the X-Factor is a little more complex and subversive than you may have thought. It operates on both a high and low road, but mainly, the low road.

The key message for us here as teachers, is the huge value of using this low road. It facilitates the transmission of an emotion from person to person without anyone consciously noticing. It could be the slightest of sarcastic tones in your voice, the movement of a foot towards the door, a beaming smile or a 'dirty look'.

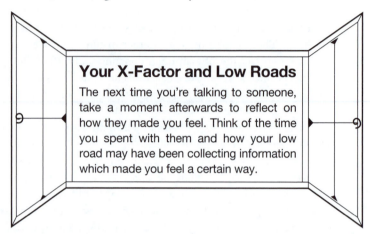

Your X-Factor and Low Roads

The next time you're talking to someone, take a moment afterwards to reflect on how they made you feel. Think of the time you spent with them and how your low road may have been collecting information which made you feel a certain way.

FIGURE 3.2 Can you tell how this teacher is feeling?

The X-Factor and catching emotions

Our X-Factor makes emotions contagious. We all know of people who make us feel good or bad. Think of the expression: 'One look from her would turn milk sour.' It is well known that people can make us feel a certain way. But how do they do this? A team led by Elaine Hatfield in 1992 provides us with some very valuable insights into emotions and how they can be 'caught'. They advanced what is known as the theory of emotional contagion. This theory states that: 'people automatically mimic and synchronise expressions, vocalisations, postures and movements with others and … as a result converge emotionally' (Hatfield *et al.*, 1992, 156).

As we mimic the expressions and postures of the person we are talking to, we also 'soak up' their emotions. Interestingly, in recent years, the emotional contagion theory has been used to explain the feelings, thoughts and behaviour of autistic children and religious fanatics (Hatfield *et al.*, 2009, 26). Obviously, the emotional contagion effect is relevant to the classroom. As you teach your class, your students will synchronise with your movements, expressions, postures and vocalisations. Your nonverbal communication will imbue them with particular feelings.

FIGURE 3.3 Enthusiasm: let me tell you about the great King Lear.

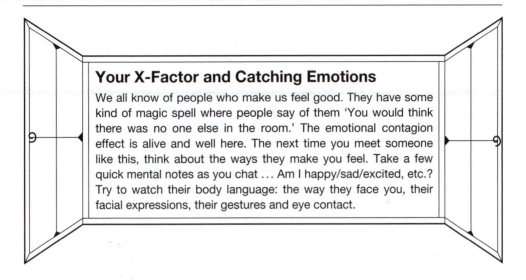

Your X-Factor and Catching Emotions

We all know of people who make us feel good. They have some kind of magic spell where people say of them 'You would think there was no one else in the room.' The emotional contagion effect is alive and well here. The next time you meet someone like this, think about the ways they make you feel. Take a few quick mental notes as you chat ... Am I happy/sad/excited, etc.? Try to watch their body language: the way they face you, their facial expressions, their gestures and eye contact.

So how does this theory stuff fit into the classroom? Research by Mottet and Beebe (2000) has found that among university students, emotions may be contagious. They found that students' emotional responses were connected to the manner in which the teacher interacted with them nonverbally. A small-scale study of primary teachers by White (2008) found that teachers perceived the conveyance of emotion nonverbally as being significant and important to their teaching. Other work on what is known as the 'teacher immediacy effect' places significant emphasis on nonverbal communication. We shall discuss that in Chapter 4, but for the moment we want to stay with emotions.

Exemplar 1: Navigating the High and Low Roads as we Teach

You are teaching a History lesson on the Holocaust. Do your facial expressions reveal your disgust at the events that happened? Do your gestures and movements and, in particular, your voice intonation reveal the horror and ghastliness of this event? If you manage to convey these emotions, you will not only travel the high road but also the low road giving students an emotional perspective on the events. You will give them an insight into the raw feelings of that event (low road) but can also look at a considered understanding of what actually went on during the holocaust (high road). Of course, the next phase in the development of this lesson has to do with your exploitation of this dimension of the emotional learning. Do you discuss the event as a class? For example, do you ask the students how they felt as you described the life of a prisoner in Auschwitz? Do you use drama, mime or role play to allow students to use nonverbal means to examine and delve into the emotions surrounding this event?

Research by Paul Ekman (which incidentally involved work with tribes, cannibals, primates and, of course, non-cannibals like most literate people!) has found that we have six basic emotions. These are anger, disgust, sadness, happiness, fear and surprise. Ekman (2003) found these to be universal for all humans (including the cannibals!). What is significant for the X-Factor is that such emotions can be triggered by our automatic appraising systems, which are continuously scanning the world around us. This scanning takes place without our conscious knowing in milliseconds and collects a large amount of information from nonverbal signs and signals. It then correlates this information with what Ekman (2003, 30) calls our 'emotion alert data base'. As we go about our daily interactions, our data base is fully switched on. This data base prepares us to deal with important events connected to our welfare and survival without us having to think about what we are going to do. Where did the data base come from? Ekman argues that this data base is written in part by our biology (through natural selection and our ancestral past) and also by our individual experience.

So, what has this got to do with your X-Factor? It reminds us that what we convey nonverbally can be interpreted in a number of ways. The X-Factor is also governed by signs and signals which are relevant to our welfare and survival. We must be aware that in tandem with the educational content we try to teach, there is another channel of communication which is 'wide open' and 'switched on'. Hence, the necessity to locate educational teaching within contexts which can be judged as 'safe' for the student.

So far we have covered...

You are hard-wired to communicate nonverbally. Your X-Factor is largely innate, but knowing how it works can enable you to develop it! Sometimes this communication can happen unknown to you. You can collect or convey lots of information nonverbally in split seconds while you converse with someone else. Other times you are aware of it. Emotions are contagious and are often leaked nonverbally. We transmit a wide range of emotions which can be caught by our students.

Exemplar 2: Ways We Give Messages

A class teacher is asking students about the character Heathcliff from the novel *Wuthering Heights*. The teacher believes Heathcliff to be a troubled soul, but not altogether unlikeable. A student advances a theory that perhaps Heathcliff could have been connected to the underworld given the novel's links with the afterlife. The teacher acknowledges the response describing it as interesting. However, her eye contact is poor, her body directs away from the student and the tone of the response is flat. These nonverbal signals may well arouse feelings of discontent in the student at the teacher's lack of nonverbal excitement or may cause the student to despair at 'missing the point'. More significantly, the student may also pick up that what really counts is the correct answer, and not the discussion of alternative theories. The point here is simple – the teacher provokes an emotional reaction in the student through her nonverbal communication.

Using your X-Factor to spark feelings in yourself

There is another side to the work of Ekman (2003) and Hatfield *et al.* (1994) which we think is most fascinating and which in our opinion has yet to be more fully utilised in classrooms. Along with nonverbal communication provoking emotions in another individual, it can also work in reverse. We can do things with our hands, faces, body language, etc., which can then provoke a feeling within ourselves. For example, by smiling and presenting open body language, we can induce feelings of relaxation in ourselves. Let's take another example in the classroom. If you were studying tectonic movement in Geography, describing how the crushing and forcing of such movements can lead to underground earthquakes and indeed tsunamis, it might be possible to give such a phenomenon some emotional meaning. For example, asking students to clasp and thrust their hands against each other, and then to pull them apart may enable them to experience the strain involved, and also to emotionally experience the release of tension.

It is here that some of the most fascinating work of Paul Ekman (2003) emerges. He argues that by doing certain things we can make ourselves feel a certain way. In the above example, the stretching and straining of the hands would have produced a feeling of tension. Along with others, for example Davidson (1994), Ekman found that making people smile produces many of the changes in the brain that occur when they smile naturally. Edgar Allen Poe, writing in *The Purloined Letter* (1844) puts it very well:

> When I wish to find out how wise or how stupid or how good or how wicked is anyone … I fashion the expression of my face as accurately as possible, in accordance with the expression of his and then wait to see what thought or sentiments arise in my mind or heart.

As Poe mentions above he 'fashions the expressions on his face' to see 'what sentiments arise'. Although he wrote the letter in 1844, Edgar Allen Poe may have been ahead of his time. His reference to the specific use of the face to ignite 'sentiments' considerably predates some of the work by Blairy and her colleagues in 1999 who came up with what is now known as 'facial feedback theory'. Again, this theory has to do with provoking emotions in yourself through the manipulation of your facial expressions. We will discuss this theory in greater detail in Chapter 14.

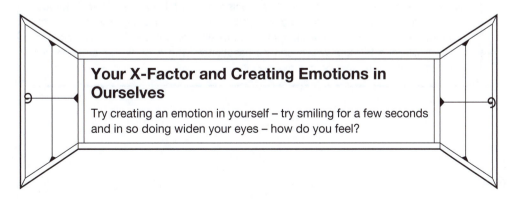

Your X-Factor and Creating Emotions in Ourselves

Try creating an emotion in yourself – try smiling for a few seconds and in so doing widen your eyes – how do you feel?

Exemplar 3: Using Actions to Help with Emotional Understanding

You are studying the life cycle of the butterfly. The lesson has come to the part where the butterfly emerges from the chrysalis. Obviously, a magnificent moment for the former caterpillar. Ask the students to crouch down low, to smile and then to slowly stretch up from this position to one where they are standing tall. This will also involve them stretching out their arms and staring around at their 'new world'. Now ask them how they feel.

The X-Factor is the emotional factor

You may ask why this chapter has devoted so much attention to emotion. There are three main reasons for this. First, as Ekman (2003, xvii) observes: 'emotions are what motivate our lives'. Second, emotions play an important role in the creation of knowledge and memories. Third, developing your classroom X–Factor is inextricably linked with emotional expression and nonverbal communication. When we think back on our school days, we inevitably smile, frown and perhaps feel a pang of sadness and so on. You will note that your memories of school days are filled with emotional highs and lows. We think it is fascinating that while you may remember De Moivre's theorem in Mathematics, and perhaps the poem 'Daffodils' by Wordsworth, your first thoughts about school days may not be about knowledge, but rather, feelings. For example, feelings you had as you entered the front gates, waited outside the principal's office, awaited an essay review or received a prize. In other words, classrooms are filled with emotion. However, it is intriguing to observe that it is only in recent times that the significance of emotion has been recognised.

So far we have covered...

Emotions are contagious as you probably know. But your X-Factor, the way you communicate nonverbally, is a critical component in making these emotions contagious. As humans we are continually scanning others for their 'emotional output'. Such scanning has deep roots in our psyche. Along with making emotions contagious to others, have you ever thought about trying it on yourself? By adopting particular physical attributes which can be associated with a particular emotion, we may then ignite that emotion in ourselves.

4

The X-Factor on the Education Stage of Today's World

Knowledge and emotion

You may be familiar with the poem, 'The Village Schoolmaster' by Oliver Goldsmith. It is about a 'village schoolmaster' who 'taught his little school' and the village 'all declar'd how much he knew'. In the poem we come across the well-known lines:

> While word of learned length and thund'ring sound
> Amazed the gazing rustics rang'd around;
> And still they gaz'd and still the wonder grew,
> How one small head could carry all he knew.

> (Oliver Goldsmith, 1728–1774)

It is thought that this poem was about Goldsmith's own teacher, Thomas (Paddy) Byrne in his own village of Lissoy, Athlone, Ireland. One of the key things we glean from this poem is the 'local' awe of this man and 'all he knew'. There is a strong celebration of the intellectual and of knowledge.

This gives us an insight into the historical arrival of emotion on the modern educational landscape. As we can glean from the poem above, there was once a time where the intellectual mind was highly valued. It was considered the primary force for creating human learning experiences. People talked of the village schoolmaster and the 'knowledge he knew'. Emotion and intuition were 'relegated' to the lower divisions, being awarded what Derry (2005) regards as secondary status. However, we now recognise that 'teaching and learning involve emotional understanding' (Hargreaves, 1998, 838). This is where the X-Factor comes in. The X-Factor is about using emotions in learning.

There is little doubt that knowing your X-Factor has a central role in improving your communication abilities. Nonverbal communication is central to all human communication. In the general media, there is one place we are sure to find nonverbal communication, and that is in the world of romance. Newspaper shelves are full of magazines with headlines like: 'Does she love you? Watch her body language' or

'Flirting Skills: Ten easy ways to get the man of your dreams'. Such articles typically cite statistics which reveal the power of nonverbal communication. So how powerful is nonverbal communication?

The power of nonverbal communication

There is considerable debate about the reliability and validity of statistics which 'measure' nonverbal communication. For example, Geoffrey Beattie (2004), a psychologist in the UK, who was involved in the analysis of participants' behaviour in the *Big Brother* TV shows, questions studies which focus exclusively on nonverbal behaviour because they do not really examine in a close manner the language in use.

That said, however, let us look at some of the statistics that are 'out there'. In 1972, Michael Argyle concluded that nonverbal communication is 12.5 times more powerful than language when we are conveying interpersonal attitudes (e.g. friendliness/hostility). It is ten times more powerful than words when we are communicating norms of superiority and inferiority. For example, think of someone you know who fits the title 'Boss'. The crucial question here is your perception of the person as boss. If we were then to examine how you interact with this person, nonverbal factors such as the amount of time the boss talks, the loudness of such talk, eyebrow movements, physical assertiveness, use of touch, arm and leg positions, gaze and proximity all come into play in establishing the boss 'as boss' (Aries *et al.*, 1983; Schwartz *et al.*, 1982).

From a number of his research studies, Mehrabian (1969, 1972, 1981) estimates that only 7 per cent of what we communicate arrives via the verbal channel. In more recent times, Weare (2004, 114) connects both nonverbal and verbal communication as follows:

Communication does not of course have to be verbal, indeed the evidence is that most of it is not, and that we gather about 90 percent of what others tell us about what they think and feel through their nonverbal communication.

These kinds of statistics are very relevant to our work as teachers. They indicate strongly that there is hard evidence showing the X–Factor as a major player in human interaction. But what about its prevalence in the classroom? As stated in the introduction of this book, we are a little worried that nonverbal communication is not given the lead role on the classroom communication stage. Indeed, as Weare (2004, 115) points out: 'Given how little words count in communication, and indeed in learning, it is ironic that so much of what happens in schools is based on words rather than other media.'

FIGURE 4.1 Nonverbal communication is like the submerged part of an iceberg.

Think about it for a moment. Our schools are surrounded by words. Typically, we receive reports via the channel of words. We ask students to write essays, comprehension questions, reports and so on. This book uses words! In most classrooms in the Western world, students have at least one exercise book for each subject, not to mention the plethora of workbooks and supporting texts that chase these exercise books. So, we believe that to a large degree, classrooms are word rich – they serve the W-Factor (Word Factor) very well, but maybe not the X-Factor as well. Thankfully, with a growing awareness of the need for 'emotionally literate schools' and with increasing recognition of what Hargreaves (2001) calls the 'emotional geographies of teaching', the value of nonverbal communication in examining the emotional terrain of classroom communication is becoming increasingly relevant.

Such burgeoning awareness has been buoyed by a greater awareness of varying learning styles and intelligences which are prodding the focus of communication away from a preoccupation with the verbal. Weare (2004, 32) makes the point very clearly, arguing that classroom communication now needs to 'appeal to all the learning styles'. In so doing, she notes that this communication should give greater consideration to other modes of communication such as art, music, dance, drama and movement. Do these ring any bells? Yes, they would all appear to be part of *The X-Factor* TV show!

The 'pzazz' factor

We may be the first to coin the term 'classroom X-Factor', but actually we are not the first to entertain the notion. In 1993, two researchers, Sean Neill and Chris Caswell undertook extensive work on classroom communication and concluded that while the curriculum content of a lesson is delivered almost entirely verbally, the automatic conclusion that well-prepared and well-verbalised lessons can guarantee success is questionable. They came up with the term 'nonverbal pzazz' and argued that while the use of verbal language is important, 'nonverbal pzazz gets the message across' (184). Such 'pzazz' relates to teacher emotional messages such as enthusiasm. The big question to ask here is how important is this 'pzazz' in getting the message across?

Neill and Caswell pointed out that the spontaneous nature of nonverbal signals coupled with the complex manner in which signals can be combined means that 'we cannot … expect a clear one-to-one link between outcomes and signals' (185). This pzazz factor obviously bears close resemblance to our X-Factor, except we think our term is better! But the 'pzazz factor' also has strong links with an educational research movement which started in the USA in the 1980s and concerned teaching styles and their expression. It could be said that this movement had its origins in a famous and amusing study known as the Dr. Fox study. Arguably, this Dr. Fox study was the first time the classroom X-Factor emerged on the scene! And this emergence was by virtue of deceit!

Dr. Fox

In 1973, Natfulin *et al.* decided to examine the significance of expressive teaching styles. So they hired an actor, and called him Dr. Fox. This fictional Dr. Fox, with a fake PhD, was given the role of lecturer in education. He had no real knowledge of the content he was to teach, but he had the ability to act! Dr. Fox delivered lectures to the participating pre-service teachers in a charismatic, interesting and funny manner. Amusingly, while the lectures were gripping and entertaining, they were devoid of any consequential content. However, when asked to evaluate the lecture, these students praised Dr. Fox as much for the academic aspects of the lecture as for his expressive style! In other words, the fake Dr. Fox fooled the audience into accepting he was competent on the academic content of his lecture through his highly engaging and expressive style of communication.

Now we can all think of people like this. You attend a lecture or class and someone asks you later: what was it about? Your reply might go something like: 'Yes, I really enjoyed that talk', but when you try to retrieve the main information of the lecture, you may find out that all you have is the emotional memory, the style of the speaker and perhaps a few key points. So what is it that makes teachers stand out? What helps them connect to an audience in the same way Dr. Fox did? To answer this question, we need to examine terms such as charismatic and enthusiastic. According to Babad (2005), we all know teachers who are 'charismatic', 'buoyant' and 'enthusiastic'.

The X-Factor and charismatic teachers

Your X-Factor is closely linked to terms such as 'charismatic' and 'enthusiastic'. Researchers such as Rosenshine (1970) and Friedman et al. (1980) note that nonverbal expressiveness (your X-Factor) is a key variable in the explanation of these terms. As you can probably guess, and have no doubt learned from experience, expressive people are perceived as being more likeable (Friedman et al., 1980). Think of the last person you met who gesticulated wildly while talking.

DePaulo (1992) points out that people who are expressive are perceived as having a social advantage. In particular, it has been shown that people who are expressive are more likely to influence other people's moods. They are also perceived as being more likeable when introduced to new people. Needless to say this has obvious implications for your classroom X-Factor. So what does the classroom literature tell us about expressiveness and the X-Factor?

In the United States, the 1980s witnessed the manifestation of two parallel lines of research which examined teacher expressiveness. One strand involved analysing 'teacher enthusiasm', while the other involved the analysis of 'teacher immediacy'. Strangely, although both strands were closely linked conceptually, they ploughed separate furrows for quite some time. 'Teacher immediacy' was championed by the work of Andersen (1979). It was based primarily on the theory that teachers could create an immediacy with their students through nonverbal communication (Andersen and Andersen, 1982). Such immediacy resulted in what Titsworth (2001) termed 'psychological closeness'. An immediate teacher made effective use of eye contact, leaning forward, vocal intonation, gestures, smiling and humour. On the other hand, non-immediate teachers were characterised by what Ikeda and Beebe (1992) called 'aloofness'. Their expressiveness was characterised by monotone delivery, aloofness and poor nonverbal communication. We can all think of teachers who fit both categories.

The other strand was entitled 'teacher enthusiasm'. Championed by the research of Murray (1983) it described enthusiastic teachers as speaking in a dramatic and expressive way, using varied vocal intonation, maintaining eye contact, using varied facial expressions, smiling, laughing and gesturing. One is immediately reminded of our Dr. Fox! Obviously, 'teacher immediacy' and 'teacher enthusiasm' are remarkably similar. It would appear that the reason for their differing alignments had to do with the cohort of teachers and learning contexts used to derive them. However, no matter which breed of expressive style you choose – either teacher immediacy or teacher enthusiasm, the research findings for both styles were clear and unequivocal. Teaching style can and does have an effect on pupil behaviour (Babad, 2005).

Recently, while we were discussing teacher expressiveness with a colleague, he asked us two simple questions: 'How good are students at reading this teacher expressiveness "thing"?' and 'If they're good at it, how does it affect their learning?' These two questions lead us appropriately to the next two chapters.

So far we have covered...

Teachers who are perceived as enthusiastic or charismatic owe much of this to 'nonverbal pzazz', or what we would call their X-Factor. They leak their emotions through their voice, their bodies and their movements. Once, emotions were seen more as substitutes on the bench, rather than key players on the pitch of learning. However, this has changed. We are now more aware of the need for emotionally literate schools.

5

How Good are Students at Reading your X-Factor?

Even babies can read your X-Factor!

Sensitivity to nonverbal communication begins within hours of your arrival into this world. Even babies are aware of the X-Factor! Research by Johnson *et al.* in 1991 found that within hours of birth, we are sensitive to nonverbal communication. New-born babies will look longer at stimuli that appear face-like. They will also track these stimuli with their eyes. Indeed, after just a few days of life, babies will imitate certain facial expressions and gestures (Field *et al.*, 1982). One of the great studies in this area concerned the 'over the cliff' study by Sorce *et al.*, in 1985. Undertaken with babies who were one year old, the study involved presenting babies with a visual cliff. The majority of babies crossed the cliff when their mothers posed happy expressions. However, no infants crossed the cliff when their mothers posed fearful expressions. Needless to say, the experiments did not actually involve babies crawling off cliffs! The point here is simple. The ability to perceive and detect nonverbal signals is innate and starts from your first week on this earth.

Moving beyond the baby stage, it appears that we develop our skills in reading nonverbal communication until about the age 30 (but can stop earlier – even as low as 20 years) (Knapp and Hall, 2002). There is good news if you are a woman. Much of the research indicates that women are better than men at reading nonverbal 'cues', especially when they come from the face (Briton and Hall, 1995).

One of the main messages coming from the literature on children's abilities to read nonverbal communication centres on their happiness. A range of studies show that children in preschool and elementary school who score highly on tests to do with their skills in reading the face, posture, gesture and tone of voice are also popular, less anxious, more socially competent, less emotionally disturbed, less aggressive, less depressed and most significantly for the classroom, have a high belief that one's outcomes are controlled by oneself rather than by other people or simple chance (for example: Baum and Nowicki, 1998; Izard *et al.*, 2001; McClure and Nowicki, 2001). In simple terms, if the child is good at reading nonverbal communication, then there is a good chance he/she will be happier.

Children and the X-Factor

Not only are they happy, work by a number of researchers has found that children scoring higher on tests which rate their abilities to read nonverbal communication also score higher on academic achievement. It is here that the most interesting twist in the tale occurs. Research by Halberstadt and Hall in 1980 found that students who scored highly on the PONS test, which rates their abilities to read nonverbal communication, were perceived by their teachers as being smarter. But the fascinating thing is that such teacher perceptions of the child being smarter did not always match their IQ tests.

In 2001, Izard *et al.* undertook research on five year olds. They examined their abilities to read facial expressions and found that children's abilities to read facial expressions at that age predicted teachers' ratings of their academic competence a full four years later (when they were aged nine). It is most likely that young children who are sensitive to nonverbal communication create such a good impression that adults actually attribute more intelligence to them than they actually have (Knapp and Hall, 2006, 78). This then creates a self-fulfilling prophesy. As teachers we think they are smarter so we tend to teach towards them more, and therefore they learn more!

There is also another twist in the tale of pupils' abilities to read nonverbal communication. Perhaps, at some point or other, you have joked with a child that if they watch too much television they will get square eyes. As children we were always told to go outside and get some fresh air, etc. However, work by Feldman *et al.*, in 1996 found that elementary school children who watched more than 14 hours of television per week were more accurate at decoding facial expressions of emotion than their counterparts who only watched seven hours or fewer per week.

In examining students' sensitivity to nonverbal communication itself, DePaulo and Rosenthal (1979) found that children are very adept at deciphering nonverbal clues about adults' emotional states. Using the PONS test, they examined children's perceptions of various nonverbal behaviours among adults. Their findings were very interesting. They found that as children develop, so too does their capacity and accuracy in making judgements about adult nonverbal behaviour. In particular, they found that children use the face and voice as key indicators of adult intentions and messages. Although the speed at which children process facial expressions improves with age, it varies according to different facial expressions of emotion. For example,

FIGURE 5.1 Children are quick to detect happiness.

happiness is detected more quickly than sadness, anger or fear (Boyatzis *et al.*, 1993). Beyond the age of ten, children's accuracy in decoding facial expressions is nearly comparable with adults (Feldman and Tyler, 2006).

Some studies provide some stark and indeed fascinating findings which ultimately indicate that your X-Factor is a 'fast factor' in predicting students' evaluations of your work (for example: Ambady and Rosenthal, 1993; Babad *et al.* 2003, 2004). These studies show that if students were exposed to just ten seconds of a teacher's nonverbal communication, without any reference to educational content, the expressive behaviours they witness during those ten seconds provide them with enough information to predict their end-of-course evaluations of the teacher.

Within the primary classroom, some very interesting work has been undertaken by Neill (1989) which shows that students, particularly in the more senior classes, are able to detect how a teacher can betray their feelings nonverbally. Take for example the 'uncertain teacher'. In this case, the teacher expressed confidence verbally; however, his nonverbal behaviour, such as hand movements or a tendency to pace and rock, betrayed his real feelings of insecurity. In these situations, the students' abilities to differentiate between teachers' verbal frontage of confidence and their nonverbal leakage of uncertainty and insecurity revealed the sophistication and accuracy of students' abilities to read nonverbal clues.

Now that we have established that children are very good at reading your X-Factor, the next chapter will look more closely at the question as to whether students' abilities to read this X-Factor actually makes any difference to their achievement.

FIGURE 5.2 Does this teacher give messages of confidence?

So far we have covered...

From an early age, children are adept at reading nonverbal communication. Research indicates that the better the child is at reading this communication, the stronger the chances are that they are happy. We must remember that from early childhood, particularly after the age of ten years, students read adults' nonverbal communication perceptively and can make inferences about you as a teacher within seconds of meeting you. They can make astute observations about your intentions, telling for example whether you are putting on a brave face. On the other hand, as teachers we also make assumptions about pupils' abilities based on their capacities to read nonverbal signs and signals. These assumptions are not always accurate.

The X-Factor and Pupil Achievement

Does the X-Factor make a difference to learning?

As we mentioned earlier, one of our colleagues stumped us one day with perhaps one of the biggest questions of this book – 'It's all well and good having an X-Factor, but what difference does it make to pupils' learning?' It was a big question, and we hope we have a big answer. The problems with 'measuring classroom nonverbal behaviour' and indeed in 'measuring' pupil achievement make such a question most difficult to answer. There are a large number of studies which analyse the connections between teacher nonverbal communication and pupil achievement. Recently, Klinzing and Aloisio (2004) analysed a significant number of these studies and collated research data spanning almost half a century. So what did they find?

Their work found that there is a significant connection between teacher nonverbal expressiveness and pupil achievement. They also made the important finding that teacher nonverbal expressiveness is 'comparable with other variables found to be related to achievement' (9). In their trawl of the research they found that there were significant positive effects on pupil achievement in those studies which examined frequent gesturing (Rosenshine, 1970), occasional teacher gaze (Breed, 1971), frequent teacher gaze (Otterson and Otterson, 1980), high rates of eye-contact (Driscoll, 1969), high rates of gesturing (Driscoll, 1969), dynamic voice tone (Driscoll, 1969) and high enthusiasm (Ware and Williams, 1975, 1977).

Other writers have found similar connections between nonverbal communication and learning, with some even claiming that nonverbal communication is more powerful than verbal communication when it comes to learning. For example, McCroskey *et al.* (2006, 425) argue that 'the instructional research to date suggests that nonverbal factors may have a much stronger impact on learning than do verbal factors'. In this regard, some authors point to the importance of nonverbal communication in arousing feelings and attitudes in the learner towards what they are learning and towards who is teaching it. The nonverbal communication of the teacher stimulates what McCroskey *et al.* call 'affective meaning'. This means that the students develop an emotional connection with the subject and with the teacher. Take, for example, the scenarios where students select subjects to study. If a student likes a teacher, and the subject he or she teaches, there is a good chance they will take another class from that teacher. These students will have a greater chance in this subject area as opposed to students who do not respond positively to the teacher.

Long-term v. short-term learning

Researchers also make a very important point here. When we teach, we usually have a set lesson to cover, say, for example, photosynthesis at Year 7. We have definite objectives for the lesson which are often short term. Do they know what chlorophyll is? Can they name the stages in the energy conversion process? What role does the sun have in the process? And so on. We often check for this learning at the end of the lesson. Our educational goals are focused on the short term. This mirrors many of the educational approaches across the globe – the focus is on short-term learning. Can they identify, name, summarise, classify, organise, argue, synthesise, reason and so on? It is probably a product of the manner in which we assess, with the strong emphasis on cognitively measurable outcomes as opposed to long-term affective predispositions.

You may remember that we started this chapter with the question: Does your X-Factor make a difference to learning? The answer is yes. The emotional connections our students make with school last a long time. There are some theorists who argue that because we spend the start of our lives in school (as opposed to the end of our lives!), then long-term learning must be an important part of the schooling process. It has to last a lifetime! For example, McCroskey (1998) argues that long-term learning is the most important form of learning. While schools are seen as teaching the content of many disciplines, they are also involved in the development of positive attitudes to learning and equipping us with lifelong learning skills. It is here that the X-Factor really comes into play. Because nonverbal communication has been shown to have a major influence on our emotions and affect (how we feel about the teacher, the subject and so on) it is therefore critical in the formation of these long-term memories (McCroskey *et al.*, 2006). In short, your X-Factor while being relevant to the classroom on a daily basis will also have an impact long term, influencing your students' attitudes and emotional connections with learning on a long-term basis.

An earlier chapter considered teacher immediacy. Here again the X-Factor is important and has been shown to have a powerful impact on instructional outcomes. McCroskey *et al.* (2006) point out that teachers with strong nonverbal communication skills have been found to influence learning outcomes, but not necessarily in a direct manner. Their influence extends into other domains beyond the typically 'measurable' learning objectives. Students have increased 'affinity' for the teacher, they have a greater liking for the subject being taught and they have better perceptions of themselves as learners. These teachers also provide their students with more 'referent power'. What is referent power? People with referent power are people who are seen as positive models. Students may or may not wish to emulate these people. They are perceived as credible and most importantly, 'task attractive'. Thus there are a wide range of benefits from the development of your X-Factor ranging from increased cognitive to affective learning. Are these benefits the same for all pupils? What about students with special educational needs?

So far we have covered...

Nonverbal communication is a significant variable related to achievement. Teacher expressiveness impacts on learning and some research suggests that nonverbal factors may have a much stronger impact on learning than do verbal factors. Students develop an emotional connection with what they learn and with you as a teacher. Of importance here is the possible influence of your X-Factor on 'task attractiveness' and in arousing feelings and attitudes in the learner towards what they are learning and towards you as their teacher.

7

The X-Factor and Special Education

Children with special educational needs and reading nonverbal communication

Pupils who have special educational needs may not always read nonverbal communication as effectively or as accurately as other pupils. Their teachers need to be more conscious of the manner in which they communicate with them. Perhaps one of the most poignant examples of this comes from a quote by the author Oliver Sacks who described the experiences of an autistic girl as follows: 'something was going on between other kids, something swift, subtle, constantly changing – an exchange of meanings ... a swiftness of understanding ... she wondered if they were all telepathic' (Sacks, 1993, 116). This quote indicates the turmoil and indeed bewilderment which autistic children must experience as they endeavour to communicate in a world where nonverbal communication is so important. Autistic children are not as adept as their peers in reading nonverbal communication, most especially when such communication concerns the face and voice intonation (Rutherford *et al.*, 2002). For example, they show severe gaze avoidance and tend to communicate with adults if they are sure that there will be little eye contact. This tendency to avoid eye contact also arose in Puttallaz and Gottman's studies of depressed children (1981). They noted that there was a distinct tendency for depressed children to avoid gaze and to avoid eye contact. Obviously this affected their abilities to communicate nonverbally.

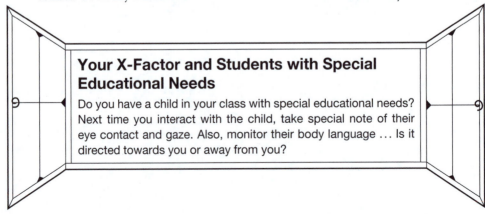

Your X-Factor and Students with Special Educational Needs

Do you have a child in your class with special educational needs? Next time you interact with the child, take special note of their eye contact and gaze. Also, monitor their body language ... Is it directed towards you or away from you?

Almost across all domains of special education, it is evident that these children process nonverbal signs and signals differently. It is quite notable in relation to students who are disruptive. McCuller's (1983) classroom observational work with disruptive children yielded some very remarkable insights into their abilities to decode nonverbal signals. He found that disruptive children may read nonverbal signs and signals inaccurately. Furthermore, by comparison to others, these children were found to be less sensitive to signals of annoyance or control from the class teacher. Interestingly, teachers' nonverbal messages for these kinds of students were clearer than with non-disruptive children.

These findings also resonate with the work of Russell *et al.* (2003) who found that disturbed, delinquent and abused children were less adept at identifying facial expressions of emotions than were their nondisturbed counterparts. This ability to read and decode facial signals accurately also arises with aggressive boys. In their work with these kinds of boys, Dodge and Newman (1981) found that aggressive boys may tend to see aggressiveness in neutral stimuli. For example, these boys, relative to non-aggressive boys, over-attribute hostile intent to their peers in situations where the peer's intent for a frustrating outcome is ambiguous.

Early life experiences

It appears that having damaging experiences in early life may affect the accuracy with which people can decode nonverbal signals. In their work with college students, Hodgins and Belch (2000) found that those college students who had been exposed to parental violence while growing up were worse at judging happy signals than their counterparts. Pollak and Sinha (2002) found that children who were abused and maltreated when young, were quicker than their peers in identifying anger in the face. Cooley and Triemer (2002) found that for boys with severe emotional disturbance, improvements in nonverbal decoding skills influenced interpersonal effectiveness in a positive way.

Reading nonverbal cues as the child grows older

Difficulties with reading nonverbal cues and signals do not necessarily improve as the child grows older. In his work, Neill (1991) established that for some special needs children, the progressional development of their communication skills did not keep pace with their peers. He noted that these children may fail to develop normal sensitivities to nonverbal signals as they grow older. Within the classroom context, Neill (1991) argues that such behaviour has two implications for the teacher. First, the teacher must be aware of the impact of their own nonverbal behaviours on these students. Second, the teacher must be aware of the specific needs of these students with respect to nonverbal communication.

Exemplar 4: How do Students read Nonverbal Communication?

How often have we 'spoken' to boys or girls who are 'acting up'? Perhaps if you have worked as a form teacher, there have been occasions where a student is sent to you because of some incident. But the question is: do you ever think of asking the student how they think the injured party feels based on their facial expressions? We always presume that their skills in reading and detecting the nonverbal communication of the 'offending situation' are accurate. Often, students will tell you 'he was looking at me funny' or 'I could tell from the look of her that she was jeering me'. If it is a group interview, should we establish whether the other party was actually 'looking funny'? Moreover, as we disentangle the 'offending incident' in an endeavour to clarify the pupils' understanding of it, we need to watch our own body language. Do you smile? Folding the arms, frowning, glaring, leaning forward and staring may be interpreted more aggressively than you think. Moreover, in the 'interview' with the 'offender', watch their body language and facial expressions. What is their eye contact like? Their gestures? Their posture?

So far we have covered...

Pupils with special educational needs do not always read nonverbal signs and signals as accurately as their peers. In some cases, they may avoid certain forms of nonverbal communication. For example, autistic children can avoid eye contact.

Part Conclusion

Nonverbal communication is woven into many aspects of psychology and pedagogy. Your X-Factor is hard-wired into your psyche and plays an important role in how we learn and how we teach. We collect information nonverbally on a continuous basis, with such information playing a key role in the formulation of emotional responses and memories. These can last a long time and accordingly are critical when we think about short- and long-term learning objectives. Part I hopefully has shown you that nonverbal communication has been around since our early ancestors and that there are solid reasons for exploiting it in the classroom context. Students are adept at reading nonverbal communication and such reading does have an impact on educational achievement. Having covered the educational value of developing your X-Factor, the next section looks closely at a number of specific features of nonverbal communication, such as smiling, eye contact, body language, use of space and so on.

Part II

The X-Factor Orchestra – Getting to know the Various Instruments

CHAPTER
8
Smiling

Smiles are easily spotted

Smiling is one of the most important aspects of your X-Factor to develop. Smiling is good for you and for those around you. Politicians are constantly being told by their image consultants to smile. One amusing example of this concerns the British politician, Gordon Brown and the creation of the 'Gordon Brown smile' in 2007. Unfortunately for Mr Brown, he seemed to overdo it, and while in parliament in November 2007, Vince Cable the acting leader of the Liberal Democrats remarked: 'The house has noticed the prime minister's remarkable transformation from Stalin to Mr Bean' (Borg, 2008, 75).

On the other hand, if we think of former US president, Bill Clinton, then his 'brave smile' immediately comes to mind. This smile is not a pure expression of happiness. Knapp and Hall (2006) argue that when

FIGURE 8.1 The brave smile.

producing this smile, Bill Clinton was conveying a mixture of pride, determination, modesty and concern. This was achieved by the paradoxical combination of the down-turned mouth, the set chin and the 'smile wrinkles' around the eyes. So we must be careful about when and how we use smiles. One of the key reasons for this is that humans are particularly adept at spotting smiles.

Smiles are the most recognisable form of nonverbal communication. We can see them more clearly than any other type. Believe it or not, a smile can be perceived from a distance of 300 ft; the length of a football field (Blum, 1998, 34). Smiles are one of the key indicators of happiness and we all like to recognise happiness. We have heard of people with 'lovely smiles', 'a smile that lit up her face' and of course the expression 'a smile from ear to ear'. Smiles are very important to the human race.

Real and false smiles

While there are many variations to the kinds of smiles we see on people's faces, there are two particular kinds of smiles which deserve specific mention. These are real smiles and false smiles. In a real smile, the 'zygomatic' muscles in the face are mobilised caus-ing a movement of the lips and most importantly a crinkling at the corner of the eyes. These are real smiles and are sometimes called Duchenne smiles, after a French neurol-ogist Duchenne de Boulogne who first studied them in 1862. According to Gosselin *et al.* (2002), children as young as nine years old can distinguish between these real smiles and the false feigned ones.

FIGURE 8.2 Which is the real smile?

On the other hand, the false smile does not reach the eyes. For a false smile, 'the muscle around the eye does not obey the will; it is only brought into play by a true feeling, by an agreeable emotion. It's inertia in smiling unmasks a false friend' (Duchenne de Boul-ogne, 1990). The key to spotting the real from the fake smile rests in deciphering whether there is movement around the corner of the eyes. Have a look at the pictures of the smiles in Figure 8.2 and decide which one is the real smile. The answer is at the end of this paragraph. From an early age, we are able to produce real and false smiles. According to Fox and Davidson (1987), a ten-month infant can produce real and fake smiles. If a stranger approaches the infant, he or she will produce a smile without move-ment of the muscles around the eye. On the other hand, when the mother approaches, the infant produces a smile which involves movement of these eye muscles. The answer to our earlier question is that the real smile is the one on the left.

Smiles make us feel good

We should try to produce real smiles as often as possible. Ekman (2003, 207) notes that 'people who frequently show smiles involving the muscle around the eye report feeling more happiness, have lower blood pressure, and are reported by their spouses and friends to be happy'. Some fascinating studies have been undertaken in this area. For example, in 1997, Keltner and Bonanno found that people discussing the death of a spouse who managed to show smiles that involve the eye muscles (the real smile), had reduced grief two years later. In another study in 2001, Harker and Keltner analysed the photographs of women in college yearbooks. They found that those women who showed smiles involving the muscles around the eyes (real smiles) reported less distress and greater overall emotional and physical well-being a full 30 years later. In short, smiling is good for you!

Smiles are felt by the receiver

There is also another old expression which gives us great insight into the power of smiling and that is: 'smiling eyes'. When the human is genuinely happy, he/she pro-duces what Ekman (1997) calls a 'felt smile'. These smiles are felt by the receiver. How can this be? When you smile, the person to whom it is directed is affected biologically (Dimberg and Ohman, 1996). Their autonomic nervous system is activated causing the release of endorphins which produce a 'feel good' emotional effect. So in addition to smiling being good for yourself, it is also good for those around you. We have good reason for highlighting this, as smiling should be an important part of your X-Factor. As a teacher, it will have effects both on yourself and others, such as pupils, parents and colleagues.

Smiling in the classroom

There are a number of studies that highlight the positive impact which smiling can have in the classroom. Studies by Keith *et al.*, in 1974 found that student teachers who smiled more often and who managed to smile for longer periods of time conducted classes where their students spent more time thinking, they answered questions more often, they discussed topics more readily and their responses in the classroom were more spontaneous.

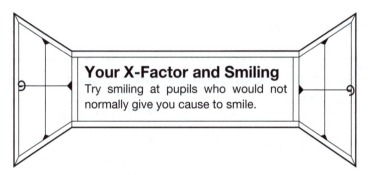

Your X-Factor and Smiling
Try smiling at pupils who would not normally give you cause to smile.

There are, however, some situational contexts to bear in mind. Studies by Neill in 1989 show that as teachers we need to be careful when and why we smile. In particular, this relates to perceptions of power. Neill showed pictures of smiling teachers to students. In some instances, these students perceived the smiling teacher as being 'weaker than frowning teachers'. This obviously relates to classroom behaviour management and constructs of power within the classroom. The studies point to the need for ground rules within the classroom before one begins 'grinning like an imbecile'!

There are other studies which provide some very interesting insights into the manner in which children are pre-programmed to respond to smiles on a gender basis. This pre-programming has its roots in what Larsen-Helweg *et al.* (2004) call 'male' and 'female language'. Basically, there are features of male language which 'work to facilitate hierarchy and dominance', while there are features of female language which work to facilitate 'cooperation and intimacy' (358). There is an interesting twist in this tale. In 1971, a team led by Bugenthal (1971) found that preschool children value father's smiles more than mother's smiles. The basis for this differentiation lay in the fact that women tend to be more expressive nonverbally than men. Therefore when a father smiled, it was more valued as it was delivered more contingently and accordingly had more informational value. Neill (1991) makes the interesting point that male teachers have an advantage over female teachers in the world of smiles because students are pre-programmed to pay more attention to male smiles.

We also need to be conscious of the manner in which we smile. Studies by Stein (1976) and Brophy and Good (1974) found that smiling can be related to teacher expectancy. In other words, we are more likely to smile towards high-achieving pupils.

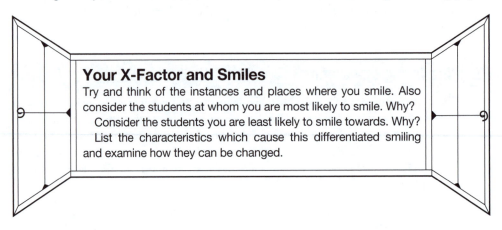

Your X-Factor and Smiles

Try and think of the instances and places where you smile. Also consider the students at whom you are most likely to smile. Why?

Consider the students you are least likely to smile towards. Why?

List the characteristics which cause this differentiated smiling and examine how they can be changed.

Exemplar 5: Using Smiles and Facial Expression in a Lesson

You are studying the following lines of Shakespeare's *King Lear*:

> Who should express her goodliest. You have seen
> Sunshine and rain at once: her smiles and tears
> Were like, a better way; those happy smiles
> That played on her ripe lip seemed not to know
> What guests were in her eyes

(Act IV, Scene III, Gentleman)

Try asking the students to act out these smiles. To make facial expressions depicting the 'guests' (tears) which were in Cordelia's eyes, to think of times in their own lives of 'happy smiles' as a means of investigating the characters and themes of the play.

So far we have covered...

Smiles are one of the most important potions in your X-Factor magic kit. The human can quickly spot a smile. There are two types of smile to focus on – real and false. False smiles do not reach the eyes and are feigned. Real smiles reach the eyes and are good for you. They are also good for those around you as they provoke a positive biological reaction in the recipient. Smiles are important in the classroom, but we must be careful that we do not differentiate our smiles, by smiling more at higher achieving pupils.

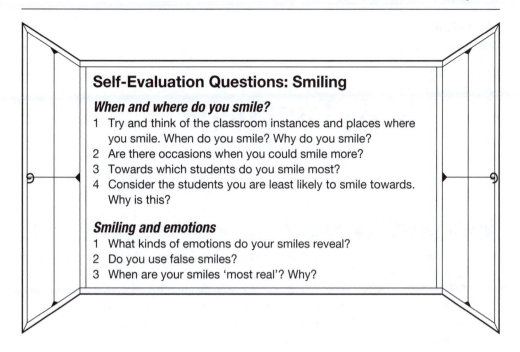

Self-Evaluation Questions: Smiling

When and where do you smile?

1 Try and think of the classroom instances and places where you smile. When do you smile? Why do you smile?
2 Are there occasions when you could smile more?
3 Towards which students do you smile most?
4 Consider the students you are least likely to smile towards. Why is this?

Smiling and emotions

1 What kinds of emotions do your smiles reveal?
2 Do you use false smiles?
3 When are your smiles 'most real'? Why?

9

Body Language

Body language is big!

Are you familiar with the action song 'head, shoulder, knees and toes, knees and toes'? Children love it. Why? Because it gives them an opportunity to rise from the chains of their desks and move about. And as we all know, children have lots of energy and like to move about. They like to use their bodies. Our bodies are continuously moving, even when we sleep. This chapter of the book looks at the messages conveyed through your use of the body – body language.

FIGURE 9.1 He said I was wet – I never heard such nonsense!

There is a multitude of books and magazines that examines body language, and in particular the body language of flirtation. For example, does she flick her hair? Did he fold his arms? Do her feet point towards him?... and so on. You may be unaware of the range of messages and emotions you can convey through your posture and body language (Neill, 1991). In their book, *Body Language for Competent Teachers*, Sean Neill and Chris Caswell (1993) identify a broad range of emotional dispositions and characteristics which teachers can reveal through their body language. Here are some of them: indifference, casualness, friendliness, strictness, interest, easygoing disposition, unfriendliness, helpfulness and dominance. As you can see, there is a wide range of emotions which we can convey through our use of body language. Surprised? This reminds us of the 'fish don't know they are wet' phenomenon. Much of what we do in terms of body language and indeed all nonverbal communication can occur without us being consciously aware of it – as far as we know, fish don't know they are wet!

A classic example of this relates to Lt General David McKiernan. In June 2003, the *Boston Globe* reported that he was taken off the list of possible candidates for the top position of Army Chief of Staff because of what Pentagon officials observed as bad body language. Why? Apparently, while Lt General McKiernan was listening to a speech being given by the Secretary of State, Donald Rumsfeld, in Iraq, he stood with his arms folded and 'did not respond in a positive way' during applause lines (Knapp and Hall, 2006). This anecdotal example highlights the manner in which body language is observed and in particular what is known as open and closed body language.

The X-Factor and open/closed body language

One of the important aspects of your X-Factor that we are going to try to develop concerns your use of body language. No doubt you have heard of the terms open and closed body language. So what are they? Basically, the study of open and closed body language involves looking at how we use the hands, the arms, the trunk and the head. For example, if someone sits down and promptly folds their arms and crosses their legs, we can describe this as closed body language. When people use their body in this way, they are in effect erecting a barrier (Lyle, 1990). Such

FIGURE 9.2 Closed body language.

actions may have a physiological basis. If you cross your arms you are protecting your upper body from attack (unless you're cold) and if you cross your legs, then similarly you are protecting your lower body from unwanted assault. Jane Lyle (1990) describes it as a form of self-preservation. When the arms and elbows are pulled tightly into the body they signal that we may be experiencing feelings of acute nervousness or chronic anxiety. So why then do we pull these limbs tightly towards us? There are a number of possible answers. We may be engaged in 'self-preservation' as mentioned earlier, or we may be giving ourselves a hug, a self-hug. These self-hugs are attempts at self-comfort. In stressful situations we may do this quite a lot (Cohen, 2007).

On the other hand, open body language is communicated when your body is exposed. There is a distinct 'lack of barriers of any sort' (Borg, 2008, 26). Your hands are usually on view, possibly the palms of your hands, your posture is free and easy and eye contact is good (Borg, 2008). By comparison to closed body language, the limbs are not brought in close to the body. Needless to say, the most appealing posture to adopt when talking to people is one which shows an open personality (Lyle, 1990). Legs are side by side, but not tightly clamped together, with hands resting in the lap or perhaps being used from time to time, to underline what is being said.

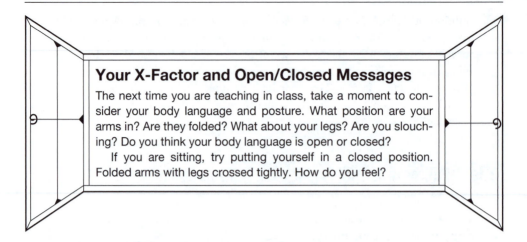

Your X-Factor and Open/Closed Messages

The next time you are teaching in class, take a moment to consider your body language and posture. What position are your arms in? Are they folded? What about your legs? Are you slouching? Do you think your body language is open or closed?

If you are sitting, try putting yourself in a closed position. Folded arms with legs crossed tightly. How do you feel?

Body language and likeability

By developing an open body language, you are also developing your 'likeability factor'. In 1972, Albert Mehrabian conducted a number of experimental studies on immediacy, or behaviours that generate closeness and prompt people to say: 'I like him' or 'I like her'. His work identified the following aspects of nonverbal communication, and in particular body language, which are connected with the likeability factor: forward leaning, close proximity, eye contact, openness of arms, possible exposed palms, openness of body, postural relaxation and positive facial expressions. Obviously it is important for students to like their teachers, as you will recall in the discussion about the 'teacher immediacy effect' in Chapter 2. (Remember – teacher immediacy has to do with the 'psychological closeness' teachers establish with students. Aloofness can best be associated with non-immediate behaviours.)

What about leaning towards students? The first question we want to ask you is whether you are aware of the way you lean as you interact with students? In 1987, a team led by Richmond looked at how teachers use their bodies in the classroom and found that teachers who leaned forward, who used direct eye contact and who used purposeful gestures were perceived as likeable and approachable by their students. Other work by Neill (1991) found that a teacher leaning forward towards a child can be interpreted as teacher enthusiasm for the answer. On the other hand, the same movement with a frown would be interpreted in a threatening manner. Patrick Miller (2005, 47) points out that 'we lean forward when we like someone' and 'we lean away from individuals we have negative attitudes toward'.

The manner in which we move is also relevant to the classroom. Perhaps one of the most widely known studies on movement and open/closed body language was the 'Shakespeare Study' by Aronoff

FIGURE 9.3 Smooth and graceful movements depicting warm and sympathetic characters.

and colleagues in 1992. In this study the researchers identified two groups of characters in classical ballet. The first group played dangerous roles, such as Macbeth or the Angel of Death while the second group adopted warm and sympathetic roles such as Juliet and Romeo. Their analysis of the various ballet performances indicated that threatening characters used much more angular and diagonal postures while sympathetic and warm characters adopted rounded and curved motions. This study is very valuable as it highlights the importance of the manner in which we use our bodies. As teachers we may use sharp, sudden and angular movements of the body which can be interpreted as threatening – remember the alert data base from Chapter 2 and the manner in which we are acutely aware of signs and signals which may threaten our welfare and survival.

On the other hand, rounded and curved movements can be envisaged as sympathetic and less threatening. Miller (1979) gives us the great example of kneeling close to a pupil to offer help. For example, kneeling beside the desk of the pupil. Here the teacher's posture and body position is on a par with the student, and in particular indicates a non-threatening and helpful stance. We will discuss this in greater detail in the chapter on teacher use of space.

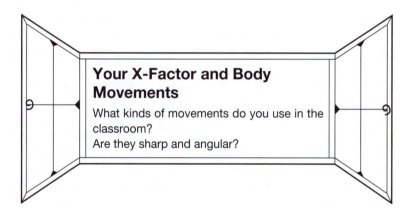

Your X-Factor and Body Movements

What kinds of movements do you use in the classroom?
Are they sharp and angular?

So far we have covered…

Body posture and orientation convey a huge range of emotions. Forward leaning, close proximity, eye contact, openness of arms, possible exposed palms, openness of body, postural relaxation and positive facial expressions are all connected to your likeability factor. Two particular types of body language also stand out – open and closed. When open, our bodies are more exposed and there is less 'closing off' or erecting of barriers such as folded arms. The way we move our bodies is also important. Is it angular and sharp or smooth and flowing? As you would expect, the sharper moves have undertones of more threatening emotions.

Using the body to mirror what we say

FIGURE 9.4 Raise your hand if you know the answer.

Perhaps one of the most potent ways in which you can develop your classroom X-Factor relates to the use of the body to augment or even supplement the words we use. Think of the manner in which a match referee can point to the line without using any words and yet the player knows he has been sent off. When we consider our use of body language in the classroom, there are a number of instances where it replicates or augments the words we use. Grinder (1996) points to the value of using body language to communicate classroom rules. So for example, the teacher might say: 'Raise your hand if you know the answer' while also raising his/her hand to show how to do this.

This brings us to the topic of using the body to mirror what we say. As far back as 1966, it was shown that our speech and movements are rhythmically co-ordinated (Condon, 1976; Condon and Ogston, 1966). So how does this happen? We may give a slight jerk of the head or the hand to stress particular points in our speech. We sometimes gesture at the most significant parts of what we are saying and then there are movements of the head and the hands around the beginning and end of sentences or phrases. One of the interesting aspects of such movements is a tendency to turn the head to one side, to flex the neck or to extend the neck after we have made a point, indicating the point is made and that transition to a new one is imminent.

There are other markers which we can also use. We may use eye blinks at the beginning or end of words. We may make minuscule movements of the head from side to side when using words which we hyphenate when writing. Our posture can also shift. For example, leaning back while you listen and then leaning forward when you talk. Postural change can happen when we are moving to a new stage of the interaction, especially at the beginning and end of speech segments (Bull and Brown, 1977). For example, our body movements can change before we say something. We make more extensive movements when the impending speech unit is large.

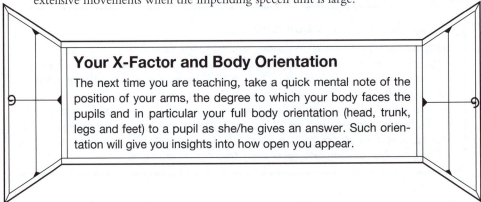

Your X-Factor and Body Orientation

The next time you are teaching, take a quick mental note of the position of your arms, the degree to which your body faces the pupils and in particular your full body orientation (head, trunk, legs and feet) to a pupil as she/he gives an answer. Such orientation will give you insights into how open you appear.

Your X-Factor is just like mine! – mimicry

Grinder (1996) suggests that when a teacher wants to acquire pupils' attention, they should remain still, prompting the students to mimic this behaviour in what is known as mirroring. Have a look at the picture alongside this paragraph – what do you notice about the people in it? Yes, they are mirroring each other. Also known as the chameleon effect, there are a

FIGURE 9.5 Mirroring.

number of situations where humans mimic the mannerisms, posture and facial expressions of the people they interact with. This is a good thing! It indicates that when we are communicating at a meaningful level, we mimic each other's body language – in a subconscious way. One particular breed of such mimicry is postural congruence. This occurs when both speaker and listener exhibit the same behaviour at the same time (Knapp and Hall, 2006). It can involve crossing the legs, crossing the arms, sitting in a particular position, leaning and head propping. When you do this you either match the person with whom you are talking or mirror their posture. Researchers such as LaFrance (1985) and Trout and Rosenfeld (1980) note that postural congruency occurs during periods of positive speech, and is rated as an indicator of cooperation and rapport.

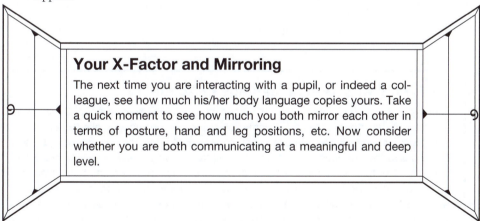

Your X-Factor and Mirroring

The next time you are interacting with a pupil, or indeed a colleague, see how much his/her body language copies yours. Take a quick moment to see how much you both mirror each other in terms of posture, hand and leg positions, etc. Now consider whether you are both communicating at a meaningful and deep level.

So far we have covered...

Our bodies and voice punctuate and act like mirrors for what we say. When we are engaged in a deep conversation our bodies also mirror or mimic the posture, facial expressions and mannerisms of the other person.

Lower body and feet

FIGURE 9.6 Do you think Carol is happy with Peter's choice of TV viewing? Look at her lower body.

When we think of the lower body and body language, it is important to look at the overall direction of the body. Have a look at the cartoon on the left and see if you can guess the messages! Some writers such as Pease and Pease (2004) and Lyle (1990) comment that the orientation of the body and the direction of the feet 'give away' a person's true intentions. For example, if the lower body is pointing away from you towards the nearest exit, there is also a good probability that the person in question would prefer to be somewhere else! (Lyle, 1990). Barbara and Alan Pease (2004, 279) describe it succinctly as follows: 'the direction in which a person points his body or feet is a signal of where he would prefer to be going'. It is important to note here, however, that body orientation which is too direct and exceeds expectations can cause discomfort and 'compensatory shifts' by the other person (Hargie and Dickson, 2004, 54).

Do you tend to move your feet and legs as you interact? What does this mean? Mehrabian and Williams (1969) undertook a number of experiments to examine leg movements. One of their findings was that leg and foot movements occur more frequently when the communicators are of a higher status than their addressee or also if the communicators are more relaxed. Interestingly, leg and foot movements were found to be more frequent when the communicator was truthful rather than deceitful. Again, more leg and foot movements were observed when the communicator talked with someone who was non-threatening as opposed to threatening.

Exemplar 6: Body Language in Action

Thomas and Paul have once again managed to find themselves in trouble, this time for charging headlong into Ms Carpenter on the school corridor! While the collision didn't result in any injuries, Ms Carpenter's 'displaced' briefcase has catapulted their behaviour to the attention of the 'school authorities'. The collision was their *coup de grâce*, as they had been fighting earlier in the toilets. The problem has been brought to your attention, and once again you have to try to get to the bottom of the incident. As you talk to the two students and encourage them to be open about discussing the fight and the incident, is your body language open? Do you face them both equally, or is your body directed towards Paul because you think he is more of a victim than a perpetrator? Do you fold your arms when you hear them complain that the incident would never have happened if your last lesson had not run over time causing them to charge down the corridor? Do you nod your head as they answer? Are you within a close distance of the students or are they on the other side of a large desk? Are your gestures soft and flowing or angular and sudden? Do you engage in postural congruency? Do you lean forward or backwards as they speak?

Walking and movement

Have you heard the song: 'Walking back to happiness, woopah, oh yeah, yeah' (Helen Shapiro, 1970)? Even if you haven't heard the song, from the words above, you can probably imagine the singer. We bet you imagine them skipping along. Unconsciously we pay more

FIGURE 9.7 Who do you think has a confident walk?

attention to walking than you may think. Now think of yourself. How do you walk? Do you look at the pavement? Is your walk brisk or slow? As you walk into the classroom, is it bristling with enthusiasm or strangled by nervousness or apathy? Jane Lyle (1990, 20) points out that 'a brisk pace and upright posture indicate a confident individual who has a secure sense of direction'. She also takes the example of happy people. They have a lightness of step and as she points out, are 'eager' to 'move forwards' (20).

On the other hand, there is the dejected individual who shuffles slowly with bowed posture and heavy feet. The X-Factor question for you rests in your awareness of your walking and the emotional messages you convey when so doing. Miller points out that our body movements are often indicators of our self-confidence, energy levels, fatigue, mood and even status. He argues that a happy person will carry a more erect posture than someone who is depressed or shy. Indeed, some researchers suggest that muggers are looking for victims who walk with their shoulders and heads down (2005, 46). These messages are not missed by students. Of course, this is not new news. In the Shakespearean play, *Troilus and Cressida*, Ulysses makes the remark: 'Nay, her foot speaks, her wanton spirits look out,/At every joint and motive of her body' (Act IV, Scene V).

There are good reasons for you to develop a confident walk. By consciously walking in a more confident way, which is relaxed, but with an upright posture, you may notice a difference in yourself. As we mentioned earlier, by actually adopting the physical attributes of a particular emotion we can develop that emotion in ourselves. Lyle (1990) argues that if you walk in an erect, confident, yet relaxed style, people will respond positively towards you. Moreover, it has been shown that correct posture aids voice projection and breathing. Being able to breathe more deeply also helps overcome tension and anxiety.

It is important to note that posture can also be used to communicate dominance. The twist in this tale is that by adopting a relaxed postural style, one can accentuate one's dominance in the group. Mehrabian (1969) found that by adopting a postural position where there are asymmetrical arm positions, a sideways lean, asymmetrical leg positions, backwards lean and relaxed hand movements, we are actually communicating dominance. Indeed, Gallagher (1992) has associated dominance with 'energetic and animated behaviour' where fluid and graceful walking, 'peppy', vigorous behaviours, erect posture and quick or non-lethargic movements can be observed. In this case, 'peppy' refers to energetic and spirited movement. The key point to note here is that these behaviours connote a high degree of actual or potential energy expenditure (Burgoon and Dunbar, 2006). Hence, while it is important to adopt postures which are relaxed, it is also important to note that overdoing such relaxation can convey dominance.

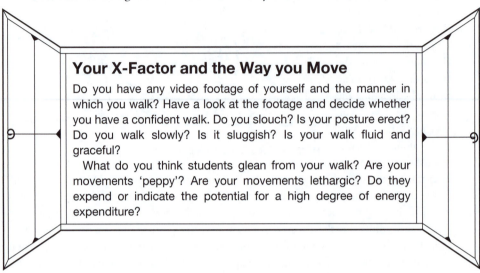

Your X-Factor and the Way you Move

Do you have any video footage of yourself and the manner in which you walk? Have a look at the footage and decide whether you have a confident walk. Do you slouch? Is your posture erect? Do you walk slowly? Is it sluggish? Is your walk fluid and graceful?

What do you think students glean from your walk? Are your movements 'peppy'? Are your movements lethargic? Do they expend or indicate the potential for a high degree of energy expenditure?

Exemplar 7: Using the Feet in a Lesson

You are studying musical beats with an elementary school class. One of the rhymes you use goes as follows:

Music has a beat,
Feel it in your feet
Clip, clop, clip clop,
Like soldiers in the street.

Ask the students to stand up and march like soldiers to the beat of this rhyme, in particular emphasising how they 'stamp' their feet to the beat in the rhyme. This 'walking' will serve as a springboard to analysing beat and rhythm.

Hands

According to Cohen (2007), approximately 12.5 per cent of your brain space is devoted to the use of the hands. The way we use our hands is a fascinating field of study. Take, for example, catwalk models. Naomi Campbell and numerous others learn to strut their stuff, but they also learn where to place their hands. According to Lyle (1990), one hand or perhaps two are resting on the hip bones, drawing attention to the erogenous zones.

As teachers, we are obviously not on the catwalk, but the manner in which we use our hands can give away signals. Hands on your hips can communicate dominance, especially when accompanied by expanding the chest (Argyle, 1988). In some cases, FBI agents take serious note of the hands on the hips or thumbs in the pockets pose, describing them as gunslinger poses and ones to be wary of in criminals. The point here is simple. There are a number of movements we can make with our arms and hands which may cause anxiety in the classroom – or staffroom! However, there are other ways in which we use the hands which also play a key role in conveying confidence and assuredness.

We pay closer attention to the use of the hands than we may realise and we use them a lot. Think of the last sports event you attended or viewed on television. The referee typically uses the hands to give signals to the players. Of course, sometimes the players give signals back! In terms of the actual way in which we use the hands, we are going to pick a few typical uses which arise in the classroom. First, there is the open palm. This is an important signal and as Borg (2008, 111) remarks: 'the palms up position wins hands down'. We associate the use of open palms with openness, honesty and friendliness. Indeed, in ancient times, empty palms indicated that one was not carrying a weapon. So for us as teachers, if we want to present ourselves as open, it is important to use our hands with the palms facing up.

Another type of hand gesture involves joining the hands together and pointing them upwards to look like a church steeple. Steepling is associated with the portrayal of confidence. There are two kinds of steeple – the raised steeple and the lowered steeple. The raised steeple occurs when you place your two palms together and then gently touch the fingertips together. Your elbows are resting on the table. Borg (2008) argues that this type of formation conveys the message of confidence. Indeed, Pease and Pease (2004) comment that when we place the steeple in front of our faces, it gives us a God-like appearance. The lowered steeple arises when the palms and fingertips are once again touching, but this time, the elbows are not propping the steeple, they are resting

FIGURE 9.8 Raised steeple.

FIGURE 9.9 Lowered steeple.

on the table. This type of formation is regarded as giving messages of self-assuredness but also cooperation (Borg, 2008). The use of steeples is fascinating. Pease and Pease (2004) argue that it can often be found in scenarios where a superior and subordinate are interacting, with the superior using the steeple and perhaps also pointing.

There is one other type of communication, involving the hands which humans use quite a lot. It dates back to the Romans, and the gladiators. However, it is also quite prevalent in the modern colosseum of the classroom. We have also encountered it in our own research – the 'thumbs up' signal. It is used to indicate approval. As you would expect, the thumbs up signal also conveys confidence (Borg, 2008). This is a clever use of the hands as one can speak to the entire class, yet also direct messages at specific students at the same time. Sometimes, it can be quite subtle. Think of the late John F. Kennedy and his tendency to have a thumb (or two) sticking out of his pocket. Some commentators note that this was no accident (Borg, 2008).

So far we have covered...

Your feet and body orientation can communicate signals of where you would like to go. We are more inclined to move our feet and legs in situations where we do not feel threatened, where we have higher status and where we are telling the truth. Our walk can communicate messages of eagerness and confidence. Our body movements are often indicators of our self-confidence, energy levels, fatigue, mood and even status. Proper posture assists voice projection. We associate the use of open palms with openness, honesty and friendliness. Steepling is associated with the portrayal of confidence. Thumbs up is a signal of approval.

Where are your hands as you move?

FIGURE 9.10 Projecting confidence: hands clasped behind the back.

There is also the question of what you do with your hands while you sit or walk. For example, while walking, do you take note of where your hands are? We have all seen the archetypal commander inspecting his troops, a policeman on patrol or perhaps even a school inspector walking the school grounds. Where are their hands? Yes, sometimes they are gripped behind the back. You might think that because the hands are behind the back in these cases, we are hiding something. However, Borg (2008) points out that here the hands are not being hidden, rather they project confidence because the individual is happy to expose the vulnerable front of the body.

Also, have you ever thought about the manner in which people clasp their hands behind their backs? Think of the last time you were on 'patrol' in the school yard. Where were your hands? The manner in which we clasp our hands behind our back can give away a lot. Borg (2008) argues that if one of the hands behind the back is gripping the wrist, rather than the hands being clasped together, this could indicate annoyance or frustration. Here you are 'gripping' the wrist of the other hand in a controlling manner, to prevent it being unleashed! Does this sound familiar? The further up the arm you go (e.g. gripping the elbow instead of the hand), the more nervousness/frustration you are feeling. When we think of nervousness there are other things we do with our hands which fall into the category of self-touching.

The X-Factor and self-touching

Think of the occasion when a student asked you for the second time for his exam script, and you remembered it was still in your bureau at home – you probably instantly scratched your head and apologised. This is a classic self-touching exercise. In some of the literature such self-touching behaviours are also described as 'displacement activities'. So why do we do these things? Borg (2008) argues that they help us deal with emotions. They are things we do to help us when we experience inner conflict, torment or frustration of some kind. When we engage in self-touching we are really trying to displace the feeling that is causing us concern. Self-touching is an important part of your body language. We can quickly read if someone is nervous or frustrated by the types of self-touches they engage in. Really, what they are trying to do is displace the feeling.

Self-touching can be associated with anxiety or stress (Knapp and Hall, 2006). Incidentally, baboons also engage in self-touching in situations of stress or anxiety. Other speculations and hypotheses about self-touching include the possibility that we rub ourselves to give ourselves self-assurance. But there are other dimensions to self-touching. Covering one's eyes can be associated with shame or guilt. Self-grooming, such as straightening your hair, or fixing your tie indicate concern for one's self-presentation. The most common thread in explaining self-touching exercises centres on their use as an outlet for nervous energy (Knapp and Hall, 2002). We have all noticed presenters who fix themselves before speaking.

There is little research from the field of education which closely examines the effects of self-touching. Perhaps the closest is Neill's (1991) depiction of an 'uncertain' teacher. This teacher was probably 'self-touching' in a way which revealed anxiety and nervousness. While there are no distinct links with the classroom, the work of a number of researchers in the field is relevant to your classroom 'self-touches'. Desmond Morris (1971) divides 'self-touches' into four categories: shielding, cleaning actions, specialised actions and self-intimacy actions.

The first of these actions is shielding – it can be illustrated by the child or even teacher who puts their hands up to their ears and declares 'I'm not listening'. These kinds of actions are undertaken to reduce information coming in through the senses. Think of our two young friends, Mark and Paul, being frog-marched to the school principal – this time for using Jenny's rag-doll as a goalpost. We have often seen principals cover their eyes in apparent disbelief when 'young offenders' are presented for interview. This serves as a very effective action, signalling to the two

FIGURE 9.11 I have seen enough!

boys that the principal cannot believe that they are once again in the firing line, and communicating long before words are exchanged that this is a tiresome matter for the principal.

Cleaning actions include hair grooming or straightening clothes – a kind of preening. Women apparently do more of this than men. It is also much more prevalent in the early stages of an intimate relationship (Daly *et al.*, 1983).

Specialised actions are used to convey specific messages. For example, we may cup our ear to show we cannot hear someone. We may put our hand under the chin to indicate 'I'm fed up here' (Knapp and Hall, 2006, 284).

Finally, self-intimacy actions, which are very important. These are comforting actions. What is key about these is that we often do them subconsciously. They represent comforting touches by someone else. Examples of these kinds of actions include holding one's hands, folding the arms and crossing the legs. Ekman and Friesen (1969b) undertook some fascinating research in this regard. They asked people to judge a set of films. The films involved a depressed woman who wanted to be discharged from hospital. This woman was pretending to be cheerful and friendly so that the hospital would discharge her. The judges who saw films of the woman's head only thought she was friendly and cheerful. However, it was a different story when the same judges only saw her body actions. When viewing these actions, they concluded that the woman was tense, nervous and disturbed. The key point here is that her body betrayed her real emotional state.

There is one interesting type of self-touching which we stumbled upon in the work of Heaven and McBrayer (2000). Their work suggests that mental concentration can be a cause of self-touching. These kinds of self-touches relate to movements which can be associated with your thinking. In their research, they read a passage to a group of adults. They found that these adults touched themselves more when asked questions about the passage they had just heard, by comparison to just listening to the passage. This brings us to the next piece on self-touches or, as they are sometimes called, adaptors.

We use the expression adaptors here as it relates to things we do which may not necessarily involve self-touching, but do involve touching. As a teacher, you are most likely very aware of these kinds of 'adaptors' as they are frequently the bane of teachers' lives – for example fidgeting. Mehrabian and Friedman (1986) managed to find 40 different variations and looked at scenarios where people tend to fidget. These included watching TV, listening to music, eating and drinking, smoking and last but not least,

daydreaming. This work noted that fidgeting indicated a high need for stimulation, which is no surprise to any of us. Everyday experience in the classroom brings up many examples of students fidgeting with pens, tapping their fingers, manoeuvring books and so on.

Finally, there is one form of self-touch which most of us have witnessed or even done at some point or other. Have you ever noticed people scratching themselves, say, for example, picking at an old scar on their arm. Ekman and Friesen (1972) argue that such scratching is related to one's hostility or suspicion of another person. Theoretically, what is happening here is that these picking and scratching actions are manifestations of aggression. This aggression may be directed at oneself or it may be felt towards

FIGURE 9.12 Manifestations of aggression.

another person. What you do then is direct this aggression inwards to yourself in the form of picking, etc.

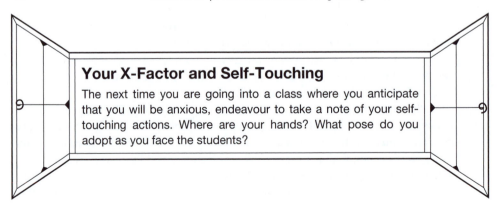

Your X-Factor and Self-Touching

The next time you are going into a class where you anticipate that you will be anxious, endeavour to take a note of your self-touching actions. Where are your hands? What pose do you adopt as you face the students?

Head nodding

When we think of head nodding, there is one story that always comes to mind – it concerns a horse called Clever Hans. He had the X-Factor! In 1900, a man called Wilhelm von Osten purchased a horse called Hans in Berlin. When Von Osten was training his horse, he taught him to count by tapping his front hoof! Yes unusual, we agree, but Hans proved to be fantastic at counting. He was a fast learner. He also learned to add, subtract, multiply, divide and even moved on to solving problems involving fractions and factors! Needless to say, Hans couldn't talk, so the only way he could communicate his answer was by tapping his hoof. He could tell the time, use a calendar and when Von Osten taught Hans an alphabet that could be coded into hoof beats, he began to use the German language. He could answer almost any question – either oral or written. It seemed he had an intelligence which was beyond the human mind.

And so Hans was brought to public audiences where he displayed this profound and unusual ability. People were agog. Needless to say, the world's media became aware of Clever Hans and an investigating committee was established. Professors of psychology and physiology, veterinarians, the Director of Berlin Zoological Gardens and a number of others formed this committee to unlock the magical talents of Hans. Of course, they also wanted to unravel the gimmick at play. The committee decided they would set up an experiment with Hans and, as part of this experiment, Von Osten, his owner, was deliberately excluded. Now with Von Osten absent, how would Clever Hans perform? To everyone's amazement, Hans, once again, astounded the intelligentsia with his answers. The committee announced there was no trickery involved. Hans was a sensation. In fact, we believe he was the first X-Factor sensation!

However, a second commission was established, this time with a new and very clever experiment in mind. Von Osten was asked to whisper one number into Hans' left ear while an experimenter whispered a number into his right ear. Hans was asked to add the two numbers. Neither the experimenter, Von Osten or the assembled crowd knew the answer in advance. Hans looked at the assembled crowd but tapped out the wrong answer. This marked the end for the celebrity status of Hans. More tests of a similar nature ensued and Hans continued to fail. Hans could only tap the answer when someone in his visual field knew the answer and was attentive to the situation. It emerged that Hans could detect human head movements as slight as one-fifth of a millimetre. Head movements accompanied by reduced body tension and a more relaxed disposition changed when Hans reached the correct number of taps. Put simply, he was able to read the body language of the crowd as a signal to stop when he reached the correct number of hoof taps.

What can we learn from this story? Think of the chemistry teacher explaining why ions have positive or negative charges. The teacher has a diagram on the whiteboard and the students are listening. But are they understanding? You ask the question 'Do you understand the explanation?' and, like Hans, check the 'assembled crowd' for head nods or body movements indicating an affirmative answer. Head nodding is a typical response we look for when checking whether students 'are with us'. It is thought to be a nearly universal sign of agreement, similar to bowing and has been shown to be more common in women than men (Larsen-Helweg et al., 2004). There is substantial research which indicates that nodding provides powerful reinforcement to the listener in the amount and type of information he/she is conveying (Matarazzo *et al.*, 1964; Forbes and Jackson, 1980). For example, Forbes and Jackson examined the behaviours of 17–19 year old interviewees for places on an engineering training scheme. They found that eye contact, smiling and nodding were characteristics common to all successful applicants.

Of course there are other head movements too. Shaking your head is the first obvious one which comes to mind. From the work of Hadar and colleagues (1985) we learn that when we shake our heads we may be signalling a query, saying 'no' or perhaps laughing. Of course, it is important to remember that in some parts of India and Bulgaria, the side to side head wobble means 'yes' not 'no'. Head shaking can also be used to underscore intensity or impossibility in what we are saying. Take, for example, when someone says 'You just wouldn't believe how ignorant he was'. We should also watch out for 'slight jerks of the head' when someone is speaking as Knapp and Hall (2002, 244) point out that these slight jerks of the head (or sometimes the hand) often accompany the primary stress points in what we are saying.

Head nodding and back-channel responses

Head nodding falls into the more general category of nonverbal communication known as 'back-channel responses'. Argyle (1988, 111) notes that these responses have a 'powerful effect' on the speaker. So what are they? Back-channel responses are like reinforcements for the speaker and typically take the form of head nods, as discussed already, short vocalisations (e.g. mmm-hmmm), glances and facial expressions. Can you think of another one? Here's a clue – think of the last section! Hopefully you have remembered posture as the answer.

Posture can give messages of agreement or disagreement. Bull (1987) found that when we are listening, agreement can be accompanied by a sideways lean (presumably

FIGURE 9.13 Mirroring.

because we are relaxed) while disagreement can be signalled by defensive, body-closing gestures such as folding the arms. Of course, you may also remember from the last section that we talked about postural congruency (when the two people who are interacting exhibit the same behaviour – it can be a form of mimicry). This too is a form of back-channel response. Postural congruence and non-conscious mimicry have been observed during periods of positive speech, when we want to be liked by others and when we want to talk with the other person as opposed to 'at' them (Knapp and Hall, 2006).

What about students? How perceptive are they of head movements? Some of the educational literature indicates that students are finely tuned to head movements when and if they occur. For example, Allen and Feldman (1978) examined the nonverbal feedback responses of 11 year old children tutoring eight year old children. They found that 'successful tutors' (as rated by their tutees) shook their heads less, nodded more and leaned towards the tutee to a greater degree. Furthermore, these back-channel responses were also found to be closely linked to other specific aspects of nonverbal communication such as eye contact and gazing. These are discussed in Chapter 12.

As a teacher, this chapter has hopefully given you an insight into the many different ways you can 'leak' how you really feel in the classroom. From self-adaptors to hand movements, we can engage in a wide variety of actions which leak our true feelings about a situation. As we discussed in an earlier chapter, our students are alert to these kinds of actions. This chapter has looked largely at how we use our bodies, our limbs, our hands and our posture. While we did look at the use of hands in this chapter, the next chapter looks more closely at the use of gestures and their communicative function. This deserves specific attention as gesture has been the focus of much study and debate in recent times.

 So far we have covered…

The way we carry our hands can communicate messages such as confidence (e.g. holding the hands behind the back) and also restraint (gripping the hands behind the back). We can also give off messages by the way we use our hands in 'self-touching' activities. We may do this if we experience inner conflict, torment or frustration of some kind. They are an outlet for nervous energy. We can quickly read if someone is nervous or frustrated by the types of self-touches they engage in. Sometimes we may rub ourselves to give ourselves self-assurance. Other times we can use the hands to shield and reduce the information coming into the senses, or we may use them in cleaning/grooming actions. Interestingly, some research indicates that mental concentration can be a cause of self-touching. Finally we have the displacement activities well known as fidgeting – a signal that there is a high need for stimulation on the part of the owner.

Self-Evaluation Questions: Body Language

Open and closed body language

1 Is your body language typically open or closed?
2 Is your posture and use of your arms and legs free and easy? Or sharp and sudden? Does it reveal relaxation? Are you sympathetic and warm? Nervous and anxious?
3 Do you frequently make closed body language statements by, for example, folding your arms a lot?

Body language and interaction

1 Are your actions open, conveying that you like the person to whom you are talking? Do they give messages of approachability? Of enthusiasm?
2 Do you lean forward in an enthusiastic manner as you talk to students?
3 Do you orient yourself properly when speaking/listening to students, e.g. do your head, trunk and feet face the student?
4 To what degree do you mirror students as they speak?

Walking

Examine your walk:
Do you have any video footage of yourself and the manner in which you walk? Have a look at the footage and decide whether you have a confident walk.

1 Do you slouch as you walk?
2 Does your walk convey messages of confidence and 'eagerness of step'?
3 Is your posture erect?

Seated position

1 Do you have a vertical sitting posture?
2 Do you slouch? Does this convey confidence?

Movement

1 Are your movements energised, leaking enthusiasm and a high degree of actual or potential energy expenditure?
2 How would you describe your body movements? Are they smooth or sudden?
3 Are they quick or sluggish?

continued

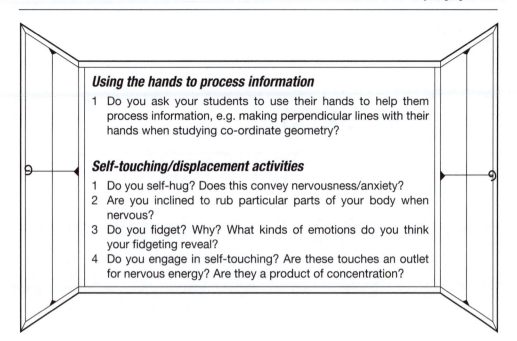

Using the hands to process information

1 Do you ask your students to use their hands to help them process information, e.g. making perpendicular lines with their hands when studying co-ordinate geometry?

Self-touching/displacement activities

1 Do you self-hug? Does this convey nervousness/anxiety?
2 Are you inclined to rub particular parts of your body when nervous?
3 Do you fidget? Why? What kinds of emotions do you think your fidgeting reveal?
4 Do you engage in self-touching? Are these touches an outlet for nervous energy? Are they a product of concentration?

10

Gestures

Everyone gestures

We all use gestures – think of the last time you accidentally pulled out in front of another car and the passing driver waved a clenched fist at you – or something similar! Even baboons gesture! In classrooms, we often see teachers gesturing, for example, they put their fingers to their lips, they raise a hand in the air as a signal for silence, they point to the door and so on. Sigmund Freud (1905/1953, 52) once said about the human: 'if his lips are silent, he chatters with his fingertips'. Gesturing is a key part of our work as teachers and an important component of your X-Factor. Of course, gesturing is as old as the human race. Some gestures can be traced back to southern Italy in the year 690 BCE where we get the image of 'horns' for a bull from bull worship and the head toss for 'no'. The great Roman statesman and philosopher, Cicero, talked about the body being a musical instrument with an eloquence which involved gesticulation as well as speech. Indeed, there are some who argue that the ancient Greeks and Romans relied more on gestures in everyday life having a more 'lively feel for the meaning of gestures' than we do (Wundt, 1921/1973, 66). Indeed, Wundt contended that they were better at reading them than we are today. The X-Factor was alive and well in the villas of Rome and Athens.

Of course, the fact that gesture existed back then and long before is not surprising. There is a neurological basis for gesture. Recent research by Krauss *et al.* (1995), Hadar *et al.* (1998) and Wagner *et al.* (2004) in the field of gesture indicates that gestures are closely related to cognitive processing. They have an impact on your working memory and help you recall both visuo-spatial and verbal items. When we accompany gestures with speech it has been shown that the combination affects our memory storage systems (Cohen, 1977; Hadar *et al.*, 1998). Also, when you are speaking, gestures are particularly useful as they help you to 'organise spatial and motor information into packages appropriate for speaking' (Wagner *et al.*, 2004, 406). In short, gesture 'confers a cognitive benefit on the speaker' (404).

Perhaps some of the most fascinating studies on gesture come from research on blind people. Since they cannot see, you would imagine blind people would not be inclined to gesture. This is not the case. In 1998, Iverson and Goldin-Meadow examined videotapes of blind people and showed that they gestured despite the lack of a visual model. Moreover, they even gestured when speaking to another blind person. Another fascinating study by Cohen in 1977 looked at the manner in which we use gestures and asked participants to give directions over an intercom and also face to face. What do you think happened? Even when participants could not see the listener, they still used hand gestures! A not uncommon behaviour when people are speaking on the phone.

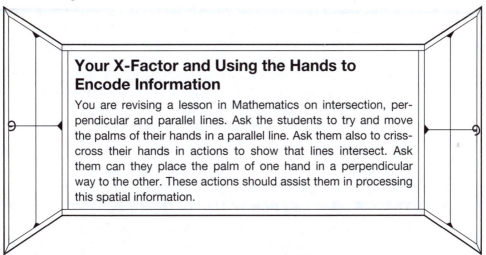

Your X-Factor and Using the Hands to Encode Information

You are revising a lesson in Mathematics on intersection, perpendicular and parallel lines. Ask the students to try and move the palms of their hands in a parallel line. Ask them also to crisscross their hands in actions to show that lines intersect. Ask them can they place the palm of one hand in a perpendicular way to the other. These actions should assist them in processing this spatial information.

Your X-Factor and information processing

Curiously, gestures are mainly done by the right hand in right-handed people, whereas left-handed people use both hands (Argyle, 1988). Why are gestures such an integral part of our communication? The reason they are important is that they allow us to present information in a multi-dimensional manner. McNeill (1992) gives us the great example of the 'running fingers'. We use the 'wiggling fingers' to portray someone running. Now we know that the fingers are just fingers, but we can also use them in representational format, where they become a character. Perhaps you have used this example at some stage or other. For example, 'Little Red Riding Hood ran away from the wolf as fast as she could'. Here your fingers wiggle to show poor Little Red Riding Hood escaping

FIGURE 10.1 Wiggling fingers.

the big bad wolf. Such symbols give us a complete expression of meaning. Let's take a further look at the example of Little Red Riding Hood running away from the wolf. If you wiggle your fingers quickly, it shows she is running fast and is moving along briskly. However, you may slow down this wiggle at the part where she is getting tired having been running for a long time. While you may never have used the words 'she is getting tired', the slower wiggle in itself can indicate this. The use of the simple wiggle conveys a multitude of information in terms of time, trajectory, space, form and as a result this one image can present multi-dimensional meaning. It can exist with your use of words, but may also give additional meaning in its own right without accompanying words. McNeill (2000, 139) puts it powerfully: 'utterances possess two sides, only one of which is speech; the other is imagery, actional and visuo-spatial. To exclude the gesture side as has been traditional is tantamount to ignoring half of the message of the brain'.

Research undertaken by Rimé in 1982 points to the fact that gestures can on occasion be used to supplement words. This is especially true when we are trying to convey a mental image or a cognitive concept. In his research, Rimé chose a topic on which we all have opinions – the movies. He asked participants to explain to each other their opinions on the movies and quite simply to express what they liked to find in the cinema. Participants were asked to give these opinions face to face and also through an opaque block (blind situation). While participants did use more gesture in the face-to-face situation, it was not significantly different from the 'blind situation'.

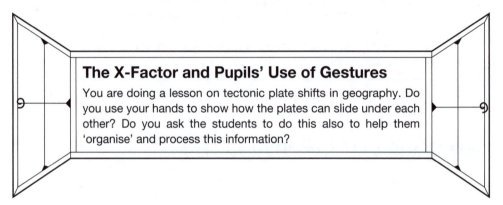

The X-Factor and Pupils' Use of Gestures

You are doing a lesson on tectonic plate shifts in geography. Do you use your hands to show how the plates can slide under each other? Do you ask the students to do this also to help them 'organise' and process this information?

Gestures are important as they help us convey semantic information. How is this? Wagner and her colleagues (2004), make the important point that there are aspects of our thinking which are more grounded in images than words. Accordingly, gestures provide us with a representational 'medium' for such images. The value of using gestures in this way should not be underestimated, as the work of Beattie and Shovelton show (1999a, 1999b). They have undertaken extensive research on the use of gestures to provide semantic value to the spoken word. In a series of research studies using cartoon strips, they found that in certain instances, the use of gesture to accompany the spoken word increased the informational value of the message by approximately 60 per cent. Indeed, Beattie (2004) reports that some gestures can be found to increase the informational value of the spoken word by up to 400 per cent! His research showed that 'when participants were presented with the gesture–speech combination they were significantly better at answering questions about the cartoon strip than when they just heard the speech extracts' (110).

Of course this should not come as a surprise. Children start to gesture at around ten months (Beattie, 2004). It happens at a time in their development 'when they are limited in what they can say, there is another avenue of expression open to them ... in addition to speaking, the child can gesture' (Goldin-Meadow et al., 1999, 118). However, with time as children develop their language skills, it is important to point out that they also become proficient users of gesture. It does not 'drop out' of their communication repertoire. McNeill (1992) argues that gestures and language are one system. As Lisa Aziz-Zadeh (2007) once remarked about language: 'it is intrinsically tied to the flesh'.

This idea that our use of language is 'tied to the flesh' is fascinating and brings us to another school of thought which has to do with 'embodied cognition'. This school of thought moves away from the idea that our brain is like a computer which governs and drives our bodies; a computer which is largely detached from the operations of limbs, arms, etc. On the contrary, embodied cognition argues that our mental processes are shaped by our bodies. Our thoughts are shaped by the types of perceptual and motor experiences we have as we interact each day with the world. Think about it for a moment. When we talk, we often use bodily actions in our expressions. Take, for example, 'the kiss of death', 'a kick in the ass', 'give me a hand' and so on. Now you have probably never thought much about these expressions; however, when we hear or say these expressions, parts of the brain which control your motor movements are activated. You may remember in our earlier chapters that we discussed mirror neurons. Well here again, these 'tiny miracles' raise their heads! They help us understand what we read by internally simulating the actions described as if we were doing them ourselves (Iacoboni, 2008, 94).

So far we have covered...

Gestures are important for cognitive processing and have an impact on working memory. This is particularly true as there are aspects of our thinking which are more imagistic than verbal. So, gestures allow us to present information in a multi-dimensional manner. They help the speaker to organise spatial and motor information into packages appropriate for speaking.

Types of gesture

When we think of gestures, it is useful to categorise them. Typically, there are four kinds of gesture. The first is termed a deictic gesture. This type of gesture typically involves pointing and is often used by children. Indeed, children begin using these pointing gestures at around the age of ten months. They are used to indicate objects and events and are context dependent. For example, a teacher pointing to a red square on the wall when discussing shapes.

The second type of gesture is known as an iconic gesture. This happens when we use a gesture which closely resembles a concrete object or event. They capture aspects of the form of the object or action. For example, in an arts and crafts lesson, the teacher may be explaining to the children how to use paste to join together two butterfly wings. The teacher brings together the two hands in a joining motion to indicate gluing together. This is an iconic gesture. Or they might press their finger against their lips as a signal to one of the students to be quiet as another gives an answer. They might ask the students to write down one equation associated with velocity and signal this intent by raising one finger to the class.

The next kind of gesture is known as a metaphoric gesture. This happens when gesture is used to present an abstract concept. These kinds of gestures are like iconic gestures in that they are essentially pictorial, but they differ in that the content is an abstract rather than a concrete object or event (Beattie, 2004). They give us an image of the invisible. For example, let's say you are discussing gravity and you bring your hand down from a height to indicate the downward force of gravity. Or let's say you are having a debate with the class, and one person declares that Stalin was a capitalist. You might extend your hand, palm up and wave it to the right asking does anyone want to challenge this idea? Or perhaps you are talking about Macbeth and describe the devious plot he created. While introducing this devious plot, you may have your fist clenched showing tension but also secrecy.

Finally, we have the use of emblems. No doubt you are familiar with these. They involve the use of gesture to communicate a message typically recognised by the community. For example, the thumbs-up signal to indicate approval.

Gestures and beats

FIGURE 10.2 Rap artists sometimes use beats.

Do you like rap music? You may have noticed on TV how rap artists tend to use their hands a lot when they are singing or rapping. While it is not clear whether this can be put down directly to deliberate knowledge of their body language, the manner in which they use their hands to 'beat' out significant parts of their songs or sentences is intriguing. This has to do basically with using your hands to emphasise what you say. It is one of the aspects of the classroom X-Factor which many people are unaware of.

So what are these beats? No doubt when you hear the term 'beat', you immediately think of a musical beat. These types of gesture are somewhat like a musical beat. They accompany your speech, in the form of a simple flick of the hand, or moving your fingers up and down, or perhaps moving your fingers back and forth. They are not that noticeable, as they are quite quick and usually quite short. You might make these movements against your lap, or on the armrest of the chair as you talk. So they can seem quite insignificant. However, they are not! They happen at the most significant parts of your speech and occur at those moments where you use the most significant words from your point of view. They demarcate those parts of the discourse which the speaker thinks is most important. That is why they are so important – 'they give a clue as to the inner workings of the mind of the speaker' (Beattie, 2004, 75). To illustrate, we refer to the work of Geoffrey Beattie and his analyses of Bill Clinton's statements during the Monica Lewinsky trial. While giving testimony, Bill made his protestations with quite a number of beats. Take the quote: 'I did not have sexual relations with that woman.' While saying the four words 'not have sexual relations', Bill made four sharp and rapid downwards movements of his pointed index finger for each of these words.

Exemplar 8: Using Beats as You Speak

As teachers we often use beats. For example, take the annual primary school tour to the zoo. The bus is bubbling with excitement, children are singing and so on. Finally, the teacher gets attention (perhaps through using a hands-up signal) and begins to explain the rules of the day. While saying 'you must not leave the group' she points in the children's direction and wags her finger for each of the words 'must not leave'. Sound familiar? This emphasises the message. We can use it in lots of other scenarios too.

The use of gesture in classrooms

A number of studies have found that lessons which are characterised by the use of gesture are more effective than the same lessons without their usage (Perry *et al.*, 1995; Valenzo *et al.*, 2003; Goldin-Meadow, 2004; Church *et al.*, 2004). For example, in 2004, Susan Goldin-Meadow asked eight teachers to teach 49 third and fourth grade primary students in one-on-one contexts. The instruction centred on strategies for solving mathematical equivalence problems. The problems were ones that this age group typically found difficult, e.g. $4+5+6=6+\_\_+\_\_$. The research found that students could better repeat the mathematical strategies if the teachers' words and gestures were congruent. Furthermore, pupil repetition of these strategies was better when the teacher gestured, as opposed to not gesturing at all. Not surprisingly, students performed less well when the teacher's physical movements conveyed contradictory information. For example, in the aforementioned problem, some teachers would point to all the numbers (4, 5 and 6) but only talk about the digits 4 and 5.

There is also considerable research evidence to show that learners who gesture spontaneously on a task are more likely to retain what they have learned about the task than learners who do not gesture (for example, Alibali and Goldin-Meadow, 1993; Cook and Goldin-Meadow, 2006). Moreover, teaching which includes gesture has been found to facilitate learning by such researchers as Church *et al.* (2004), Singer and Goldin-Meadow (2005) and Valenzo *et al.* (2003). Finally, when children use gestures to help them recall an event, they report more details about the event than children who are not instructed to gesture (Stevanoni and Salmon, 2005). It is important to also point out that gesturing can also hinder performance. In some instances, gesturing on tasks that do not lend themselves to gesture is likely to disrupt the performance (Schooler *et al.*, 1993).

Gesture and mathematics

We can use gestures in a wide range of curricular areas. Think of using your hands to demonstrate the effects of forces in physics, or the staccato effect in music. The possibilities are endless. Flevares and Perry (2001) argue that lesson content in Mathematics is particularly suited to gesture. They point to their own research which involved video analysis of teachers in instructional settings across a number of lessons. Their work led them to observe that teachers tend to use gesture more frequently in Mathematics lessons than in other lessons. In particular, they found that Mathematics teachers used from five to seven unspoken representations of mathematical ideas per minute, with gesture being the most common form of unspoken representation. Within the literature, a number of commentators are united on the point that mathematical concepts lend themselves to the use of gesture (Goldin-Meadow *et al.*, 1992; Perry *et al.*, 1995; Goldin-Meadow *et al.*, 1999). In 1998, a team led by Shavelson argued that when explaining mathematical concepts, teachers need to translate the concepts into many symbolic forms. The concept, where possible, needs a representational format. Mayer and Andersen (1991) make a similar point noting that the advantage of using gesture is that it can be used to accompany the explanations of a concept thereby providing multiple representations, but in a unified manner. So where could you use gesture with maths? Let us start with angles, symmetry, area, volume, weight, measure, data, shapes, numbers (e.g. counting fingers, counting in multiples, etc.) and so on.

Gesture and culture

Throughout this chapter we have talked about gestures as they relate universally to all of us. This may be a little inaccurate! It is important to say that gesture can vary according to culture. Beattie (2004) points to the 'extravagant gesticulations' of the Italians compared with the 'inhibited gesticulations' of the English. The type of culture you live in has an impact on your degree of gesturing. It has been shown that Arab students when moving to the USA will attempt to inhibit some of the gestures they would normally use back home (Beattie, 2004, 83). Indeed, it has often been noted that Arabs are the 'world leaders' in terms of the vast variety of gestures they use. They respond and react to situations with their hands and their bodies. As Barakat (1973, 751) once wrote: 'So intimately related are speech, gesture and culture, that to tie an Arab's hands while he is speaking is tantamount to trying to tie his tongue.' This leads us to our next section which has to do with the use of the tongue, namely voice intonation.

So far we have covered...

There are a number of gestures we can use. The deictic gesture is used to indicate objects or events. Iconic gestures are used to capture aspects of the form of the object or action. Metaphoric gestures are also pictorial, but they are used to depict an abstract idea rather than a concrete object or event. Finally, emblems are used to communicate a message typically recognised by the community. A number of studies have found that lessons which are characterised by the use of gesture are more effective than the same lessons without their usage. Indeed, the nature of mathematical concepts can lend themselves especially well to the use of gesture. Gesture is important in facilitating students' learning and also in assisting with the recall of stored knowledge.

We also make use of beats. They happen at the most significant parts of your speech and occur at those moments where you use the most significant words from your point of view. Needless to say, culture plays a role in your predisposition to using gestures.

Self-Evaluation Questions: Gesture

Gestures and your teaching

1 To what degree do you use gesture as you teach?
2 What do your gestures reveal about your emotions as you teach?

Gestures and meaning

1 To what degree do you ask students to use gestures to help them process concepts?
2 Do you use gestures to create specific images for the pupils?
3 To what degree do you use iconic (resembling objects)/metaphoric (presenting abstract concepts)/deictic (indicating objects or events)/emblems (e.g. thumbs-up) gestures?

How you use your hands

Open palms
1 Are your palms open as you gesture? Do they show openness?

Using the hands to process information

2 Do you ask your students to use their hands to help them process information, e.g. making perpendicular lines with their hands when studying co-ordinate geometry?

Beating

1 To what degree do you use beats (movement of the hands or fingers at significant parts of your speech) to mark out or emphasise what you are saying?

11

Vocal Expression

Introduction

We have all heard the expression, sometimes even in schools: 'Now, say sorry like you mean it.' The child then has to have another go at saying sorry, with the proper vocal intonation and accompanying facial expressions, etc. The way we use our voices often gives away the true meaning of what we want to say. The character Desdemona in Shakespeare's *Othello* gives us a good idea of this: 'I understand a fury in your words, but not the words' (Act IV, Scene II). Long before Shakespeare, the human race was intrigued by the possible uses of the voice. For example, the Romans were fascinated by oratory and the use of voice. Cicero (1942/*c*.55 BCE, Section 216) once wrote 'for nature has assigned to every emotion a particular look and tone of voice and bearing of its own'.

Of course, the ability of the voice to convey emotion is not a new phenomenon. From the mother on the savannah lands who exclaimed 'yeuk' to dissuade her child from climbing into a carcass, to last year's winner of *The X-Factor*, our voice impregnates our words with emotional meaning. Michael Argyle (1988, 145) makes the point that 'the voice is a leakier channel than the face, i.e. it is not so well controlled and is more likely to reveal true feelings'. You will recall from Part I of this book that the emotional meaning we attach to the content we teach is very important. You are also probably thinking – great – we are now going to get a neat list of voice sounds and associated emotional meanings. Unfortunately, the literature on that particular topic is inconclusive. It appears that a paradox exists. While listeners seem to be accurate in decoding emotions from voice cues, scientists, on the other hand, have been unable to identify a 'neat' set of voice cues which one can tag to particular emotions (Cowie *et al.*, 2001; Murray and Arnott, 1993). However, if we go back to 1986, and look at the work of Scherer, we can see some links between particular uses of the voice and associated emotions. Before we examine this work, it is necessary to give you an explanation of the term 'pitch'.

Pitch has to do with the number of vocal vibrations of the vocal folds. These vibrations are dependent on the length and thickness of the vocal cords, as well as the tightening and relaxation of the muscles surrounding them. This explains why women generally have higher voices than men do – they have shorter vocal cords. The sound of your voice changes as the rate of the vibrations varies. As the number of vibrations per second increases, so does the pitch, meaning the voice would sound higher. Faster rates form higher voices (higher pitches) while slower rates elicit deeper voices, or lower pitches. To illustrate this, think of situations where people become frightened or excited. The muscles around the voice box (or larynx) unconsciously contract, putting strain on the vocal cords, making the pitch higher. We also change the pitch of our voice to imitate someone.

Returning to the work of Scherer, he found that joy and elation can be associated with raised pitch and pitch variability. Depression can be associated with lowered voice pitch and intonation intensity. Anxiety can be associated with raised pitch, breathy quality and longer more silent pauses. Fear can be associated with raised pitch and high energy at higher pitches. Anger can be associated with higher speech rate and sudden increases of pitch and loudness on single syllables.

Voice intonation and the classroom X-Factor

Within the classroom, there is extensive commentary on the importance of vocal variety. Richmond *et al.* (1987) argue that when it comes to the use of the voice (also known as paralanguage or vocalics), vocal variety is the factor which students associate most positively with learning. And, by corollary, they associate vocal monotone as the behaviour most negatively associated with learning.

So, are you aware of the kinds of vocal variety you use in the classroom? One of the antidotes to monotone expression has to do with pitch variation. This is another important dimension of your V-Factor (voice factor). Extreme pitch and what are known as 'up contours' produce ratings of 'highly pleasant active and potent emotions such as happiness, interest, surprise and also fear' (Scherer, 1979, 251).

As you may remember in Chapter 2, we discussed vocal monotone as one of the characteristics which is associated with a lack of teacher immediacy. Pick up any textbook on teaching skills and you will find references to the necessity for varied vocal intonation. How do we get this vocal variety?

Miller (2005) provides us with some insightful advice. He argues that teachers need to take the following steps:

1   ensure there is a proper quality of projection;
2   monitor the rate at which you speak;
3   vary the kinds of intonation you use.

These suggestions are very useful. But there are other factors which are important in your use of the voice. These factors are associated with gender and personality types.

Your V-Factor and gender

There are some notable differences in the genders when it comes to voice intonation. Michael Argyle (1988) points out that men tend to have louder and lower pitched voices, which is not entirely due to anatomical differences. On the other hand, he points out that because women tend to smile more while they speak, the voice quality gains a higher pitched sound. Furthermore, women make more use of voice intonation and of specific voice intonation patterns (Brend, 1975). What are voice intonation patterns? When speaking, women tend to use a downward glide with surprise or with cheerfulness – think of them talking to children. They are also more inclined to place a rising note at the end of a sentence, like when asking a hesitant question (Lakoff, 1973). On the other hand, men tend to interrupt more when in conversation. When women interrupt, it is to ask a question or to ask the speaker to elaborate (LaFrance and Mayo, 1978).

Vocal fluency and persuasiveness

One of the big differences in the genders in connection with the use of voice centres on fluency. In 1973, Lalljee and Cook found that men are less fluent than women, making more speech errors in general. In particular when men are uncomfortable, there are more filled pauses. This is important and is relevant to your 'V-Factor'. A study by a team led by Burgoon in 1990 found that verbal fluency is a strong predictor of persuasiveness. Your rate of speech and its volume is also connected to persuasiveness. People are fluent when they know what they are talking about (Eggert, 2010). Mehrabian (1972, 71) comments that 'higher speech rate and volume' are some of the variables associated with persuasiveness. Other factors connected with persuasiveness are 'facial pleasantness and activity' and 'less direct shoulder orientation'. Indeed the rate of speech is a matter that frequently gives rise to self-reflection for teachers. Do I speak too fast? Too slow? What does this tell me? It is important to be fluent in your speech, but not to speak too quickly. When you speak too quickly this may cause you to take rapid shallow breaths. Your body can then interpret such actions as anxiety and this anxiety can cause you to speak even faster.

One of the preconceptions about rate of speech has to do with gender. It is often thought that women speak faster than men. There is little difference. Tusing and Dillard (2000) have found that speech rate is negatively associated with dominance. The faster the rate of speech, the lower the estimation of dominance.

When one analyses speech rate, one of the factors to bear in mind has to do with the number of pauses in each utterance. There are two kinds of pause – a silent one (we say nothing) and a 'filled' pause (we might add in something like 'um' or 'er'). Believe it or not, pauses can take up 30–40 per cent of our 'speaking time' (Argyle, 1988). Also, as you would expect, we pause more when the topic in hand is more difficult – often twice as often (Goldman-Eisler, 1968).

Silent pauses (when we say nothing) represent thinking time, allowing us to plan the words and sentence clauses to come. Spontaneous speech usually has a rhythm which incorporates these clauses. We alternate between fluent and hesitant phases. So how do we interpret these pauses? Lalljee (1971) found that people who use 'filled' pauses a lot (i.e. adding in things like er, um) were interpreted as anxious or bored. On the other hand, users of silent pauses can be interpreted as angry, contemptuous or anxious. These emotional characteristics are often segregated into extroverted and introverted personality types. People who are characterised as being more extroverted (as compared to introverted) are more fluent, allow for shorter pauses in conversation turn taking, have shorter silent pauses in their own speech, fewer hesitations, speak faster, in a louder tone and with more variable pitch (this term will be explained later in the chapter). Finally, extroverted people have been shown to talk more.

So what can you do about these 'ums' and 'ers'? Max Eggert (2010, 165) argues that in order to appear confident, it is better to allow yourself 'small periods of silence between your words when you are thinking rather than filling the gaps with ums and ers'. He also observes that pausing after making a major point and 'sweeping the room' with your eyes gives emphasis to the point.

The fluency of your speech and how you use your pauses is an important dimension of your X-Factor. Of course associated with pause is what is known as prosody.

So far we have covered...

There are some who say the voice is a leakier channel than the face for our true emotions. It is not possible to identify a neat set of vocal cues which can be tagged to specific human emotions. Vocal variety is the factor which students associate most positively with learning. Vocal monotone is one of the characteristics which is associated with a lack of teacher immediacy. How can you develop your vocal variety? First, you must ensure there is a proper quality of projection. Monitor the rate at which you speak. Vary the kinds of intonation you use. If you are a man, you may have to work a little harder at this as women make more use of voice intonation and of specific voice intonation patterns. The fluency with which you speak is also important. Verbal fluency is a strong predictor of persuasiveness. But remember, the faster the rate of speech, the lower the estimation of dominance. What about 'ums' and 'ahs' in sentences? Teachers who use 'filled' pauses a lot (i.e. adding in things like er, um) can be interpreted as anxious or bored.

Prosody

One aspect of vocal intonation which deserves specific mention concerns what is termed in the literature as prosody. Prosody is the term used to describe the use of vocal variations to change the meaning of what is being said. Take the following sentence for example – 'Mark is coming with me.' We can give this sentence additional meaning by emphasising certain words as follows:

'Mark *is* coming with me.' The emphasis on the 'is' here is definite, meaning this is happening presently.

'Mark is coming with *me*!' Here the emphasis is on 'me'. He is coming with me and no one else!

'*Mark* is coming with me.' Here the emphasis is on 'Mark' and no one else.

As teachers we make frequent use of prosody. Indeed, the obvious 'habitat' for prosody rests in our use of questioning. Hargie and Dickson (2004, 116) argue that there are certain nonverbal signals which should accompany a question, with the 'raising or lowering of vocal inflection on the last syllable being one of these'. As teachers we should be very aware of this. Why? We ask a lot of questions. In 1982, Dillon reported that teachers ask about two questions per minute. On the other hand, this work found that, on average, a pupil asks about one question per month! You're probably saying to yourself – maybe that's because children don't ask that many questions? Not so. Tizard *et al.*, 1983 recorded four year old girls in the home and found they asked an average of 24 questions per hour! There is an obvious imbalance here. But the key point centres on the use of voice intonation as we ask questions. As we mentioned earlier, our own personalities are also connected with our use of voice intonation.

Personality and your V-Factor (voice factor)

The word personality comes from the Latin word 'persona'. This word has in fact two meanings. It can describe a theatrical mask. On the other hand, when we split the word in two, you have 'per/sona' which means 'by sound'. Our abilities to recognise each other from the sound of our voices is very strong. Think of the last time you picked up the phone and instantly recognised the speaker. By way of an aside, Joseph Stalin was very aware of this unique human ability. He selected a number of prisoners who were scientists and engineers to develop speaker recognition technology so his police could identify 'enemies of the state' (Hollien, 1990). Several studies also show that we are very capable of judging social class on the basis of the voice alone (Knapp and Hall, 2006). So what are these connections between our 'persona' and the sound of our voice?

In 1968, Addington made some interesting connections between personality and vocal expression. Before considering these connections, think of some recent male and female voices you have heard and try to recall the emotions they conveyed. Say, for example, a voice that sounded flat. Now have a look at Table 11.1 (Addington, 1968) which connects vocal cues with personality stereotypes and gender (see p.77).

As Table 11.1 indicates, we make a number of stereotyped calculations about people's personalities based on their voice attributes and also their gender. As we have already discussed gender, let us now look at personality.

There are a wide number of studies which connect voice attributes with personality. For example, Zuckerman undertook extensive research on voice attributes and found that people whose voices are considered more attractive are believed to have personality traits such as dominance, competence, industriousness, sensitivity and warmth (Zuckerman and Driver, 1989). Indeed, there is considerable research to show that people with attractive sounding voices are in general rated as having better personalities. They are less neurotic, more open, warm, agreeable, powerful, honest and conscientious (Knapp and Hall, 2006). So what makes the voice attractive? How do you develop your V-Factor?

The V-Factor and attractive voices

Attractive voices are rated as having more resonance, being less monotonous and less nasal. What is resonance? The best way to explain resonance is to think of the two stringed instruments: the guitar and the violin. Both have different resonances. Why? The sound from these instruments is determined not by the string that is played, but rather the space where the vibration takes place. The size, shape and material of the box over which the string plays affects the resonance of the note being played. In the same way, humans have a 'box' for resonating sound. This box is made up of our throat, chest, mouth and nasal cavities. Because we all vary in size, we all sound different – we have different resonances. Singers often vary their resonance. Take, for example, jazz and opera singers.

TABLE 11.1 Simulated vocal cues and personality stereotypes.

VOCAL CUE (TYPE OF VOICE)	MALE SPEAKER AND STEREOTYPED PERCEPTIONS	FEMALE SPEAKER AND STEREOTYPED PERCEPTIONS
Breathiness	Younger more artistic	More feminine; prettier, more petite, effervescent, high-strung; shallower
Thinness	Did not alter the listener's image of the speaker; no significant correlations	Increased social, physical, emotional and mental immaturity; increased sense of humour and sensitivity
Flatness	More masculine, more sluggish, colder, more withdrawn	More masculine, more sluggish, colder, more withdrawn
Nasality	A wide array of socially undesirable characteristics	A wide array of socially undesirable characteristics
Tenseness	Older, more unyielding, cantankerous	Younger; more emotional, feminine, high-strung; less intelligent
Throatiness	Older; more realistic; mature; sophisticated; well adjusted	Less intelligent; more masculine; lazier; more boorish, unemotional, ugly, sickly, careless, inartistic, naïve, humble, neurotic, quiet, uninteresting, apathetic
Increased rate	More animated and extraverted	More animated and extraverted
Increased pitch variety	More dynamic, feminine, aesthetically inclined	More dynamic and extraverted

Source: Addington (1968).

In addition, a number of studies point out that for males only, lower pitch is also considered attractive (e.g. Zuckerman and Driver, 1989; Zuckerman and Miyake, 1993; Bloom et al., 1999). Within the domain of affection, the importance of pitch gains significance. Both men and women are rated as showing more affection when their voice varies in pitch. But here again there are gender differences. For men, greater affection is associated when the average pitch level is low. On the other hand, women are perceived as more affectionate when their average pitch level is high (Floyd and Ray, 2003). In addition, extremes of pitch, pitch range, shrillness and squeakiness produce more negative impressions (Zuckerman and Driver, 1989; Zuckerman and Miyake, 1993).

In relation to loudness of voice, the work of Siegman (1987) and Weaver and Anderson (1973) shows that dominant individuals tend to have voices which are louder than less dominant individuals. Once again, there are some masculine and feminine factors to bear in mind here. Lippa (1998) undertook extensive studies of college students to establish differences in vocalics according to gender. His work found that among men, those who were more masculine had less expressive, lower pitched, slower and louder voices than their female counterparts. If you are a student teacher, this finding is of importance to you when you examine your vocalics. Finally, there may be reason to avoid engaging in loud, vigorous and explosive speech. According to Hall et al. (1984) there is a danger that you fall into the category of a person who may suffer from heart disease.

Your voice and breathing

In developing your X-Factor as a teacher, it is important to be aware of the manner in which the voice produces sound. How you breathe affects your voice projection. So when you are tense for example, your diaphragm may tense up and distort the tone of your voice, causing its pitch and volume to fluctuate. Think of the sensation of having butterflies in your stomach. This is caused by a 'fluttery diaphragm' which causes the voice to shake (Lyle, 1990, 63). Feelings of severe strain reveal themselves in a hoarse and strained voice as tension in the neck and throat muscles affect our vocal resonance.

When we are anxious, we can also produce more speech errors, especially in the early stages of interaction. These kinds of speech errors are called 'dysfluencies'. However, as you get more familiar with the situation which caused the anxiety, the frequency of these errors decreases (Scott et al., 1978).

The final matter we wish to consider about the voice concerns something we all have to a greater or lesser degree – an accent.

Your V-Factor and your accent

Extralinguistics is the term used to refer to one's accent. Accent can be a 'powerful catalyst for prejudice' (Hargie and Dickson, 2004, 78). Your accent and how you express your emotions are connected to what is known as 'emotion dialects'. Emotion dialects relate to the manner in which your cultural identity affects the way you express emotions nonverbally. Different cultures have their own nuanced ways of expressing emotions nonverbally. As you would expect, this means that we are better at judging emotions on the faces of people who share our own cultural, ethnic or national identity (Elfenbein and Ambady, 2002, 2003).

But did you know that when we converse with someone who has a different accent and are seeking their approval or trying to make ourselves as comprehensible as possible, we bring our speech more into line with the accent of the person to whom we are talking (Willemyns *et al.*, 1997)? In short, we imitate their accent. This may also extend to our voice qualities as we 'play' to different audiences (DePaulo, 1992). These alterations in our voice do impact on the impressions we make. For example, LaPlante and Ambady (2003) contend that we make judgements about someone's politeness based not only on the content of their language but also on the tone of their voice. While this may seem obvious, it is important for the multi-cultural classrooms of the modern world. To what degree do you share the ethnic and cultural identity of your pupils?

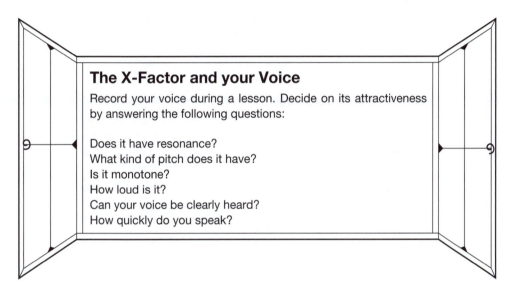

The X-Factor and your Voice

Record your voice during a lesson. Decide on its attractiveness by answering the following questions:

Does it have resonance?
What kind of pitch does it have?
Is it monotone?
How loud is it?
Can your voice be clearly heard?
How quickly do you speak?

So far we have covered...

Attractive voices are rated as having more resonance, being less monotonous and less nasal. In addition, for males, lower pitch is also attractive. Generally, people with attractive sounding voices are rated as having better personalities. People whose voices are considered more attractive are believed to have personality traits such as dominance, competence, industriousness, sensitivity and warmth. Dominant individuals tend to have voices which are louder than less dominant individuals. We also make judgements about someone's politeness based not only on the content of their language but also on the tone of their voice. Prosody is the term used to describe the use of vocal variations to change the meaning of what is being said. How you breathe affects your voice projection. So when you are tense, for example, your diaphragm may tense up and distort the tone of your voice, causing its pitch and volume to fluctuate. When we are anxious, we can also produce more speech errors. Accent can be a 'powerful catalyst for prejudice'. We tend to bring our speech into line with the accent of the person to whom we are talking.

Self-Evaluation Questions: Vocal Intonation

Is my voice attractive?

Record your voice during a lesson. Decide on its attractiveness by answering the following questions:

a Does it have a pleasant quality?
b Is it monotone?
c Has it appropriate loudness for all students to hear?
d Do you speak too quickly/too slowly?
e Do you vary the intonation of your voice?
f Are there extremes of pitch/shrillness/squeakiness?
g Do you have clear voice projection?

Your voice and your emotions

1 What kinds of emotions do you hear in your voice? Do you think the students will be stimulated/engaged by these emotions?
2 Do you make sure your voice registers your enthusiasm?

Prosody

To what degree do you place emphasis on particular words in your sentences, e.g. Mark *is* coming with me?

12

The X-Factor and 'Classroom Eyes'

FIGURE 12.1 Anxiety/dismay.

You have probably heard terms such as 'beady eyes', 'snake eyes', 'icy stares', 'shifty eyes' and 'bedroom eyes' at various points throughout your life. When considering people's attributes, we often speak of their eyes. Indeed, eyes have been the focus of attention for centuries. For example, we have *Mona Lisa*'s eyes, Medusa's eyes (she had snakes coming out of her head and could turn you into stone!) and the great Clint Eastwood stare. In this chapter we are going to introduce you to a new term: 'classroom eyes' and show you its relevance to your X-Factor. In fact we think we are the first to coin this term!

Classroom eyes and interaction

FIGURE 12.2 Anger.

Have you ever heard an adult admonish a child with the words: 'Stop looking away while I am talking to you'? Indeed, you may also have heard it within the walls of a school. One type of eye contact which is often referred to in research is described as gazing. You have probably heard the refrain: 'What are you looking at?' Sometimes couched aggressively and sometimes simply inquisitively, this could be re-termed as 'What are you gazing at?' as gaze basically involves our looking behaviours. In this book, we use the term gaze to mean 'looking at another, especially in the facial area' (Hargie and Dickson, 2004, 64).

Gazing is an important component of your X-Factor. You may think that when you are engaged in a conversation with someone you are both gazing directly at each other – this is not the case. During fluent speech, the person listening does more of the gazing, while the person speaking does less. Believe it or not, when we are engaged in conversation, we only gaze at the other person about half of the time (Knapp and Hall, 2006).

FIGURE 12.3 Gazing or looking.

In developing your 'classroom eyes', there are a number of important things to remember about how you look or gaze at someone while in conversation. First, your gazing serves a 'regulatory' function. You give responses by the way you look back at the person. Sometimes you suppress a reaction and give no response. Second, when you converse with someone, you engage in a lot of monitoring. You look at the other person to check their attentiveness and also to give them messages that certain units of thought are concluding. This relates to an aspect of 'looking' which is known as grounding. As people talk they look for evidence that they have been misunderstood (as opposed to understood) and then set about 'repairing the damage' (Goodwin, 1981). The listener and speaker's use of eye contact is an important feature of this tango of communication. Third, we tend to look away when having difficulty processing information or deciding what to say. Finally, the way we gaze gives off expressive messages. For example, how does the conversation interest you? How involved are you in the discussion? Of course it is important to point out that in giving feedback by the way we look, we may also, at the same time be giving feedback through other nonverbal channels such as smiling and head nodding. When these various forms are combined in symphony, the result is a strong cocktail of messages indicating either positive or negative nonverbal feedback.

Gazing and the initiation of conversation

The use of gaze serves many important functions. As teachers, one of the primary functions which gazing serves has to do with the initiation of interaction. We use eye behaviour to regulate the flow of conversation. Sometimes we look at the listener at the end of a sentence or a thought unit to indicate to them that it is their turn to start talking or alternatively we may look at them to establish whether they have understood what we have said. Schmid Mast (2002) has undertaken some interesting research in this regard which shows that in small groups (e.g. three people), the leader makes widespread use of this gazing to invite others in the group to speak. This control of the group through the use of gazing allows the leader to orchestrate who speaks next and also how much time they get to speak. Needless to say, we should not engage in staring. Looking too much can cause discomfort. A gaze of longer than ten seconds is likely to induce irritation (Knapp and Hall, 2006).

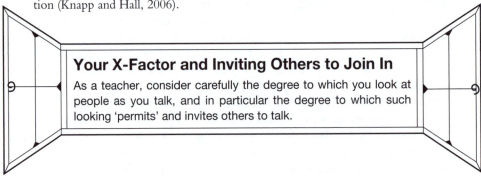

Your X-Factor and Inviting Others to Join In

As a teacher, consider carefully the degree to which you look at people as you talk, and in particular the degree to which such looking 'permits' and invites others to talk.

Looking away is not necessarily a 'bad thing'

In developing your 'classroom eyes', it is important for you to be aware that when people look away from you, it is not always a bad thing. As teachers it is important for us to remember that people tend to look away when they are trying to process difficult or complex ideas. When this happens, what the person is really trying to do is shift their gaze from external matters (the world) to internal matters (inside the head). As teachers we ask a lot of questions and we should expect students to 'look away' while engaged in thought and in some cases to signal that they are actually thinking.

The type of questions we use can also have an influence on this inclination to 'look away'. Reflective questions as opposed to simple factual questions cause people to 'avert their gaze' as they endeavour to think about the matter. Some work by Glenberg *et al.* (1998) provides us with some fascinating insights into the manner in which we ask questions. Their work showed that when asked to answer factual questions, participants who had their eyes closed performed better than participants who were asked to look directly at the questioner. Excluding external stimulation when engaged in difficult cognitive activity can have benefits. It suggests to us as

FIGURE 12.4 Mr Fox: My eyes are closed. Can't you see I am thinking?

teachers that there may be merits in allowing or suggesting to students that they close their eyes when endeavouring to process or interrogate a tricky concept.

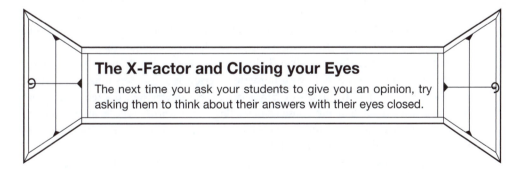

The X-Factor and Closing your Eyes

The next time you ask your students to give you an opinion, try asking them to think about their answers with their eyes closed.

Of course looking away can also give us clues to other things which are at play. When people are embarrassed, humiliated, feel shame or guilt they look away more. We all know of students who look away. For example, when a class is asked for a volunteer to read at assembly, some students look away for fear of being asked. Another example is when students look away to signal they do not wish to be questioned by the teacher.

FIGURE 12.5 Tell-tale signs when lying!

There are also some occasions where we look away or 'avert our gaze' when lying. But this can depend on the liar in question. In 1970, Exline set up an intriguing experiment to investigate whether people gaze more when lying. In the experiment, a group of participants were given a task to do. Amusingly, they were also encouraged to cheat on the task. When the task was over, and the dust had settled, the participants were then invited to an interview to discuss how they got on in the task. The results were fascinating. As they discussed the task, some of the participants looked away when lying about how they did it, while other cheaters looked more while lying. Why? The answer emerged when participants were cross-referenced using a 'Machiavellian scale'. Basically this scale measured how unscrupulous and cunning each participant was. Those cheating participants who scored high on the Machiavellian scale, looked more, using gaze to present the appearance of innocence. On the other hand, the low-scoring Machiavellian cheaters looked away much more when being interrogated. In other words, if you are the Machiavellian type, there is a good chance you will stare as you lie.

Classroom eyes and 'the look'

You may or may not have seen the recent comic film entitled *Zoolander* where Ben Stiller plays a male model with a unique ability to present the 'blue steel look'. This is a type of fixated look, which in the film had a type of spellbinding effect. Although just a comedy, the film reminds us of the importance of 'being looked at'. People often talk about the ways in which people look – we have song lines such as 'the look of love' (ABC, 1982) and movie lines such as: 'if looks could kill, I would be a dead man by now'. So looking at people is a significant feature of human interaction. This may seem obvious, but there are solid reasons for this.

Being seen is a 'profound form of social acknowledgement' (Knapp and Hall, 2006, 343). A number of studies from the world of psychology highlight the significance of 'being looked at' (e.g. Kleinke, 1986; Exline and Winters, 1966; Bernieri *et al.*, 1996). For example, studies on people with borderline personality disorders sometimes report that they feel invisible. In studies on physician–patient interaction, the use of gaze has been shown to have dramatic consequences. Physicians who engage in more patient-directed gaze have been reported to be more accurate at recognising psychosocial distress in their patients (Bensing *et al.*, 1995).

One of the most fascinating places in which we see the 'being looked at' factor arising comes from sport. If you follow sport at all then you are probably aware of the 'home team advantage'. This seemingly 'unathletic' advantage of the home team is quite intriguing. The ball is the same, the pitches are not any bigger or smaller and there are no magical fitness advantages when a team plays on home soil. Yet the home team is often the winner. The statistics are fascinating – home teams are the winner in 58 per cent of professional football games, 60 per cent of college football matches, 67 per cent in professional basketball, 64 per cent in professional hockey and 53 per cent of the time for professional baseball (Knapp and Hall, 2006). Marsh *et al.* (1978) have also reported that glancing at the supporters of the other team can be the spark for occasions of violence between opposing supporters, with the 'He looked at me' rationale being employed for such outbreaks.

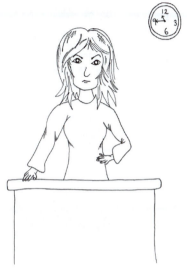

So what has this got to do with your classroom X-Factor? The key point here is that friendly and also unfriendly support (unfriendly hometown support can, needless to say, increase performance errors) are likely to have a 'profound effect on performance' (Knapp and Hall, 2006, 114). This is important for our students both young and old.

Think of the child playing in the playground saying 'look at me; I am going on the climbing frame'. Knapp and Hall (2006, 343) make the important point that being watched 'infuses meaning into the child's actions'. This is an important dimension of human psychology. Children like to be supported. Harkins and Szymanski (1987) call it the 'social facilitation' effect, where our performance is enhanced merely by the presence of others. Now there are no specific studies that we are aware of which examine the effects of actually

FIGURE 12.6 I'm watching.

'being present and observing' children in the classroom; however, that is not to say that it does not exist. What we can glean from some studies is that children are susceptible to the 'social facilitation effect'. In one of social psychology's first experiments we are given a simple, yet classic insight into this effect. Triplett (1898) asked boys to wind line on a fishing reel. The amazing finding was that they wound it faster when there were others present with them, even though it was not a competition and there were no prizes for the speed at which they wound the line.

Of course, on the other hand, the famous 'when the cat's away, the mice will play' metaphor can also come into play when people think they are not being watched. Harkins and Szymanski (1987) call this 'social loafing'. This occurs when people slack off while working with others. They are especially inclined to do this when they think their contribution will not be evaluated.

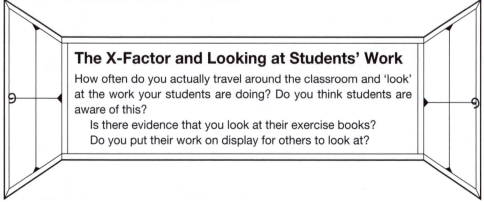

The X-Factor and Looking at Students' Work

How often do you actually travel around the classroom and 'look' at the work your students are doing? Do you think students are aware of this?

Is there evidence that you look at their exercise books?
Do you put their work on display for others to look at?

So far we have covered...

During fluent speech, the person listening does more of the gazing, while the person speaking does less. We use eye behaviour to regulate the flow of conversation. When we engage in conversation, we look for evidence that we have been misunderstood (as opposed to understood) and then set about 'repairing the damage'. We may look away when having difficulty processing information or deciding what to say. Leaders can control the group through the use of gazing, thereby orchestrating who speaks next and also how much time they get to speak. Needless to say, we should not engage in staring. Looking too much can cause discomfort. However, being looked at is important as it is a 'profound form of social acknowledgement' and infuses meaning into the child's actions. Excluding external stimulation by closing your eyes can help when engaging in difficult cognitive activity.

Looking means liking

A number of studies show that we gaze at people and things we perceive as rewarding (e.g. Efran and Boughton, 1966; Efran, 1968; Kleinke, 1986; Modigliani, 1971). But did you know that increasing your gaze is also connected with increasing how much people perceive themselves as being liked by you? In other words, we look more at people we are getting to like – and of course on the other hand we look less at people we dislike. This is an important factor to consider when thinking of behaviour management. If you have a disruptive and/or challenging pupil in your class, do you tend to avoid looking at them?

There are other dimensions to 'looking' which are connected with the important words of trust and honesty. Think of the last time you helped a colleague or student in your class. When we engage in these 'helping' tasks the use of gaze serves the important function of signalling trust, liking and honesty (Foddy, 1978).

You are how you look

The way you look or 'gaze', as it is often put in the academic literature, can give away important messages about your personality. Here is a short exercise for you. Have a look at the characteristics in Table 12.1 and decide which ones you would like to have associated with yourself.

The characteristics in the boxes below are all traits which have been found to be linked with people 'who look more' (Kleinke, 1986; Mehrabian and Williams 1969). The literature on gazing is fascinating because it highlights something simple we can do

TABLE 12.1 Characteristics of people 'who look more'.

Competent	Credible	Persuasive	Truthful
Assertive	Socially skilled	Informed	Friendly

which affects how people perceive us. For example, Argyle (1988) has found that 'gaze levels are higher' in those who are dominant, extroverted, assertive and socially skilled. In a well-known study, Kleck and Nuessle (1968) decided to examine how much we look at people and as a result how they perceive us. They showed a film of people looking at their partners. In the film, some of these people looked at their partner for 15 per cent of the time, while some of the people looked at their partner for 80 per cent of the time. Guess what? The 15 per cent people were labelled as cold, pessimistic, defensive, immature, evasive, submissive, indifferent and sensitive. On the other hand, the people who looked at their partner for 80 per cent of the time were judged as friendly, self-confident, natural, mature and sincere. Indeed, the amount we look has also been associated with nervousness and a lack of self-confidence. In a study by Cook and Smith (1975), people with low gaze were seen as being nervous and lacking in confidence.

Would you like to be perceived as more intelligent? There is some research evidence to indicate that people who perform highly on IQ tests also look more and engage in more interpersonal gazing (Knapp and Hall, 2006). This has obvious relevance for the classroom. But like all patterns of human behaviour, there are upsides and downsides to looking. It has been found that some Machiavellian types tend to look more as they have a greater need to control their environment (Murphy *et al.*, 2003).

So far we have covered...

Increasing your gaze is also connected with increasing how much people perceive themselves as being liked by you. People who gaze more are often perceived as being competent, credible, persuasive, truthful, assertive, socially skilled, extroverted, informed, dominant and friendly. The use of gaze serves the important function of signalling trust, liking and honesty. There is some evidence that those who perform highly on IQ tests engage in more interpersonal gazing.

Looking and social attitudes

While we are obviously advocating that 'looking more' is an important part of your X-Factor, we do want to caution the manner in which you do so. Here 'the amount we look' and 'who we look at' are important factors for us to bear in mind as we work in multi-cultural and multi-ethnic classrooms. We often leak messages by way of our nonverbal communication and because of this we can sometimes reveal social attitudes, such as negative feelings towards minority groups (Knapp and Hall, 2006). In a study undertaken by Dovidio *et al.* in 1997, on interview situations, a group of interviewees were set a task to establish whether they had some implicit attitudes concerning racial prejudice towards African American and white American interviewers. Then they placed these people in interview situations. Those interviewees who displayed more racial bias in the task blinked and gazed less towards the African American interviewer than the white interviewer with such blinking being associated with negative arousal and tension.

Classroom eyes and the anxiety factor

In our work with student teachers we have often heard them say: 'I was very nervous on my teaching practice.' Social anxiety is another factor to consider in gazing patterns. People with social anxiety gaze less. Matthews *et al.* (2003) note that some socially anxious individuals are especially attuned to evidence of threat in their environment. You may remember our chapter on the 'alert data base'. In this particular chapter we discussed how the human is continuously scanning the environment for nonverbal signs and signals, many of which are picked up in milliseconds. There are some who argue that this 'alert data base' is governed by our biology but also by our own individual experiences (Ekman, 2003). This may also be the case for socially anxious individuals who are 'especially visually attuned to evidence of threat in their environment' (Knapp and Hall, 2006, 354).

This brings us to the next part of 'classroom eyes' which has to do with giving feedback.

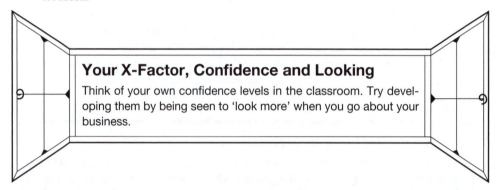

Your X-Factor, Confidence and Looking

Think of your own confidence levels in the classroom. Try developing them by being seen to 'look more' when you go about your business.

The way we use our classroom eyes

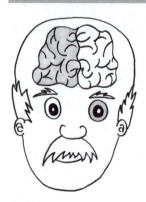

FIGURE 12.7 Your right brain is linked to the left eye – and vice versa.

You have probably heard of 'looking someone in the eye' and, indeed, no doubt have been advised before going into interviews, etc., to 'look them straight in the eye'. The interesting thing is, we do not actually stare directly into the other person's eyes for extended periods of time when we engage in 'looking someone in the eye' (Knapp and Hall, 2006). What actually happens is we do look at their face, but do not fixate on a single point. Rather, we make a series of glances of about one-third of a second at different points of the face, but especially the eyes and the mouth (Yarbus, 1967).

The way we use our eyes can sometimes give clues as to the side of the brain we are using. A set of fascinating studies which looked at electroencephalic activity (EEG) in the brain, gives us other insights into the manner in which we move our eyes.

When you move your eyes in a certain direction, it is thought that such movement indicates activity in the opposite side of the brain. So, for example, if you move your eyes to the left (a leftward glance), it indicates activity in the right side of the brain. Here you may be accessing or processing emotional or spatial information. On the other hand, if you move your eyes to the right (rightward glance), then you are often undertaking tasks associated with the left side of your brain, such as intellectual and linguistic tasks (Knapp and Hall, 2006).

Classroom eyes and teacher expectations

On the international stage, one particular study in 1968 catapulted the value of classroom nonverbal communication to centre stage and has specific relevance to your X-Factor. The well-known 'Pygmalion in the Classroom' study by Rosenthal and Jacobson (1968) demonstrated that teacher expectations of student academic potential could have an influence on their educational performance. The study highlighted that teachers' judgements of students' abilities could become self-fulfilling prophecies. More significantly, although teachers believed they treated all students equitably, this was not the case. The term 'teacher differential behaviour' was born.

Teacher differential behaviour concerns the mediation of teacher expectations in an inadvertent manner by the classroom teacher. The research indicates that these 'leaked' (Babad, 2005) expectations are internalised by the student and have a definitive effect on their school performance. Of key significance for educationalists were the findings by Harris and Rosenthal in 1985 that teacher differential behaviour, in the form of communicated expectations, was prevalent and potent in terms of pupil self-belief and application.

In analysing the mediation of such expectancies, Harris and Rosenthal found that teacher expectations are mediated through very fine and often hidden nuances, and not through gross and obvious behaviours. More significantly, they also noted that such nuanced and covert transmission of expectation had a very strong nonverbal component (Babad, 1993). For example, teacher eye contact was one particular dimension of nonverbal communication which was identified as revealing teacher expectations. Brophy (1983) measured the duration of teachers' eye contact with different students. He discovered that when a student responded incorrectly to a question, the teacher maintained eye contact for a longer period if they had high expectations of the student. On the other hand, the teacher maintained shorter eye contact if they had low expectations of the student. More significantly, Weinstein (2002) found that although the difference in length of eye contact was often not even noticeable to the casual observer, it was to the student in question. Students were found to be very perceptive of this nonverbal behaviour, correctly interpreting the hidden messages of eye contact as a revelation of teacher expectancies.

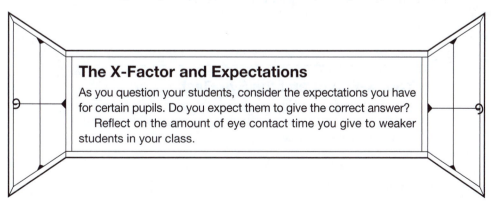

The X-Factor and Expectations

As you question your students, consider the expectations you have for certain pupils. Do you expect them to give the correct answer? Reflect on the amount of eye contact time you give to weaker students in your class.

Blinking

Blinking is sometimes associated with what Birdwhistle (1966, 244) called 'kinesic markers'. These are nonverbal markers we may use to accompany what we are saying. We may use these kinesic markers in terms of micro-movements of the head. Say, for example, if we were saying a hyphenated word. In some cases, we may use an eye blink at the beginning and end of some words. Excessive blinking has been shown as a sign of anxiety. The human should normally blink between six and ten times per minute. Some psychiatrists have noted patients blinking by up to 100 times per minute (Knapp and Hall, 2006).

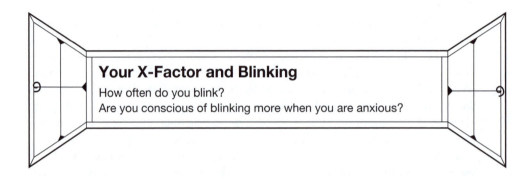

Your X-Factor and Blinking
How often do you blink?
Are you conscious of blinking more when you are anxious?

The eye flash

Sometimes we use our eyes without much conscious awareness, but other times we use them very deliberately. The example often cited in this scenario is the 'eye flash'. This flash is important as we usually use it to emphasise particular words as we speak, typically adjectives (Knapp and Hall, 2006). The 'eye flash' consists of the opening of the eyelids for less than a second *without* the involvement of the eyebrows (Walker and Trimboli, 1983). This is an important feature of your X-Factor. How aware are you of the adjectives and key words you use in a sentence? Do you emphasise certain words as you speak? Think of our last chapter on hand movements – do you use the eye flash and beats to emphasise the key words of your sentences?

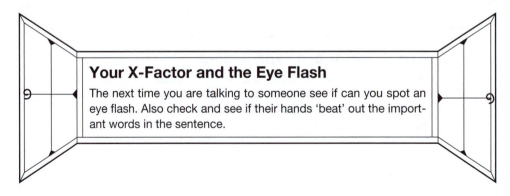

Your X-Factor and the Eye Flash
The next time you are talking to someone see if can you spot an eye flash. Also check and see if their hands 'beat' out the important words in the sentence.

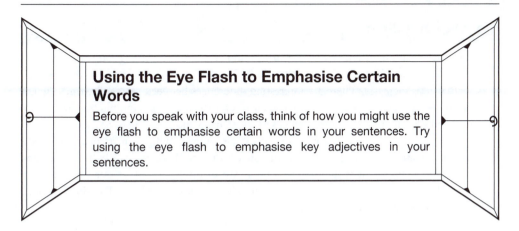

Using the Eye Flash to Emphasise Certain Words

Before you speak with your class, think of how you might use the eye flash to emphasise certain words in your sentences. Try using the eye flash to emphasise key adjectives in your sentences.

Pupil dilation and flashbulb eyes

It is impossible to discuss the topic of eye contact without making some reference to pupil dilation. Within the world of romance, there is considerable evidence to show that when people are attracted to each other their pupils dilate (pupil dilation means the pupils actually get bigger). Beyond the boundaries of flirtation, there is also evidence to show that pupil dilation occurs in other contexts. Pupil dilation is associated with attentiveness, mental effort, interest and perceptual orientation. Positive emotions and contentment are indicated by dilation and may often be accompanied by rising of the eyebrows, widening of the eye area and making the eyes look larger. As Joe Navarro (2008, 179) puts it 'the brain is essentially saying, I like what I see; let me see more'. Now whether we can control this dilation is another matter, but we can certainly recognise it in others. It is important to say here also that just because someone else's eyes are not dilated does not mean that they are not attentive or positively disposed.

Indeed, in some contexts, we may also dramatically expand on this further by opening the eyes as wide as possible and creating an effect that is known as flashbulb eyes. This is a wide-eyed look often associated with surprise or positive events. We encountered this in our own research, with one of our participants drawing a picture which depicts perfectly this flashbulb look of surprise and amazement (White, 2008, 124). You have probably noticed the big ears in the picture too. We'd better explain! Using flashbulb eyes does not make your ears bigger! In the case of this picture, the participant was explaining how she listened to pupils' answers (hence the symbolic big ears) and classroom comments, etc., and responded in a positive manner through the use of facial expressions and enlarged eyes.

FIGURE 12.8 Teacher's drawing – conveying amazement and encouragement.

Looking and distance

Distance is an important factor to bear in mind when we consider gazing and eye contact. What the theory tells us is that mutual gazing actually increases as the distance between us increases. There are interesting differences between men and women when it comes to gazing distance. Up to a distance of 10 ft, men will continue to gaze, while women's gazing reduces after distances of 6 ft (Knapp and Hall, 2006, 352).

We are also inclined to stare more at people with disabilities, particularly if we do not anticipate having to make conversation with them (Thompson, 1982). In developing your X-Factor, it is important to be aware of how we look at our students with special educational needs, particularly those with physical disabilities. The simple advice here is to be careful that you do not stare.

So far we have covered...

The further you are from someone, the more you gaze. Is this a good thing? Well, we can often leak negative feelings towards minority groups via our nonverbal communication, with blinking and reduced gaze being particularly relevant here. Indeed, our use of the eyes has also been found to be particularly relevant to the mediation of expectations in the classroom. Teacher differential behaviour which has a strong nonverbal component can leak our real expectations of the students we question. Other eye behaviour such as excessive blinking can leak feelings of anxiety. But what about the positive ways in which we can use our eyes? The eye flash is one such example, where opening of the eyelids for less than a second emphasises particular words as we speak, particularly adjectives. The direction in which we gaze can also give clues as to the side of the brain we are using. If you move your eyes to the left (a leftward glance), it may indicate activity in the right side of the brain. Here you may be accessing or processing emotional or spatial information. On the other hand, if you move your eyes to the right (rightward glance), then you are often undertaking tasks associated with the left side of your brain, such as intellectual and linguistic tasks.

Self-Evaluation Questions: Eye Contact

Am I being understood?

As people talk, they tend to look for evidence that they have been misunderstood rather than understood. This searching process is an attempt by the talker to identify moments when they are misunderstood and then to 'repair the damage'. Called grounding, it involves checking for understanding. Do you actively engage in 'grounding'?

Looking/gazing

1 To what degree do you look at students as they work?
2 How often do you move around the classroom and 'look' at the work your students are doing?
3 Is there evidence that you 'look' at exercise books?
4 Do you put pupils' work on display for others to look at?

Interaction

1 Do you use eye contact to initiate interaction?
2 Do you use eye contact to regulate the flow of conversation in class discussions?
3 Do you maintain appropriate eye contact with students for whom you have lower expectations?
4 How often do you use eye contact to check whether the student has understood what has been said?
5 In group situations, do you use eye contact to ensure all students are invited to contribute?
6 Do you try to ensure you make eye contact with all students?

Blinking

1 Do you blink a lot? Is this a sign of anxiety?

The eye flash

The eye flash involves opening the eyelids for less than a second without involvement of the eyebrows to emphasise particular words as we speak, e.g. adjectives. Are you aware of the value and possibilities of using the eye flash?

Students' thinking

1 Do you ever think of allowing students to close their eyes as they process or interrogate ideas/comments?
2 In what ways do you interpret students who look away? Do you view this positively as 'thinking' time?

13

Our Use of Space

Signs in our world

FIGURE 13.1 Territorial markings.

The world is governed by territorial rules. Our occupancy of space is much more important than we think and is flagged almost everywhere you look. If you are sitting down reading this book, in say a library, you will probably see territorial signs everywhere – 'No talking' – 'Private' – 'Staff Only'. You may also notice that people have strewn their bags, pencils and folders across desks, putting down the markers of their territories. Similarly, schools are quite territorial. Think of the sign on the staffroom door that has great significance for students – this is the staffroom, and, by corollary, not a student room – stay out! School car parks are adorned with signs such as 'Staff Cars' and other subtle territorial guides such as 'Please report to the school secretary'. If you ask any junior infant about grass in a school, they will probably say 'it is not for walking on'! We can also claim territorial areas by our use of objects – signals and signs of our occupancy of a particular area. Like all other species on this planet, the human is a territorial creature. We manage our use of space carefully, swiftly and often astutely.

Territories

Have you ever noticed the way birds gather on a wire? The next time you are out for a walk, look up and you will see that there is almost exactly the same distance between them (Argyle, 1988). The human also has space requirements. This chapter of the book considers your S-Factor (space factor)! Think of the student who says: 'get away from me' to another friend. His friend is standing too close and he is looking for more space. Like the birds on the wire we too have space requirements. In order to develop your S-Factor, it is important for you to be aware of the manner in which we are attuned to territory.

Basically, we can divide the human world into three kinds of territory. The primary territory is one which you yourself own. For example, your home or your bedroom. You can also have primary possessions such as a watch, or handbag and so on. We have an inbuilt need for our primary territory. Indeed, there is some research which suggests that those who have appropriate primary space have better levels of adaptation. In Japan, where there can be considerable overcrowding in the home, a study of Japanese women by Omata in 1996 found that those who had few private spaces of their own in the home, showed poorer levels of adaptation than those who did.

Secondary territory is not as central to the human as primary territories. An example of these kinds of territories are places where you tend to go regularly such as the local pub, or the same seat on a train. Schools tend to fit into this category. As teachers we occupy our secondary territories in quite a territorial manner. Do you sit in the same place in the staffroom? Do others? Do you always put your briefcase in the same place in the classroom? Do you always teach from the same place? The next time you are doing a course, notice that after break, you tend to return to the same seat, and so do the other participants! Similarly, students tend to occupy the same spaces. They are very aware of their territories. One of the fascinating pieces of work in this area involved a study by Gress and Heft in 1998 where they gradually increased the number of students who were forced to share a room. As the number increased, so too did the territorial behaviour of the occupants! In particular, they created barriers and arranged the room in certain ways which prohibited interaction. Interestingly, earlier work on the crowding of students by Sinha and Mukherjee (1996) found that where students are in crowded conditions, such as sharing a room, they actually come to need larger personal space and begin to dislike sharing even more than would be expected.

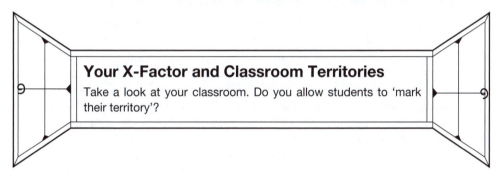

Your X-Factor and Classroom Territories

Take a look at your classroom. Do you allow students to 'mark their territory'?

The third type of territory we have is public territory. This is the kind of space that is available to all of us in the public domain, but only for a limited amount of time. So, for example, we have park benches, telephone booths, car park spaces and so on. The fascinating thing about public space is that we have clear rules about its occupancy. One of the classic ways in which we do this is to leave markers. So we find library books on desks, or jackets on seats. This is relevant to the classroom. From the seats of infants to the desks of PhD students, classrooms are alive with 'markers' and territorial jostling. This is an important thing to remember. Students like to 'mark', personalise and customise their own learning mini-cosmos. As a teacher do you allow for this? As students take their seats in your classroom, do you say to them: 'Are we all ready to start? Are we organised and settled into our seats?'

Finally, there is an aspect of 'territorial space' which relates to interaction territory. This is a special kind of space that we create around us. For example, how often have you spotted two teachers having an 'after-school chat' in the school car park? We 'walk around' these teachers as they have gathered in a public space and accordingly we have no real remit transgressing their own personal space (Hargie and Dickson, 2004). These kinds of interaction spaces have to do with our own personal spaces, they are a bit like bubbles which we carry around with us.

So far we have covered...

Like all other species on this planet, the human is a territorial creature. We manage our use of space carefully, swiftly and often astutely. Basically we can divide the human world into three kinds of territory. The primary territory is one which you yourself own, such as your bedroom. Secondary territory is not as central to the human as primary territories. Examples of these kinds of territories are places where you tend to go regularly such as the local pub, or the same seat on a train. Third, there is public territory. This is the kind of space that is available to all of us in the public domain, but only for a limited amount of time. So, for example, we have park benches, telephone booths, library seats. So how do we defend these public territories? One of the classic ways in which we do this is to leave markers. From the seats of infants to the desks of PhD students, classrooms are alive with 'markers' and territorial jostling.

The X-Factor and personal bubbles

There is a well-known song about a teacher and his student by the band The Police which has the chorus line 'Don't stand so close to me'. We all have personal space requirements; sometimes we like to have them invaded, sometimes not. Why do we need personal space? One theory from Dosey and Meisels (1969) quite simply suggests that it has to do with protection. This could make sense. For example, violent offenders need more personal space than the rest of us. They also seek more space behind them than in front of them, which contrasts with the rest of us, as we need more personal space in front of us (Hayduk, 1981, 1983).

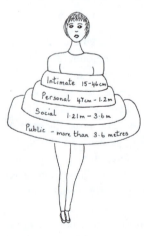

FIGURE 13.2 Our portable space–bubble requirements.

Put simply, personal space has to do with what Pease and Pease (2004) call the 'portable bubbles' we carry around with us. Hall (1966) gives us the most explicit and probably the simplest version of these bubbles. He describes the human space bubble in terms of four zones. The first zone is the intimate zone distance of 15–46 cm. As its name suggests, this relates to occupancy of the space by individuals very well known to the person in an intimate way. The second zone is the personal zone of 47 cm to 1.2 m. This zone relates to people who are very well known to the person and with whom the person is 'comfortable'. The third zone is the social zone of 1.21–3.6 m. This zone relates to social interaction, such as dinner party interaction. The fourth and final zone is the public zone, which is more than 3.6 m. This zone relates to interaction in the public domain and concerns meeting total strangers. Which zones do teachers occupy? Neill (1991) points out that on a typical school day, we tend to occupy the personal and social zones. Interestingly, as teachers, we are the primary architects of who occupies what bubbles. While it may seem obvious that we occupy certain bubbles, there are important distinctions to be made in terms of personality.

Sometimes the size of the personal space bubble depends on the individual in question. Argyle (1988) points out that Type A personalities which can be people who are very driven, time conscious and competitive, and also includes introverts, highly anxious people and violent offenders, need to have larger personal space bubbles than others. This will be discussed further in the next section.

In developing the S-Factor, it is important to know what kind of personal space we require as there are times when personal space distances are connected to our abilities to function cognitively. In particular, people who require more personal space have been shown to perform less well in recall and information processing tasks when they are placed in situations with a 'high social density' (Sinha *et al.*, 1999). This is of importance for your X-Factor and the X-Factor of your students. Some students may require more space than others. Do you like a lot of personal space?

On a typical school day, our occupancy of space tends to be within the personal and social zones. But the way we move between personal and social spaces with our students can leak our considered levels of intimacy with certain students (Neill, 1991). Indeed, research by Miller in 1979 suggests that we are inclined to preserve more distance between ourselves and students we dislike. There are also connections between the way we move towards students and the effectiveness of reprimands. Van Houten *et al.* (1982) found that reprimands delivered from a close distance (e.g. a metre) were more effective than those delivered from a long distance.

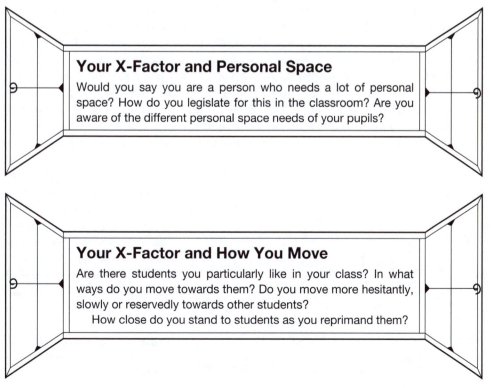

Your X-Factor and Personal Space

Would you say you are a person who needs a lot of personal space? How do you legislate for this in the classroom? Are you aware of the different personal space needs of your pupils?

Your X-Factor and How You Move

Are there students you particularly like in your class? In what ways do you move towards them? Do you move more hesitantly, slowly or reservedly towards other students?

How close do you stand to students as you reprimand them?

So far we have covered...

As humans we have four zones in our personal space bubble. The first zone is the intimate zone distance of 15–46 cm. We know the people very well and intimately. The second zone is the personal zone of 47 cm to 1.2 m. This zone relates to people who are very well known to us and with whom we are 'comfortable'. The third zone is the social zone of 1.21–3.6 m. This zone relates to social interaction, such as dinner party interaction. The fourth zone involves interactions of more than 3.6 m. This zone relates to interaction in the public domain and concerns meeting total strangers. Typically, as teachers, we tend to occupy the personal and social zones. But the size of these personal space bubbles can depend on your personality. People who require more personal space have been shown to perform less well in recall and information processing tasks when they are placed in situations with a 'high social density'. Also, as teachers, there is some research to show that we are inclined to preserve more distance between ourselves and students we dislike. Moreover, reprimands delivered from a close distance have been found to be more effective than those delivered from a long distance.

Interaction distances and personality

Have you ever noticed how close some people stand to you? Do you like this? Are you inclined to stand close to other people? There is considerable evidence to show that the closeness with which we stand to someone gives off messages about our personalities. Argyle (1988, 178) makes the point that proximity is 'decoded in terms of personality qualities'. If we think someone is going to be friendly towards us, we are more likely to interact with them at a closer distance. And while we converse, if we are still friendly, this distance can be further shortened. Introverts and anxiety-prone individuals tend to stand further away than extroverts. On the other hand, people who have a high concept of themselves, have affiliative needs, are high on interdependence, are self-directed or are low on authoritarianism tend to stand closer than others. The human is acutely aware of this. Even preschool children are perceptive of how close we stand to each other (King, 1966).

It is probably no surprise to learn that we stand closer to people we like (Mehrabian, 1968). Not only do we stand closer to people we like, but we also make a whole host of calculations about another person's personality based on distances of interaction (Patterson, 1968). Research on interview situations

FIGURE 13.3 Bunny Rabbit: Mr Fox, don't stand so close, we're not that friendly!

shows that where people choose closer distances when interacting, they are often seen as warmer, liking one another more, being more empathic and more understanding. In an intriguing study undertaken by Patterson and Sechrest (1970) an interview scenario was set up. The interviewees and interviewees sat side by side. However, the experiment instructed the interviewees to sit at different distances from the interviewer – at 60 cm, 120 cm, 180 cm and 240 cm. Those who came closest to the interviewers were judged as friendly, extroverted, aggressive and dominant. This has obvious significance for where we sit in terms of the students in our classrooms.

Indeed, dominance is one of those personality characteristics that can be clearly expressed in terms of spatial behaviour. Greater distances are chosen between persons of unequal status. Like the dominant monkeys in a troop of baboons, the higher the status of the individual, the more space they are afforded. Argyle (1988, 175) observes that the way we use rostrums and the like, serves to reinforce status by giving the 'leader extra height'. He also observes that a person can communicate dominance by select-

FIGURE 13.4 Mr Shark: On this occasion, I insist – you go first.

ing where they sit. Those with higher status or dominance go straight for the most important seat – or in some cases are allocated these seats.

In other seating arrangements, Lott and Sommer (1967) found that the higher status person usually sits at 90 degrees to the lower status person. They also point out that where there is a difference in status people do not tend to sit side by side. Dominance is also expressed by the freedom to move. Higher status people are able to choose interpersonal distances and are able to start and stop encounters. Mehrabian (1969) describes this as 'non-reciprocity' as the low status person does not have the same freedom. Teachers have the freedom to move where they wish, while students often do not (Miller, 2005).

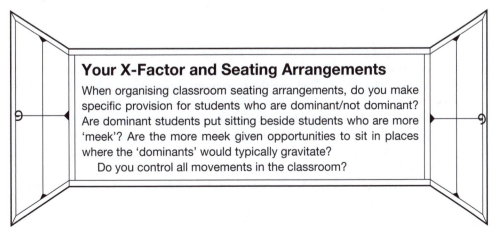

Your X-Factor and Seating Arrangements

When organising classroom seating arrangements, do you make specific provision for students who are dominant/not dominant? Are dominant students put sitting beside students who are more 'meek'? Are the more meek given opportunities to sit in places where the 'dominants' would typically gravitate?

Do you control all movements in the classroom?

Interaction distances and what we say

We are also likely to try and manage interaction distances based on our perceptions of what the person is going to say. When you meet someone, you anticipate what they are going to say. This anticipation can affect the conversational distance you maintain with the other person. As you would expect, we maintain a closer distance with someone when we anticipate that they are going to say something positive. The classic study in this area was undertaken by Leipold in 1963. Three scenarios were set for a group of students who were 'tipped off' on feedback they were due to receive from a teacher called 'Mr Leipold'. The first 'tip off' scenario involved the student being told he/she was going to receive a negative comment from Mr Leipold such as 'Your grade is poor and you have not done your best.' The second scenario involved a more positive setting involving praise, for example, 'You are doing very well and Mr Leipold wants to talk to your father.' The third scenario was a neutral one, for example, the student was told: 'Mr Leipold is interested in your feelings on the introductory course.' As you would expect, students who received the positive 'tip offs' sat closest to Mr Leipold, while those who received the negative 'tip offs' sat farthest from him.

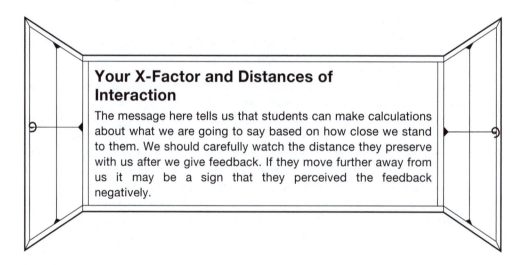

Your X-Factor and Distances of Interaction

The message here tells us that students can make calculations about what we are going to say based on how close we stand to them. We should carefully watch the distance they preserve with us after we give feedback. If they move further away from us it may be a sign that they perceived the feedback negatively.

The interesting twist in this tale is that distances between people which are too close can elicit negative attitudes when the communicator–addressee relationship is not an intimate one (Mehrabian, 1969). So the obvious question here is: at what distances do these negative attitudes begin? When do we start to feel uncomfortable? Our trawl of the literature would suggest what is known as the '1 ft distance' ($c.30$ cm). As Russo (1967) points out, straying inside this distance, in the vast majority of cases, causes people to move away. Typically, people start to feel a little uncomfortable at $c.70$ cm, moderately so at $c.50$ cm and very uncomfortable at under $c.30$ cm. Obviously people with large personal space needs will have even lower tolerance of these space invasions (Hayduk, 1983, 1981).

Approaching people and boys v. girls

There are interesting gender differences in terms of how we approach people. With strangers, males feel more stress when invaded 'head on' – i.e. from the front. On the other hand, Fisher and Byrne (1975) observe that women are more disturbed when they are approached from the side. Why is this? Fisher and Byrne advance the theory that women see invasion from the side as a need for affiliation, while men see front-on invasions as threatening. There is also evidence to indicate that women approach more closely than men. In particular, women approach women more closely than any other gender combinations (Argyle, 1988).

Interaction distances and culture

It has been shown that there are variations in conversational distance according to your culture. For example, infants reared in different cultures learn different rules of what is termed in the literature as 'proxemics' (how we occupy space). In Japan, mothers spend a lot of time with their infants by comparison to say American mothers. Indeed, in some cultures, mother, father and infant sleep in the same room (e.g. Japan) and in other cultures they sleep in separate rooms (e.g. UK), while in others, the infant sleeps in the mother's arms at night (e.g. Kenya). This has an effect on the children and their preconceptions of what are comfortable and uncomfortable interaction distances. In those cultures where the infant and mother/family are in close proximity, there is a tendency towards interaction at closer distances.

Some research shows that there are differences in interaction distances among children according to race. For example, in 1985, Halberstadt found that on entering elementary school, black children were more inclined to speak at closer interaction distances than white children. However, this tendency had almost vanished by the time they reached fifth grade. There may also be differences in interaction distances according to class. For example, Scherer (1974) found that middle-class children maintained greater conversational distances from each other. On the other hand, lower-class children, by comparison, maintained shorter conversational distances.

The space factor and the meaning of what we say

The next time you are talking to someone, carefully watch the way they occupy space as they tell you something. Our occupancy of space can vary according to what we are saying, giving additional meaning to parts of our sentences which we think are important. Erickson (1975) found that proxemic shifts may mark important segments of our encounters with someone else. For example, if we are interacting with someone and shorten or extend the interaction distance, we may be doing this to mark beginnings or endings of our encounter, or we may be doing it to change the topic or to emphasise a point in the conversation. We can also use proxemic shifts to mark the beginning and ending of the encounter.

So far we have covered…

Our occupancy of space can vary according to what we are saying, giving additional meaning to parts of our sentences which we think are important. That said, introverts and anxiety-prone individuals tend to stand farther away than extroverts. On the other hand, people who have a high concept of themselves, have affiliative needs, are high on interdependence, are self-directed or are low on authoritarianism tend to stand closer than others. Preschool children are aware of this. If we think someone is going to be friendly towards us, we are more likely to interact with them at a closer distance. People who choose closer distances when interacting are often seen as warmer, liking one another more, more empathic and more understanding. We also maintain a closer distance with someone when we anticipate that they are going to say something positive. When we expect criticism, we sit further apart. Greater distances are chosen between persons of unequal status. A person can communicate dominance by selecting where they sit. What distances do we start to feel uncomfortable at? In the vast majority of cases, the '1 ft distance' causes people to move away. The way you are approached can also cause stress. With strangers, males feel more stress when invaded 'head on' – i.e. from the front. On the other hand, women are more disturbed when they are approached from the side. It is important to remember that conversational distances do vary according to culture.

Where do you stand?

Where do you stand when you teach your class? Do you think this makes a difference? Well it does. Where we stand can affect the style of teaching we adopt. In 1980, Reid looked at the places where teachers tended to stand and found that those who confined it to the blackboard area of the classroom tended to adopt lecturing styles of teaching. This had an effect on pupil engagement. Teachers who stood in these places received less feedback from their students than if they were itinerant teachers who moved freely around the classroom.

FIGURE 13.5 Zone of participation.

Where you stand can also affect your distribution of questions. It has been established that particular areas of the classroom receive higher concentrations of teacher questions than other areas. One of the primary reasons for this is quite simply connected with the teacher's range of vision. Student participation is highest when students are located within range of the teacher's eye gaze. Where we concentrate our questions also has to do with the fact that teachers are inclined to locate attentive students closer to what Adams and Biddle (1970) call their 'teaching zone'. This zone basically looks like a kite with the teacher at the apex – see Figure 13.5. The students in the centre of the room are most affected by the questioning while those at the periphery are more likely to be left out.

In a further fascinating insight into teacher location in the classroom, Koneya (1973) found that when high, medium and low participating students were given a chance to choose the seats they wanted to occupy in a classroom, high participators were most likely to choose seats in the 'zone of participation'. So, what if we change where students sit and deliberately place the low and medium participating students in the 'zone of participation'? Koneya found that low participators did not increase their involvement in lessons; however, medium participators did increase their classroom participation. In relation to where we sit and stand in class, there is one other important finding from the work of Haber (1982). She examined students who were in the minority in five different colleges, looking in particular at students who were in the minority in terms of ethnicity, race and religion. She found that these minorities tended to pick seats which were at the periphery of the 'zone of participation'. How can we solve this? Within the classroom, the critical point to remember here is that 'teachers have the freedom to move around the classroom whereas students do not' (Miller, 2005, 59). Thus by moving to a different area of the classroom we can set up a new zone of participation and accordingly place those students who may be outside our zone of gaze back in it.

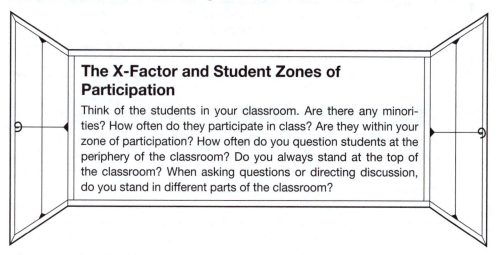

The X-Factor and Student Zones of Participation

Think of the students in your classroom. Are there any minorities? How often do they participate in class? Are they within your zone of participation? How often do you question students at the periphery of the classroom? Do you always stand at the top of the classroom? When asking questions or directing discussion, do you stand in different parts of the classroom?

Who gets to go first?

'Teacher, I was first in the line and then Mark pushed me out of the way.' Have you heard this before? Being first in the line is a big deal for elementary pupils, but it may not stop at that – precedence and who gets to go first is relevant to all of us. No doubt as a teacher you have often wondered what 'the big deal is'. But precedence is a key part of human behaviour, and indeed there may be an evolutionary basis to this (Burgoon and Hoobler, 2002). Alpha males in the animal kingdom get to feast on the prey

FIGURE 13.6 Who gets to go first can be symbolic.

first. And so too, it seems that dominant humans are the first then to get the spoils of war. We make many quick and important calculations about people based on whether they 'lead' the group or whether they follow. The next time you meet a group of teachers, see who is 'leading' the group as they walk. Are they the dominant type? Do they seem confident? We use the symbolism of the group leader in many different ways – think of the leader of the parade, the 'VIP area', the team captain leading the players on to the pitch and so on. So it is little wonder that in the world of the child, who gets to go first is 'big business'! This is an important feature of classroom behaviour. How aware are you of rotating the leader? Are different students allowed to lead the group or class? It is also relevant to your own status. Do you always lag behind others when walking? Are you first to lead as you leave the classroom? When walking with a group of your colleagues, do you lead or follow?

So far we have covered...

Student participation is highest when students are located within range of the teacher's eye gaze. By moving to a different area of the classroom we can set up a new zone of participation and accordingly place those students who may be outside our zone of gaze back in it. Who gets to go first leaks messages about leadership.

How close do you sit to a student?

In many countries, police interrogators are instructed to sit close to a suspect, with no desk between them, as the desk can be seen to provide comfort or protection for the interrogated. It is argued that the removal of this barrier coupled with the closeness of the interrogator gives them an advantage (Knapp and Hall, 2006).

Clearly, classroom scenarios are not similar to police interrogation rooms, but we want you to think of the situations where you work with small groups of students. Where do you sit? Now think of the situation where someone sits down beside you and then moves their chair closer to you. How do you feel? One of the ways in which we can stir a 'get me out of here feeling' in others is to sit beside them on a chair and then move the chair closer to them (about 30 cm – 1 ft) (Russo, 1967). This is particularly relevant to students. Russo undertook a number of studies on college students and found that sitting too close to them caused them to feel uncomfortable, but, most interestingly, they were reluctant to say anything about these feelings to the 'intruder'. Instead, when we are in these 'uncomfortable' scenarios, we try to give nonverbal signals by making defensive gestures such as folding our arms, shifting our posture and attempting to move away.

Why do we say nothing? Knapp and Hall (2006) make the astute observation that 'the norm of politeness' prevails in these situations. We make statements 'off the record'. We glare, start fixing papers, lean back, fold our arms and so on. Interestingly, there may be some relevance to status here also. Barash (1973) found that the perceived status of the intruder had a bearing on how quickly students try to 'flee the situation'. If the intruder was regarded as having high status (more formally dressed), then the students were much more inclined to flee.

Where we sit, and where others sit in relation to us, affects us in many ways. We all sit together on the tram or underground, but how do you feel when someone sits too close to you in the airport departure lounge? Did you know, that as people come close to us in 'face to face' encounters our bodies react (Finando, 1973; McBride *et al.*, 1965)? Our heart rate and galvanic skin responses increase. The next time someone approaches, try to take a moment to ascertain whether your body functions change. When we go into these states of arousal, we label the state in one of two ways. We either decide it is a positive state or a negative one. When people are confronted by an 'intrusion' which they do not like, they take measures to restore a 'proper' distance. This can involve looking away, changing the topic being discussed to one which is less personal, making a barrier by crossing one's arms, covering body parts and rubbing one's neck. Interestingly, by rubbing our neck we are engaged in a displacement activity which was mentioned in an earlier chapter, but, also, we are pointing the elbow outwards in a sharp manner which has a defensive message. Now the issue for you as a teacher is to be aware of these signs and signals, which may indicate that you are seated too close to a student. In so doing, and as we mentioned earlier, it is also important to note that personality and tolerance of interpersonal distances are related.

There is also some research to show a connection between where we sit in the classroom and how we 'dispense rewards'. In 1980, a team led by Russell conducted some fascinating research on social influence and the way we sit. They found that when giving rewards of a 'I am personally pleased' nature, then sitting beside (side by side) the person had greater effect. So, for example, in the classroom, this might mean saying that 'I think you were very kind to offer help to Fernando in doing his Maths'. On the other hand, rewards which were 'correct' as opposed to personal, were better delivered head on. For example, saying 'I have good news for you, you attended school all term and so you are one of the students who will receive an attendance prize'.

Seating and leadership

Like the precedence we talked about earlier, where you sit gives off important messages about leadership. The key factor at play here has to do with communication. For example, elected group leaders generally put themselves at the head of the table – when the table is rectangular. This has to do with the flow of communication. Other members at the table position themselves so they can see the 'leader'. The spatial position of the leader determines the flow of conversation, which in turn re-establishes the leader as leader. In 1968, Ward conducted an experiment where college students were grouped around a table for a discussion and found that those who were visually central were rated as having more leadership. Interestingly, the study also found that those who were placed in visually central positions behaved differently. They talked more. This has obvious significance for us as educators. In group work, do we place quieter students in a more visually central position to perhaps try to get them to engage more? This may be difficult. Work by Reiss and Rosenfeld in 1980 found that people choose seats based on definite mindsets. For example, they chose end positions to convey power and dominance.

FIGURE 13.7 Being visually central can affect flows of conversation.

On the other hand, we can occupy seats to give messages in terms of signalling interest and quite simply whether we like someone. We all know that students like to sit beside their friends. When we want to convey interpersonal attraction we choose seats which are side by side. And no doubt you are familiar with the back-benchers – students who pick seats which are the least visually accessible to indicate they do not wish to participate (Reiss and Rosenfeld, 1980). From studies of students in cafeterias and libraries, Cook (1970) found that when engaged in cooperation we tend to sit side by side. If we are working on different things but need to sit at the same table we seek plenty of room and where possible select the most distant seating arrangements.

Competitions are part and parcel of all classroom life. If we are competing with each other then we tend to sit opposite each other. As Argyle (1988, 173) points out, this is not surprising. From the animal world we know that when frightened they like to keep the enemy 'under surveillance'. Interestingly, in Cook's 1970 study of US students, when competition was part of the task in hand, they chose to sit opposite each other and also quite close together, thus allowing each person a chance to judge the competition and even put them off through nonverbal means (e.g. eye contact). In comparison to the USA, Argyle (1988) suggests that Britons are more inclined to sit farther apart when in competition.

Furniture

Have a look at your classroom. Where is your desk? Where are the pupils' desks? There is some research evidence to indicate that where we place our desks has an effect on others. In 1976, Zweigenhaft examined the location of American professors' desks in their offices and found that those professors

FIGURE 13.8 Where do you position your desk? Does it act as a barrier?

who put their desks against the wall or window as opposed to setting them up as a barrier between them and their visitors were rated as being more willing to give individual attention to students, to encourage the development of different viewpoints by students and they were less likely to show 'undue favouritism'. The manner in which we organise students' desks also affects different kinds of learning. This is particularly relevant to co-operative learning.

Seating arrangements and co-operative learning

In recent times, the benefits of using co-operative learning have come to the fore (Cohen, 1990; Slavin, 1989; Johnson *et al.*, 1998). One of the central findings from research in the field is that the long-term academic and social benefits of co-operative learning are overwhelmingly positive (Putnam, 1997; Slavin, 1985; Johnson and Johnson, 1989). So what does this mean for classroom organisation and seating arrangements? In order to facilitate co-operative learning, the classroom may need to be arranged so that the students within these groups are in close contact, facing each other and sitting on the same eye-to-eye level in assigned areas of the classroom. In addition, it is important to make provision for the appropriate spatial design and circulation patterns to facilitate student and teacher participation in instructional activities and to allow for communication among students and between students and teachers (Kirk, 2005).

So far we have covered...

Where students choose to sit is not accidental. It is often a subconscious choice that reveals levels of engagement, leadership or even self-awareness of difference. It gives off important messages about leadership. The spatial position of the leader determines the flow of conversation, which in turn re-establishes the leader as leader. This has obvious significance for us as educators. In group work, do we place quieter students in a more visually central position to perhaps try to get them to engage more? What about the kind of task in hand? Co-operative tasks usually mean people sit side by side. On the other hand, if we are competing with each other then we tend to sit opposite each other. What about the make up of the group? The way we organise seating arrangements is important in terms of facilitating co-operative learning.

We also make calculations about people based on where they sit. Extraverts are likely to choose seating arrangements opposite the other person. When giving rewards of a personal nature some research shows that they are delivered better when seated beside the person. On the other hand, rewards based on 'correctness' are better delivered when seated in 'head on' scenarios. Where and how we locate our desks gives off messages. For example, we can use our desks as barriers.

Self-Evaluation Questions: Use of Space

Territories

1 In what ways are the 'territories' in your classroom 'marked'?
2 Do you allow students to 'mark' their own territories?

Personal space

1 Would you say you are a person who needs a lot of personal space? Are you aware of the different personal space needs of your pupils?
2 Are there students you particularly like in your class? In what ways do you move towards them? Do you move more hesitantly, slowly or reservedly towards other students?
3 How close do you stand to students as you reprimand them?
4 Do you tend to stand closer to students you like?
5 When sitting next to pupils, how closely do you monitor their body language and facial expressions in order to ascertain that you are not too close to them or too far?

Your location in the classroom

1 Where do you stand as you teach? Do you tend to teach from the same place?
2 Do you always stand at the front of the classroom? Are there any areas of the classroom you do not occupy regularly? Why?
3 What is the kite zone of participation like around you? Do you change where you stand in order to ensure all students are within the zone of participation?
4 How often do students participate in class? Are they within your zone of participation? How often do you question students at the periphery of the classroom?
5 When directing discussions, do you stand in different parts of the classroom?

Dominance

1 Do you communicate dominance by selecting where you sit and where certain other students sit? Are some students with 'higher status' or dominance allowed to sit where they want?

Conversational distances

1 Are you aware of the conversational distances students maintain with you?
2 To what degree are you aware of the cultural variances in conversational distances?

continued

Proxemic shifts

1 How aware are of you of your use of proxemic shifts? (Our occupancy of space can vary according to what we are saying, giving additional meaning to parts of our sentences which we think are important.)

Who gets to go first?

1 Do the same people always get to go first?
2 Are you first to lead as you leave the classroom?

Being visually central

1 When organising discussion groups, do you ensure that quieter students are seated in more visually central positions?
2 Where is your desk? Does it act as a barrier between you and your students?

14

Facial Expressions

The face a book to read

FIGURE 14.1 Using the face to give messages.

We all use our faces to give messages – either wittingly or unwittingly! Think of one colleague giving a knowing wink to another at a meeting or the child who sticks his tongue out at a peer who has annoyed him intensely! This is an example of the deliberate use of the face. But sometimes, the face can betray us. It can leak what we truly feel or believe. For example, Hart (1995) found that judges' expressions can unconsciously influence jurors. Physicians' expressions can have an impact on patients (Ambady *et al.*, 2002). TV presenters may inadvertently leak their favourite political candidate (Mullen, 1986).

As humans we tend to give more weight to the face than any other channel of communication (Knapp and Hall, 2002). There is a myriad of inferences that we make about people's faces ... he looks grumpy, she looks pleasant and so on. This is not surprising. Did you know that there are over 20 muscles in the face which can produce in excess of 1000 distinct expressions? Even though we can produce all these expressions on the face, it is quite amazing that across the globe we are able to recognise six basic emotions in the face – sadness, anger, disgust, fear, surprise and happiness. There are some who say that contempt is a possible seventh. There is also evidence that we are specially attuned to the recognition of anger and threat (Esteves, 1999; Fox *et al.*, 2000).

Using your face to give messages

The recognition of faces is part of our evolutionary heritage. Believe it or not, sheep can recognise other sheep's faces (McGilchrist, 2010)! The human is especially good at reading the face. We have an 'inborn capacity' to do this, beginning from early childhood (Segerstrale and Molnar, 1997; Babad, 2005). This is not surprising, as we use our faces a lot to accompany what we are saying. Like the beats we talked about in using your hands, or the 'eye flash' to signify important words, so too the overall face is used to augment our messages. This is often termed 'syntactic display'. Here we use the face to mark words and clauses in the sentence. We use it to mark the beginning, end and restart of sentences. And, of course, we use it to place emphasis on certain parts of what we say. Sometimes this is unwitting as it happens concurrently with our talking, but sometimes it is not. On such occasions we 'manage the use of our face'. As teachers there are many ways we can successfully and deliberately use the face to 'beat out' what we are saying and to give messages (White, 2008).

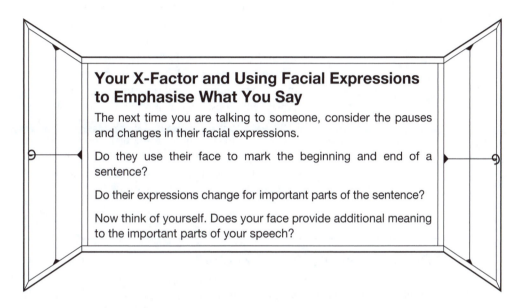

Your X-Factor and Using Facial Expressions to Emphasise What You Say

The next time you are talking to someone, consider the pauses and changes in their facial expressions.

Do they use their face to mark the beginning and end of a sentence?

Do their expressions change for important parts of the sentence?

Now think of yourself. Does your face provide additional meaning to the important parts of your speech?

Facial expression and display rules

Think of the person who receives a CD from a friend for their birthday. They open the present and exclaim 'Just what I wanted!' with a facial expression of excitement: while, secretly, rueing the fact that they had bought it themselves the previous day. Such use of the face is governed by what Ekman and Friesen (1969b) call 'display rules'. These are display rules we use to give deliberate messages. Teachers often do this. In some of our own research we came across instances where teachers used their faces to send a message. In one research situation, the teacher drew a picture (see right) to portray the use of facial expressions to give positive reinforcement.

FIGURE 14.2 Teacher's drawing – conveying amazement and encouragement.

FIGURE 14.3 The face as a lighthouse of emotion.

This teacher was responding positively to a pupil's answer, displaying what she called 'enthusiasm and support' for the child's comment. Notice the open eyes and broad expression of awe. Here this kind of response could be termed as 'overintensification of the affect' (Ekman and Friesen, 1969b). We are exaggerating our emotional response through the use of the face.

Our faces beam our emotional reactions across the classroom. Russell *et al.* (2003) give us a great description of the face as a 'lighthouse of emotion'. It beckons and beacons to all around, and as such is obviously a critical feature of your X-Factor. It allows you to imbue what you are saying and how you are reacting with emotional meaning. In addition to using the face to 'overplay' emotions, we can also use it to underplay our emotions in what Ekman and Friesen (1969b) call the 'deintensified affect'. Think of the disappointed student who is dropped from the college debating team and passes it off saying 'I don't really mind', with a facial expression of disinterest and acceptance.

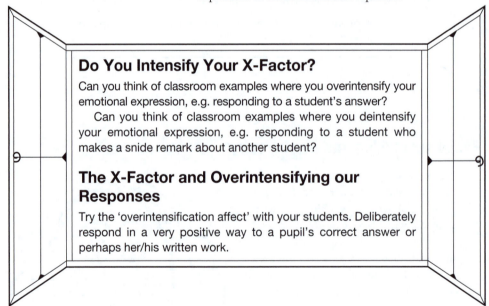

Do You Intensify Your X-Factor?

Can you think of classroom examples where you overintensify your emotional expression, e.g. responding to a student's answer?

Can you think of classroom examples where you deintensify your emotional expression, e.g. responding to a student who makes a snide remark about another student?

The X-Factor and Overintensifying our Responses

Try the 'overintensification affect' with your students. Deliberately respond in a very positive way to a pupil's correct answer or perhaps her/his written work.

A closer look at the work of Ekman and Friesen (1975) helps us understand these display types. They looked at the display of emotions in public and make the point that our displays of emotion are affected by social norms. This may explain why sports people rarely cry after losing a match and also why, for example, people in the UK were transfixed when Paul Gascoigne cried on screen after England were knocked out of the World Cup in 1990. To help us classify the various forms of social facial displays, Ekman and Friesen came up with the following types:

The withholder

This occurs when there is little facial movement, with the face actually inhibiting the expression of emotion.

The unwitting expressor

Here we express feelings which we think have been hidden – for example, 'How did you know I was surprised?'

The revealer

Here the face clearly reveals what the person is feeling.

The blanked expressor

Here we think we are portraying an emotion, but others only see a blank expression.

The substitute expressor

Here the facial expression is not what you think it is. For example, you think you showed surprise but instead, disappointment emerged.

The frozen-affect expressor

This relates to emotional expressions that tend to be permanently etched on someone's face. It may be just part of an emotional display on show at all times.

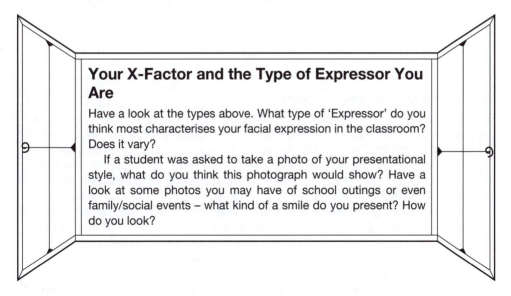

Your X-Factor and the Type of Expressor You Are

Have a look at the types above. What type of 'Expressor' do you think most characterises your facial expression in the classroom? Does it vary?

If a student was asked to take a photo of your presentational style, what do you think this photograph would show? Have a look at some photos you may have of school outings or even family/social events – what kind of a smile do you present? How do you look?

Facial expression and social setting

Social setting is important when it comes to facial expression. Without getting too deeply into neuroscience or contemporary theory on personal identity, there are a number of theories on emotional expression in the face which are worthy of consideration. Dating back to Darwin, there are some who say that facial displays of emotion have a biological origin. They argue that the face is a direct biological signalling system for what is happening inside you emotionally (Cornelius, 1996). However, there are others who think that social factors are also important players in the way we use our faces. They state that social motives and intentions influence our use of facial expressions (Fridlund, 1997). These social pressures impact on how much we want to reveal nonverbally. Knapp and Hall (2006) describe the influence of such social pressures on our use of the face as 'the audience effect'. The funny thing is that although this effect obviously occurs when we have an audience, it may also happen when we are on our own – in an 'imagined presence' (Knapp and Hall, 2006, 305). Sometimes we adopt facial expressions when we are on our own! Think of opening a letter and discovering you owe more tax than you have paid!

Indeed, some philosophers argue that all facial expressions are a form of acting or 'performance' (Nichol and Watson, 2000). You may remember that in Chapter 2 we talked about 'Early Man and the X-Factor' and how we are pre-programmed to read nonverbal communication. Fridlund (1994) argues that while we are programmed to read the face, we are not pre-programmed to readily express our emotions on our face. Such an argument is grounded in the theory that in ancient times, if our face readily expressed our emotions it could give our rivals an advantage over us. Fridlund makes the critical point that facial expressions are meant to *communicate* rather than *reveal* our emotions. This is an important distinction. It is very useful in the classroom. What kinds of messages do you deliberately convey from your face? How do you feel as you walk into a classroom?

 So far we have covered...

Your face acts as a 'lighthouse of emotion'. As humans we tend to give more weight to the face than any other channel of communication. There are six basic emotions which we can spot on the face – sadness, anger, disgust, fear, surprise and happiness. Sometimes we use the face to augment our messages. This 'syntactic display' uses the face to mark words and clauses in the sentence. We also use it to mark the beginning and end of sentences. And, of course, we use it to place emphasis on certain parts of what we say. We can also use the face to give deliberate messages. Sometimes termed display rules, we can 'overintensify the affect' by exaggerating our emotional response or we can 'deintensify the affect' by underplaying our emotions. We must also remember that displays of emotion in public are affected by social norms.

Controlling our facial expressions

To say that we can totally control the face and use it deliberately is simplistic. There are aspects of our facial displays which occur in a matter of milliseconds and we have no control over them. Keltner (1997) calls them 'micro-momentary expressions'. They are particularly associated with the expression of feelings of amusement and embarrassment. Here we reveal amusement or embarrassment in a fraction of a second and often in a very fleeting manner. Because these micro-momentary expressions are so rapid, they are difficult to control. The interesting thing is, even though they occur in milliseconds, the human can still read them. Knapp and Hall (2002, 328) note that we have an 'uncanny sensitivity' to facial expressions. Studies of minute facial expressions also show that we unconsciously mimic these expressions even when they happen so quickly that we do not have time to process them consciously. Indeed, one particular study by Murphy and Zajonc in 1993 showed that when we are exposed to just four *milli*seconds of a happy or angry face we are affected by such rapid exposures (such a fast exposure makes it too short for us to process the picture consciously).

You may remember from Chapter 2 that how we convey our emotions nonverbally is important from the point of view of the emotional contagion effect – people can catch our emotions via nonverbal channels. So, in adopting these facial expressions of interest or disinterest, we are also affecting the listener. There is also something else very important happening here. Something you may be unaware of, yet experiencing at the same time! This has to do with facial feedback theory.

Facial feedback theory and your X-Factor

Sometimes as teachers we pretend to be surprised and overawed at a pupil's work or answer, etc. In other words we adopt facial expressions which convey these messages. You may remember that in Chapter 3 we discussed how you can evoke emotions within yourself. Have a look at Figure 14.4, completed by one of the participants in our research, which depicts some of this teacher's facial expressions of emotion in the classroom. Notice the deliberate use of the eyes and mouth. Here the

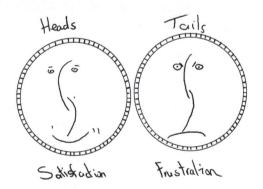

FIGURE 14.4 Teacher illustration of 'classroom emotions'.

teacher was communicating expressions of excitement in one instance and concern in another. In adopting these outward facial expressions, was the participant actually stirring any inward emotions?

If we adopt particular facial expressions there is also the chance that the outward adoption of such expressions may cause an inward realisation of the emotion. Putting on a happy and surprised face may make us happy and surprised inside. This relates to what is known as facial feedback theory. Basically it asserts that through our manipulation of our facial expressions we can then prompt particular emotions in ourselves. As we move our facial muscles we are also sending signals to the brain that we are experiencing an emotion and then we may ignite that emotion inside ourselves (Blairy *et al.*, 1999). To illustrate this, let us look at Strack *et al.*'s (1988) well-known 'pencil in the teeth study'.

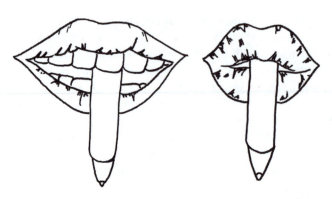

Here a group of investigators deceived participants by telling them they wanted to investigate ways to help persons with disabilities to hold a writing implement. The implement could be held between the teeth, or it could be held by the lips. Such usage of the lips and teeth were ingeniously selected. When we hold something in the teeth, we naturally expand our lips – our smiling muscles are activated. On the other hand, when we hold something using the lips, the muscles are contracted and the smiling muscles are not activated to the same degree. While holding the pencils in the teeth and in the lips, participants were also shown cartoons. Those participants who held the pencil in their teeth (which activated the smiling muscles) rated the cartoons as funnier than those who held the pencil using their lips. In other words, the facial feedback affected the participants' predispositions to particular emotional experiences.

FIGURE 14.5 Holding the pencil in the teeth activates smiling muscles.

Let us take another example – sadness. Paul Ekman (2003, 97) provides a list of instructions to make you feel sad. He suggests the following set of facial moves:

1 Drop your mouth open.
2 Pull the corners of your lips down.
3 While you hold those lip corners down, try now to raise your cheeks, as if you are squinting. This pulls against the lip corners.
4 Maintain this tension between the raised cheeks and the lip corners pulling down.
5 Let your eyes look downward and your upper eyelids drop.

Are you feeling sad yet? In undertaking this exercise, it may also be helpful to look at a sad picture.

Not only can manipulation of our facial muscles affect our emotions, it can also affect our judgements. Another fascinating study by Strack and Neumann (2000) examined how certain facial manipulations can affect judgements. In this study, some of the participants were asked to furrow their brows while undertaking a task on a computer. The participants were then told that the study was investigating how working on a computer can cause tension for the user. This was a trick and was not the real purpose of the experiment. The real purpose of the experiment was to investigate whether the participants' judgements of other people would be affected by furrowing their brows.

While working on the computer with their furrowed brows the participants were asked to rate certain celebrities according to their fame. Those participants with the furrowed brows were less generous in their ratings than the other participants who had a 'normal brow'.

The point here is simple and reminds us of the great lines from Roald Dahl's book *The Twits*. Early in the book, Roald describes how the Twits developed ugly faces because they thought ugly thoughts! He describes the phenomenon as follows:

> If a person has ugly thoughts, it begins to show on their face. And when that person has ugly thoughts every day, every week, every year, the face gets uglier … a person who has good thoughts cannot ever be ugly. You can have a wonky nose and a crooked mouth and a double chin and stick-out teeth, but if you have good thoughts they will shine out of your face like sunbeams and you will always look lovely.
>
> (*The Twits*, 7)

Indeed, Dahl's description of the sunbeams shining from the face also reminds us of Russell *et al.*'s (2003) description of the face as a lighthouse of emotion as discussed earlier in this chapter.

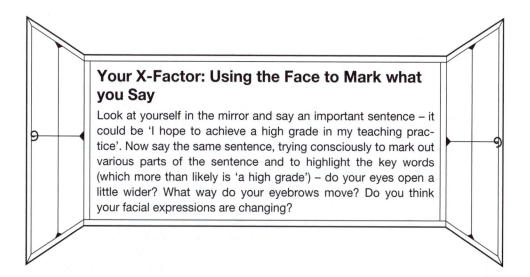

Your X-Factor: Using the Face to Mark what you Say

Look at yourself in the mirror and say an important sentence – it could be 'I hope to achieve a high grade in my teaching practice'. Now say the same sentence, trying consciously to mark out various parts of the sentence and to highlight the key words (which more than likely is 'a high grade') – do your eyes open a little wider? What way do your eyebrows move? Do you think your facial expressions are changing?

Expressing emotion is good for your health factor!

You are probably saying to yourself at this point that there are people you know who display lots of emotions on their faces and others who display none. Does it matter? Yes, it does! Expressing your emotions is good for you. It is good for the health of your X-Factor! A number of studies make connections between people who 'repress' their emotions and health problems. People who are less expressive experience a higher level of internal physiological arousal (Buck *et al.*, 1974). For example, Friedman and Booth-Kewley (1987) found that a 'repressed' style of expression is related to indicators of heart disease and even heart attacks. Other laboratory experiments by Butler *et al.* (2003) and Richards and Gross (1999) showed that short-term suppression of emotion has a negative impact on blood pressure, cardiovascular activity and even certain types of memory. Women who show less facial expressions during sad accounts of stories may have more skin problems (Malatesta *et al.*, 1987). So a healthy expression means a healthy X-Factor.

Facial expression and culture

What about facial expressions across various cultures? You may recall that the beginning of this chapter talked about the universal recognition of six basic human emotions across all cultures (sadness, anger, disgust, fear, surprise and happiness). While these can be recognised universally, it is also correct to say that facial expressions do vary according to cultures and social settings. Oriental cultures are often described in terms of people having inscrutable faces. When we think of facial expressions here, we must remember the display rules discussed earlier in this chapter (Ekman, 2003). These rules basically mean that it is not always socially acceptable to reveal what we truly feel. In a clever study aimed at examining how Japanese and Americans display their emotions publicly, Ekman (1972) asked both races to watch films about accidents and surgery in private and then with a 'scientist' sitting by their side. What do you think he found? As you probably can guess, both the Americans and the Japanese revealed the same facial expressions when they watched the films on their own. However, in company, the

So far we have covered...

We have an 'uncanny sensitivity' to facial expressions. Indeed, there are aspects of our facial displays that occur in a matter of milliseconds and we have no control over them. Sometimes we unconsciously mimic these minute facial expressions. While there are features of our facial displays which are almost instantaneous, we can also use the face deliberately. This is known as the audience effect and falls into discourse which suggests that all usage of the face has a social purpose. Our social motives and intentions impact on our use of facial expressions. We also make faces when we are alone. We can use the face to affect ourselves. If we adopt particular facial expressions there is also the chance that the outward adoption of such expressions may cause an inward realisation of the emotion. Not only can our manipulation of our facial muscles affect our emotions, it can also affect our judgements. Expressing your emotions is good for you. A number of studies make connections between people who 'repress' their emotions and health problems.

Japanese masked their negative expression more than the Americans (actually the Japanese often masked the negative facial expressions with a smile). This intriguing study tells us two things.

First, there is commonality in how we respond facially to certain life events. Second, we are aware of how we portray emotions in public. This goes back to the display rules we mentioned earlier. This awareness of the cultural variations in facial display is important for the classroom. It tells us that differing students may have different expectations and predispositions to emotional expression.

The crooked smile

If you look closely at the *Mona Lisa* painting, you will notice that her smile is not perfectly symmetrical. It seems a little bigger on the left side than the right. A quick glance at 'expert analyses' of this smile throws up a plethora of theories, but one theory concerns left and right brain thinking. As you probably know, the human brain is divided into two hemispheres. Broadly speaking, the right hemisphere is more concerned with nonverbal messages (McGilchrist, 2010). It has more to do with your X-Factor!

You are also probably aware that the right side of the brain controls the left side of the face. But did you know that the right hemisphere is longer, wider, generally larger and heavier than the left hemisphere? Did you know that the right side of the brain is deeply involved in social functioning, in empathy, emotional

FIGURE 14.6 The crooked smile.

understanding and emotional expression? McGilchrist (2010, 38) argues that it is this part of the brain which is always 'on the look out' for new experiences.

As the left side of a person's face is controlled by the right side of their brain, it means that the left side tends to be more emotionally expressive. But this really only takes effect when one engages in posed expressions. Hence, if we consider the *Mona Lisa* smile, it could be that she is actually 'posing the smile' as it is bigger on the left side of her face. When one engages in more genuine and spontaneous expressions, then the face puts on a more symmetrical display – in this case, with both sides of the face presenting the smile in a balanced manner. Hence, when you see a crooked smile, i.e. a smile on one half of the face, there is a good chance that it is posed, rather than genuine (Skinner and Mullen, 1991).

The face and multiple expressions of emotion

Shakespeare's *Macbeth* depicts a man whose ambition drove him to murderous ends. Early in the play, Lady Macbeth says to him: 'your face my thane, is a book where men may read strange matters … bear welcome in your eye, your hand, your tongue. Look like th' innocent flower but be the serpent under't' (Act I, Scene V). Lady Macbeth was well aware of the potency of the human face and its abilities to leak emotion.

FIGURE 14.7 Eyebrows reveal surprise and anger.

We often think that the face is used to express just one emotion. For example, people say 'she looked sad', or 'he looked happy'. While this may be true, we frequently convey a number of emotions in the face. Often termed 'affect blends', we can use the face to express a range of emotions. Think of the lines of the 1970 Badfinger song – 'you always smile but in your eyes your sorrow shows, yes it shows'.

For example, you can raise one eyebrow in surprise and one eyebrow in anger. This happens because we can often experience two emotions at the same time. Say, for example, a student is on Teaching Practice and their supervisor tells them that they are getting a D grade (of course this was before they read this book!). The reaction may be both surprise and anger – with the two eyebrows raised differently. This is an important distinction for the classroom. We can give messages of acceptance and reprimand in one look. Think of the teacher discussing homework and the student gives a very good answer, but also discloses that she has not completed all of the assignment. The question here is whether you give the 'double look' – depicting 'well done on your insightful answer, but you should also have completed all of the homework assignment'. Here the eyes and eyebrows convey surprise, but the mouth bears less of a smile – more of the brave smile.

Using the face without words

FIGURE 14.8 The withering look.

This aspect of facial expression is in our opinion one of the most valuable features of your X-Factor. Lady Macbeth was quick to spot the 'strange matters' in her husband's face. And so too, there are many occasions where our facial expressions do not need words – think of the 'knowing look' teachers give to students when they say 'I know people are going to behave on this trip, because we all know the rewards we got from Principal Brown after last year's trip'. In our own research we came across numerous instances where teachers used their face without words. One notable exemplar was what one teacher called 'the withering look'. This was directed at students who were misbehaving or distracted. We must remember that in using the face, without actual words, we may use other nonverbal means of communication: for example, back-channel responses and leaning forwards.

In our own work with student teachers on teaching practice, we have heard them talk about the anxiety they feel when standing up in front of a class and in particular in front of a teaching practice supervisor. Typically, we show anxiety by having more facial movements than normal, increased blinking and movements associated with fear such as the horizontal mouth stretch (Harrigan and O Connell, 1996). So how do we overcome such anxiety? Well, obviously, awareness of such facial movements may help you overcome them. But we would also urge you to think about the facial feedback theory we discussed earlier. Try 'putting on' a smile and adopt a tall posture which may then propagate feelings of greater ease and confidence.

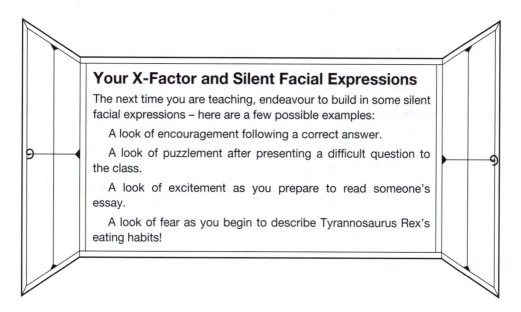

Your X-Factor and Silent Facial Expressions

The next time you are teaching, endeavour to build in some silent facial expressions – here are a few possible examples:

A look of encouragement following a correct answer.

A look of puzzlement after presenting a difficult question to the class.

A look of excitement as you prepare to read someone's essay.

A look of fear as you begin to describe Tyrannosaurus Rex's eating habits!

So far we have covered...

The right hemisphere of your brain is more concerned with nonverbal messages – it has more to do with your X-Factor! It controls the left side of the face. What this means is that the left side of a person's face tends to be more expressive. Often termed 'affect blends', we can use the face to express a range of emotions. Of course we can also use facial expressions without words. Associated with facial expression are a range of other nonverbal types of communications such as eye contact, smiling and what is known as back-channel responses. The amount of emotion one displays on one's face can vary according to culture.

Self-Evaluation Questions: Facial Expression

Your face as a lighthouse of emotion

1 Do you think there are times/occasions when your facial expressions notably change? Why is this?

Syntactic display

1 Do you think your expressions change for important parts of the sentence?

Facial responses

1 Does your face show 'overintensification of the affect', e.g. open eyes and broad expression of enthusiasm and support for a child's answer?
2 Does your face show 'deintensified affect', e.g. underplay your emotions when perhaps annoyed or disappointed by something?

Facial feedback theory

Are you aware of the potential of improving your own demeanour through the manipulation of your own facial expressions, e.g. making yourself smile to provoke that emotion within yourself?

15

Attractiveness: Dressing for the Classroom – 'Does My School Bag Look Big in This?'

Attractiveness

FIGURE 15.1 Attractiveness.

Would you say you are attractive? Most people are not so vain as to say they either are or are not and, as we all know, beauty is in the eye of the beholder. However, in the development of your X-Factor, the importance of appearing attractive should not be underestimated. Wilson and Nias (1999) point out that physically attractive people are seen as more personable, popular, intelligent, persuasive, happy, interesting, confident and outgoing. This could be particularly important if you are on teaching practice. Hargie and Dickson (2004) observe that in day-to-day evaluative decisions about the quality of people's work or their suitability for selection, bias may favour the attractive, especially in situations of limited protracted contact. So what makes one attractive? In 1997, Mehrabian and Blum examined photographs of young adults and had them rated in terms of physical attractiveness by both males and females. Those factors which caused people to describe these photographs as attractive were as follows: masculinity (e.g. features to do with strength, larger chest, broader chin), femininity (based on longer hair, make-up, larger and rounder eyes), self-care (suggested by shapely figure, well groomed, well-fitting clothes), pleasantness (based on perceptions of friendliness, happiness, babyish features) and finally ethnicity.

You are probably saying to yourself – physical attractiveness has only to do with adults. This is not correct. Physical attractiveness stereotypes also affect children. In 1986, Hatfield and Sprecher examined what children between the ages of four and six years thought about attractiveness in their peers. Their findings were fascinating. Children in this age bracket thought that attractive children are nicer, less aggressive and less anti-social. They also found that teachers also fall prey to these attractiveness influences. Teachers think that attractive children will be more intelligent, academically successful and more popular. There are indications that teachers not only make attractiveness judgements about young children, but that they also treat the 'unattractive children' with fewer and less positive communications (Knapp and Hall, 2006). What about older students? Reis *et al.* (1982) found that attractive male students are more assertive and interact more with women. On the other hand, attractive female students are less assertive.

So it would seem that the odds are stacked in favour of attractive people. But does it make a big difference to them? Because they apparently have a different social experience than less attractive people and because people are more inclined to react positively towards them are they actually any better off than the rest of us? Well a number of differences have been found. Attractive people have been shown to be somewhat happier, more self-confident, assertive and socially skilled and in better psychological health, especially in the case of women (Mathes and Kahn, 1975). But there are a number of exceptions to this of course. The fascinating twist in the attractiveness tale relates to self-esteem. The relationship between personal appearance and self-esteem is surprisingly small. Major *et al.* (1984) argue that attractive people discount praise more quickly as they fear it may be more a product of their personal appearance than the actual quality of their work. So how do we make ourselves attractive for the classroom?

So far we have covered...

The importance of appearing attractive should not be underestimated. Physically attractive people are seen as more personable, popular, intelligent, persuasive, happy, interesting, confident and outgoing. Attractive people have been shown to be somewhat happier, more self-confident, assertive and socially skilled and in better psychological health, especially in the case of women. The relationship between personal appearance and self-esteem is surprisingly small. Physical attractiveness stereotypes affect children. Teachers may think that attractive children will be more intelligent, academic and popular.

We rarely wear clothes by accident

Have a look at what you're wearing. Can you recollect putting those clothes on this morning? How did you choose? You may be surprised to learn that generally we choose the clothes and cosmetics we wear carefully. It is unusual for their selection to be random (Argyle, 1988). As James Laver (1949) once famously put it: 'clothes are the furniture of the mind made visible'. We are conscious of the messages our clothes convey. This is not a recent phenomenon.

Throughout history man has worn clothing as much for protection as for decoration. For example, in the 1830s Charles Darwin visited the islands of Tierra del Fuego, off the southern tip of South America. Here he discovered a people who wore only a small cloak of animal skin and a little cosmetic paint in spite of the cold weather, the rain and the sleet. He decided to give them some scarlet cloth, and what did they do with it? They put it around their necks! This shows the value placed on attractiveness and on using clothing as much for 'decoration' as for protection.

It is estimated that we began wearing clothes about 100,000 years ago. Indeed some argue that early humans wore clothes for two reasons – for protection and to give messages about themselves. Little has changed since then! By the end of the old stone age, about 25,000 years ago, humans had invented the needle which allowed sewing. We had learned to make yarn from some plants, from fur and from the hair of some animals. The stage was set for *Vogue*! It is fascinating to find that we only started making clothes in an industrial sense in the last 200 years. Before that most clothes were made in the home or by groups of workers commissioned to make them.

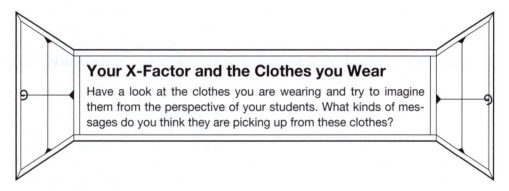

Your X-Factor and the Clothes you Wear

Have a look at the clothes you are wearing and try to imagine them from the perspective of your students. What kinds of messages do you think they are picking up from these clothes?

Self-image

Hoult (1954) suggests that it is possible to change people's perceptions of a person by changing their clothes. This relates to one of the central theories we find in relation to dress psychology – Goffman's Doctrine of Self-Presentation (1956). Goffman's theory of self-presentation is primarily based around the notion that we manipulate the impressions other people form of us. How do we do this? According to Goffman, we deliberately present ourselves in the form of a 'quasi-theatrical performance', with appearance being an important part of this performance.

So what does this performance tell us? Quite simply, the manner in which we select and wear clothes leaks information about our own self-image. What we wear waves a flag about how we want to be seen. The teenagers in our classrooms give us clear evidence of this. For example, in 1969, Gibbins undertook a study on 15 and 16 year old girls who lived in the north of England. The work examined the clothes which these teenage girls liked and how these clothes related to their own self-image. As you can probably guess, there was a definite relationship between the clothes a girl chose and her own self-image. Perhaps the most important and indeed significant study in the field of classroom clothes and teenagers came from Hamilton and Warden in 1966. They examined the achievement test scores of high school boys and their grade point averages. In this work they found that even though some boys had high achievement test scores, if they wore clothes deemed as 'unacceptable' by their peers, then they were found to have lower grade point averages than those who wore 'acceptable clothing'. The other very interesting finding emerging from this study related to conflict. Those students who wore 'acceptable clothing' found themselves in less conflict and in more school activities.

'Cool' and 'warm' clothes

When we talk of the way in which people perceive clothes, there are a number of findings which emerge consistently in the literature. These findings have to do with the terms 'cool' and 'warm' (Gorham *et al.*, 1999, 282). Now when you hear the term cool, you might think of Danny Zuko (John Travolta) in the film *Grease*! This is not quite the 'cool' we have in mind. When we say 'cool' in terms of clothes we are talking about '*cool perceptions* of clothes'.

When we have cool perceptions of clothes, we are making judgements about the wearer's knowledge, educational background, preparation, level of sophistication and competence (Harris *et al.*, 1983; Miller and Rowald, 1980). On the other hand, warm judgements of clothes have to do with perceptions of the wearer as trustworthy, sociable, likeable, enthusiastic and interpersonally attractive (Leathers, 1992).

A number of studies consistently show that the clothes you wear do have a particular effect on someone's perceptions of you as being 'cool' (Bickman, 1974; Harris *et al.*, 1983; Miller and Rowald, 1980). But not in a 'Grease Lightning' kind of way! Cool here has to do with perceptions of the wearer's knowledge base, educational background, sophistication and competence. There is also fascinating research to show that if you wear 'cool' clothes then you may decrease 'warm judgements' about you. So, for example, if the clothes you wear prompt the observer to perceive you as being competent and well educated they may be less likely to make judgements about you in warm terms, i.e. in terms of being sociable, likeable or enthusiastic. Interestingly, females tend to be more receptive to these kinds of clothing cues than males (Kuehne and Creekmore, 1971; Solomon and Schopler, 1982).

Although the terms 'cool' and 'warm' exist in the general world of clothing psychology, there is some evidence of their existence in the classroom. In 1980, an intriguing study by Rollman found that students do make judgements about teachers based on their attire which are similar to the 'cool' and 'warm' terms we discussed earlier. This study asked the same set of male and female teachers to dress in the following sets of attire:

1 casual – wearing jeans, sport shirt and sneakers;
2 moderately formal – casual slacks, skirt, turtleneck, jacket;
3 formal – classic business attire.

FIGURE 15.2
Typical casual attire.

FIGURE 15.3
Moderately formal attire.

FIGURE 15.4
Typical formal attire.

A total of 50 students were shown three photographs of the same male and female teacher in casual dress (jeans, etc.), moderately formal attire (slacks, etc.) and formal attire (business dress). The students were then asked to rate the photographs using ten adjectives: fair, sympathetic, knowledgeable, enthusiastic, friendly, flexible, clear, organised, stimulating and well prepared. So what do you think were the results? Some of the students' perceptions of the teacher were somewhat predictable – when the teacher was dressed formally, he or she was seen as more organised, knowledgeable and better prepared. Those teachers who were dressed informally were seen as more friendly, flexible, sympathetic, fair and enthusiastic than any of the teachers wearing the other two modes of dress. Broadly speaking, the results showed that warm attributes were more associated with informal dress and cool attributes with more formal dress.

The study also uncovered some fascinating insights into issues of clarity and the classroom. Male and female teachers scored highest on perceptions of their clarity when they were dressed 'moderately formally'. You are probably wondering were there any gender differences which emerged in the study? The study uncovered one primary gender difference. Males were rated as most stimulating when they wore moderately formal attire (e.g. casual slacks/jacket). Of course, one of the obvious drawbacks of this study has to do with its use of photographs. Simply showing students a set of photographs neglects the realities of interacting in context.

Although Rollman's work does give us insights into students' perceptions of attire, more recent research in the 1990s by Morris and Gorham provides us with insights into the contextualised wearing of clothes in the 'live' classroom scenario. In 1996, Morris *et al.* looked at the effects of wearing three kinds of classroom clothing: (a) formal professional dress, (b) casual professional dress and (c) casual dress. It is important to note that these studies were undertaken in university contexts. As we have learned from other studies, 'warm attributes' (e.g. sociability, extroversion) were associated with casual attire. However, formal dress did not have an impact on perceptions of teacher competence or knowledge, except when female students were judging female teachers. This work also threw up some other interesting findings which concern power dressing and student teachers.

Power dressing

No doubt you have heard the term 'power dressing'. So what is it? The term itself is supposed to have originated in an article in the New York paper the *Post-Standard* in September 1979. It has to do with clothing styles which were favoured in business and politics in the US and UK throughout the 1980s. The style was heavily influenced by influential women who were in the news at the time. For example, some of the cast of the television shows *Dynasty* and *Dallas*, the UK Prime Minister Margaret Thatcher and the Princess of Wales were seen to adopt this style. As a style, it was more associated with women, but men too had stylised types of power dressing such as wearing expensive suits. For women, power dressing had masculine overtones, frequently involving the wearing of a tailored jacket with shoulder pads. The clothes were often made from expensive materials.

FIGURE 15.5 Power dressing.

The question is: does power dressing work? There is a common assumption that beginning teachers particularly need to bolster perceptions of competence, credibility and knowledge by 'dressing up'. In their university research work, Morris *et al.* (1996) found that 'dressing up' did not help the beginning teacher. In fact, they found that 'dressing down' (e.g. wearing casual faded jeans and a t-shirt) had no effect on credibility ratings by students, but did result in high approachability ratings (as compared to teachers wearing formal dress). This brings us to our next point about classroom attire.

From their research on college classrooms, Gorham *et al.* (1999) make the point that 'there is little evidence that instructor attire has any meaningful, predictable effect on student perceptions of attributes related to either teachers' approachability or credibility' (295). Their work found that students' judgements of such attributes were influenced much more by how the teachers behaved rather than what they wore. This work does contrast with the 'dress for success' mantra which we come across in the business world. One of the points Gorham *et al.* do make, and which supports the value which is sometimes placed on formal classroom dress attire, has to do with the 'reciprocity effect'. They point out that students' respect for the teacher is related to their perceptions of how much the teacher respects their own role in the classroom; for example, having attire which is 'clean, pressed and neat'. This does not necessarily mean the attire is formal such as wearing a suit. So what do we wear? Let us first think of the moments when clothes are first perceived: the great moment of 'first impression'.

First impressions

First impressions are important. Max Eggert (2010, 36) calls it the 7–11 effect. We make 11 observations about people in the first seven seconds of meeting them. What are they?

1   Economic level: where does the person come in society? How rich are they?
2   Educational level: how intelligent are they? What is their probable academic achievement?
3   How honest are they?
4   How much can they be trusted?
5   Sophistication: what is their level of sophistication?
6   Gender: what is their sexual orientation? Availability? Desirability?
7   Level of success.
8   Political background: how likely are they to vote?
9   Value orientation: do you share the same values and principles as this person?
10   Ethnic origin.
11   Social desirability: how much would you like the person as a friend?

In forming these impressions, physical looks, speech, body shape, body language and clothes are all taken into account. And one thing to say for sure is that clothes are an important factor in this list. When we are making first impressions, Leather (1992, 242) points out that we are influenced by three factors.

1   We are most influenced by the cues that are most obvious.
2   We put more weight on negative cues than on positive cues.
3   We make judgements based on the assumptions that others are like us.

When we think of first impressions, we must also consider gender differences. Knapp and Hall (2006) point out that both females and males look first at clothes in same-sex encounters. However, they point out that when opposite members of the sexes meet, this is not quite the case. Females look at clothes first when they meet a man, but when a male meets a female he looks at clothes third, with figure and face apparently taking precedence over glances at her clothes. If you are on teaching practice or awaiting a visit from a mentor or evaluator, the research does point out that positive first impressions are established when the style of clothes you wear are similar to those who are judging you (Reid *et al.*, 1997).

Does my X-Factor match yours?

People are responsive to those with a similar appearance to themselves. This is sometimes called 'homophily'. Gorham *et al.* (1999) define homophily as the degree to which 'two people perceive themselves as similar to one another'. They also suggest that it is linked to two things:

1   the ability to influence;
2   people's willingness to communicate.

The key point here for the classroom has to do with what is known as 'optimal homophily'. This happens when people think the communicator is very similar to them in most ways but somewhat more competent on the topic in question (McCroskey *et al.*, 1974).

When we think of 'similar' appearances, the issue of social class inevitably weaves its way into the dis-

FIGURE 15.6 We have similar appearances – are we similar in other ways too?

cussion. From the work of Sissons (1971), we learn that the social class of a person can be judged by their clothes. In her research, she arranged for an actor to stop 80 people at a train station in Paddington to ask for directions to Hyde Park. For 40 of these people, the actor was dressed and behaved as upper middle class while for the other 40 he was dressed as working class. These interactions were recorded. It was found that when the actor was dressed as middle class and when the person being stopped was also middle class, the interactions went most smoothly. In these similarly dressed situations, there was instant rapport between the two people, the interaction lasted longer and the two people actually smiled more. This contrasted with the other possible combinations where middle class met with working class. Here there was less rapport and the interactions were shorter.

From the work of Harp *et al.* (1985) we can see the subtle ways in which our ideas about clothes and especially our 'solidarity' with the other speaker takes effect. Harp *et al.* examined the effects of clothing on newsreaders. They found that people thought the news was more credible and that the news was better remembered when the broadcaster wore conservative rather than trendy or casual clothes. This was especially true for viewers who wore conservative clothes themselves. Here we learn that clothes should befit the occasion.

So far we have covered...

Generally we choose the clothes and cosmetics we wear carefully. The manner in which we select and wear clothes leaks information about our own self-image. A number of studies consistently show that the clothes you wear do have a particular effect on someone's perceptions of you as being 'cool'. Cool perceptions of clothes have to do with perceptions of the wearer's knowledge, educational background, preparation, level of sophistication and competence. There is also fascinating research to show that if you wear 'cool' clothes then you may decrease 'warm judgements' about you. Warm judgements of clothes have to do with perceptions of the wearer as trustworthy, sociable, likeable, enthusiastic and interpersonally attractive. In terms of the classroom, there is little evidence that instructor attire has any meaningful, predictable effect on student perceptions of attributes related to either teachers' approachability or credibility. Students' judgements of approachability and credibility are much more influenced by how teachers behave rather than what they wear. Clothes are an important factor in first impressions. Positive first impressions are established when the style of clothes you wear are similar to those who are judging you. Why? Because this probably indicates a 'similar outlook or group membership'.

Our clothes should fit the occasion

It is important to dress for the occasion. Knapp and Hall (2006, 205) observe that 'uniforms do help people identify the wearer's probable areas of expertise. And this knowledge may be persuasive.' For example, in a study on the value of uniforms, Lawrence and Watson (1991) asked a woman to dress as a businesswoman in order to make public service announcements seeking contributions to fight leukaemia. This same woman then made the same announcements dressed as a nurse. As you would expect, when dressed as a nurse she received more pledged contributions and was judged to be more knowledgeable than the businesswoman. So the key point here is to wear clothes which befit your role and surroundings as an educator. This reminds us of the famous story of Victoria Clark, assistant secretary of Defense for Public Affairs in America. She was criticised for wearing bright colours while answering questions on Iraq, with one commentator noting that 'Pink is not an appropriate colour in the time of war' (Knapp and Hall, 2006).

It is important to remember that students do take note of what we wear. In 1984, Reeder and King undertook research in Tennessee on students' perceptions of the approachability of teachers based on what they wore. A female high school teacher was perceived as being more approachable, more likely to offer assistance in an emergency and more likely to allow students to make up work when she wore a soft feminine style of dress. On the other hand, this research also revealed that a teacher who wore a skirted and tailored suit was perceived as being more capable of maintaining classroom order and one with whom students could discuss personal problems. This teacher was also judged as having leadership qualities and as being trustworthy and capable. Those female teachers who wore a simple skirt, blouse and vest or a masculine styled pantsuit were judged as least intelligent and most old-fashioned.

Clothes and perceptions of expertise

In addition to 'fitting in' with the cultural milieu of the school, it is also important to think about the manner in which clothes can influence perceptions of our expertise. In some situations we judge the person's intelligence based on the appropriateness of their clothes for the particular social situation they find themselves in (Rees *et al.*, 1974). Lennon and Miller (1984) suggest that if you are a female and wear conservative clothes which consist of a skirted suit or a blazer then there is a stronger possibility that you will be perceived as more intelligent. In contrast, Paek (1986) argues that very dressy styles are less likely to convey an image of intelligence.

Some of the most interesting insights into clothes and perceptions of expertise comes from the work of Lapitsky and Smith in 1981. They studied the reactions of 160 female students to photographs of an author. These students gave significantly higher ratings to the author when she wore more attractive clothing. Moreover, the attractively dressed author was judged to have written a more creative essay, with better ideas and better quality than the less attractively dressed author.

So far we have covered...

Students take note of what we wear, making calculations about leadership qualities, capabilities, trustworthiness, intelligence and approachability. Thus, we should dress to fit the occasion and cultural milieu we find ourselves in. We may also judge a person's intelligence based on the appropriateness of their clothes for the particular social situation they find themselves in.

Clothes and status

There appears to be significant benefit to wearing 'high status' clothing, in the appropriate setting. For example, in 1996, Alder and Towne showed that if you are wearing 'high status clothing', then people are

1 more inclined to take orders from you;
2 accept you in taking the lead on something;
3 comply with your requests.

Obviously a number of these factors relate to your work in the classroom. There are a host of studies which indicate the 'persuasive nature' of high-status clothing. One of the most widely known of these studies concerned violations of traffic signals! In 1955, Lefkowitz *et al.* decided to investigate whether unsuspecting bystanders could be persuaded to violate a traffic signal light. This study found that pedestrians were much more likely to violate the traffic signal light if another person violated it ahead of them, but especially if that person's dress represented a person with social standing.

Clothes and their effect on your own X-Factor

While clothes can have an impact persuasively on others, they can also impact persuasively on ourselves. Like the facial feedback theory we discussed in an earlier chapter, where putting on a smile can actually make you feel happy inside, so too wearing particular kinds of clothes can change how you feel. If, for example, you wear a uniform this will affect how people act towards you and also of course how you act yourself. One example of this comes from the roller skate study by Tharin in 1981. This study looked at the number of accidents which occur at roller skating rinks. Interestingly, there were fewer accidents on nights when respectable clothes were required. On these same nights, there was also less noise and fewer confrontations.

The manner in which clothes can give you confidence should also be considered. Some studies by Gorham *et al.* (1999) and Roach (1997) have looked at what student teachers wear when going to class. Some of them wore suits to distinguish them from their students, who were often quite close to them in age. They reported that wearing these suits gave them added confidence when dealing with their students. However, the twist in the tale is that such confidence seemed to be related to the student teachers' perceptions only. The clothes they wore seemed to have little effect on the perceptions or behaviour of their students.

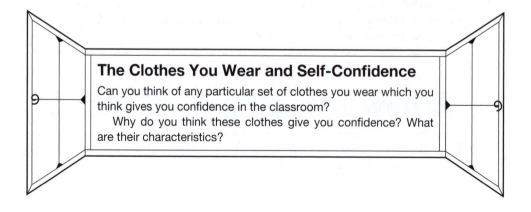

The Clothes You Wear and Self-Confidence

Can you think of any particular set of clothes you wear which you think gives you confidence in the classroom?

Why do you think these clothes give you confidence? What are their characteristics?

Do you tend to go with the latest fashions?

Do you follow fashion? Would you say you follow it closely? You may now learn some things about yourself! Some researchers such as Kaiser (1985) and Millenson (1985) suggest that followers of fashion are people who are socially anxious, conformist and other-directed. When we consider people who follow fashion, we should also think about people who go with the latest trends – these are known as early adaptors of fashion and are seen as more romantic, frivolous and even bold (Argyle, 1988). The research in relation to girls and the adaptation of fashion is notably interesting. Girls who wear more fashionable clothes have self-images which are nearer to this image than those who wear less fashionable clothes. The fascinating thing from the research of Gibbins and Gwynn (1975) is that when a fashion has been well established, not wearing it can invite scorn and rejection. Needless to say, this is particularly relevant to our teenage students.

School uniform

Many schools have a uniform. Why? The argument typically advanced is that the style of dress changes how students feel about themselves and this in turn affects how they behave. If we think about the roller skate study by Tharin in 1980, this could make sense. But is this true for school uniforms? Apparently not. Knapp and Hall point out that 'school uniforms by themselves without the support of students and parents are not likely to accomplish much' (2006, 207). A study by Brunsma and Rockquemore in 1998 seems to confirm this. They examined the effects of wearing a uniform on substance abuse, behavioural problems and attendance and found that the uniform did not have any direct effect on these matters. Indeed, in some scenarios, this study found that uniforms had a negative effect on achievement!

FIGURE 15.7 The school uniform.

So far we have covered...

Some research suggests that followers of fashion are people who are socially anxious, conformist and other-directed. Indeed, early adaptors of fashion are seen as more romantic, frivolous naughty and even bold. Also, there appears to be significant benefit to wearing 'high status' clothing, in the appropriate setting. But we must remember that along with having an impact on others, the clothes we wear can have a persuasive impact on ourselves. In some scenarios the clothes you wear can give you confidence. Finally, what about school uniforms? School uniforms by themselves without the support of students and parents are not likely to accomplish much.

Self-Evaluation: Attractiveness

Self-presentation

1 Are you well groomed?
2 Do your clothes fit you properly?

Clothes and self-image

1 Have a look at the clothes you are wearing and try to imagine them from the perspective of your students. What kinds of messages do you think your students are picking up from these clothes?
2 What image do you seek to portray in the classroom?
3 Do your clothes reflect this image?

Clothing and the cultural milieu of your school

1 Do your clothes fit the cultural milieu of your school?
2 To what degree do you think your clothes convey messages about your expertise?

Clothing and personal confidence

1 Can you think of any particular set of clothes you wear which you think gives you confidence in the classroom?
2 Why do you think these clothes give you confidence? What are their characteristics?

16

Environment and the Classroom X-Factor

The X-Factor outside you

So far in the book we have looked at how you smile, how you walk, how you gesture, what you wear and a host of other factors connected with your X-Factor. This chapter looks at other ways you can develop your X-Factor within your working environment.

Beautiful environments

Have you ever walked into someone else's classroom and experienced a 'wow' feeling? Isn't this room beautiful? Students must love it in here. Or would they notice? Well, there is evidence to indicate that they do notice these things and that being in a visually pleasing classroom is good for your learning. Studies by Campbell (1979) and Woolin and Montagre (1981) have found that students are perceptive of 'beautiful' and 'ugly' rooms. When in beautiful rooms, they rated teachers higher, did better on tests and solved problems more effectively than in the ugly ones. Not surprisingly, this 'visual-aesthetic effect' has been found in other scenarios.

Human beings are conscious and aware of their visual-aesthetic surroundings. In research by Maslow and Mintz (1956) and Mintz (1956) the effects of placing people in an 'ugly room', an average room and a beautiful room were examined. While in these various rooms the participants were given negative prints of photographs. When in the beautiful room, the participants gave significantly higher ratings of the faces in the photographs as projecting 'energy and well being' than in say the ugly room. Indeed, the beautiful room was rated by the participants as producing feelings of pleasure, enjoyment, energy and comfort by contrast to the ugly room which provided feelings of monotony, discontent, fatigue and irritability (among others).

Warm environments

Think of the expression 'this room has a warm feel'. Environments that make us feel psychologically warm may also make us feel physically warmer. In a fascinating study undertaken by Rohles in 1980, students were asked to study for two hours in different classrooms. One classroom had a neutral decor and another resembled a walk-in meat-cooler room – but without the meat and associated butchering paraphernalia! The temperature in both rooms was the same. Nearly all students reported feeling that the meat-cooler room was cooler. Then Rohles redecorated the meat-cooler room. It was panelled, carpeted, equipped with subdued lighting and other room decorations. This time two new sets of students were asked to study in both rooms. This time the meat-cooler room was in fact judged to have a warmer temperature!

Colours and emotion

One of the big factors in the creation of 'beautiful and warm environments' has to do with the use of colour. Thankfully, our world is saturated in colour. It is estimated that about ten million colours exist. According to Sharpe (1975) the normal human eye is capable of discriminating approximately seven million different colours. Colour is all around us. We have it in the sky, trees and so on. We also use it deliberately. Think of the red fire engine, the 'battenburg' police car. We even have blue moons! Colour is used more than you think in everyday conversation and is often associated with emotions. For example, I saw red, I was green with envy, I feel blue today, he is a yellow-bellied coward.

No doubt you have heard that colours can help create a 'mood'. Some of the great artists, such as Gauguin or Van Gogh talked of using colour to convey emotion and mood. Indeed, Deborah Sharpe (1975, x) argues that 'colour responses are more tied to man's emotions than to his intellect. In general people do not respond to colour with their minds.' Using Freudian psychology to explain how we respond to colour Sharpe makes the point that colour responses are normally under the control of the ego. They are controlled by the 'self-preserving, socialised and conscience controlled energy system of the human' (xi). On the colour spectrum, she observes that generally when we use adjectives to describe colour, we categorise the warm end of the spectrum (red, yellow and orange) to be exciting and stimulating, while the cool end (green and blue) is characterised as peaceful, cool and respectful.

We also make associations with particular kinds of colour. Numerous research projects have found that red, yellow and orange are associated with excitement, stimulation and aggression. On the other hand, blue and green are associated with calm, security and peace, while black, brown and grey are associated with melancholy and sadness. Yellow is connected with cheer, gaiety and fun and, finally, purple is associated with dignity, royalty and sadness (Sharpe, 1975, 55). Some of these associations are best summarised in the work of Burgoon and Saine (1978). They established the associations shown in Table 16.1 between moods and colour (see p.137).

Now the next obvious question is whether all humans respond equally to colour.

Children and colour

You may find it surprising to learn that we respond differently to colour according to our age. Of course, the key question for this book is how do students in the classroom respond to colour? Mahnke (1996) points out that children's acceptance or rejection of certain colours mirrors their own development. Perhaps one of the largest studies in

TABLE 16.1 The moods created by colour.

COLOUR	MOOD
Red	Hot, affectionate, angry, defiant, contrary, hostile, full of vitality, excitement, love
Blue	Cool, pleasant, leisurely, distant, infinite, secure, transcendent, calm, tender
Yellow	Unpleasant, exciting, hostile, cheerful, joyful, jovial
Orange	Unpleasant, exciting, disturbed, distressed, upset, defiant, contrary, hostile, stimulating
Purple	Depressed, sad, dignified, stately
Green	Cool, pleasant, leisurely, in control
Black	Sad, intense, anxiety, fear, despondent, dejected, melancholy, unhappy
Brown	Sad, not tender, despondent, dejected, melancholy, unhappy, neutral
White	Joy, lightness, neutral, cold.

Source: Burgoon and Saine (1978).

this area was conducted by Heinrich Frieling (1957) of the Institute of Colour Psychology. He tested 10,000 children and young people from the ages of five to 19 years, from all corners of the world, in an effort to establish which colours are best suited for different age groups. While the work produced lengthy statistics and analyses, we can summarise the findings generally as follows:

In the age group 5–8 years, black, grey, white and dark brown are rejected, while red, orange, yellow and violet are preferred.

In the age group 9–10 years, grey, dark brown, black, pastel green and blue are rejected with red, red-orange and green-blue being preferred.

In the age group 11–12 years, black, white, grey, olive, violet and lilac were rejected.

In the age group 13–14 years, the preferred colours were blue, ultramarine and orange.

Obviously, a knowledge of these preferred colours is important for the use of colour in the classroom, but does that mean that you now have to buy a paint brush and paint the walls of your classroom red because you teach kindergarten? Not so. Frieling's work does point out that using a child's preferred colours as the basis for a wall colour may not be as simple as it looks. Some colours are not always suitable as wall paints and may need to be modified. So while you may now have insights into the likely colour preferences of the students you teach, you may still be wondering how to create the optimum colour learning environment for your pupils. Some other studies provide possible answers.

In a series of studies on children in primary school, researchers in the institute, Gesellschaft für Rationelle Psychologie in Munich, Germany, found that children responded better to colours such as blue, yellow, yellow-green and orange. Indeed, children who were tested in these rooms scored 12 IQ points more than those tested in white, black or brown rooms ('Blue is Beautiful', 1973). It is important to note that these children thought these rooms were beautiful. These beautiful rooms also seemed to stimulate creativity and alertness. White, black and brown rooms were considered ugly. Indeed, in the orange room, the students were most friendly and smiled the most! When in these rooms, positive social reactions increased by an amazing 53 per cent, with the children smiling more and using more friendly words. Negative reactions were also reduced in the orange room by 12 per cent. There was less irritability and hostility on the part of the children.

In short, people associate serenity and calm with the colours blue and green. On the other hand, red and orange are seen to be arousing and stimulating (Ball, 1965). Indeed, it would appear that any colour which is bright is likely to be more stimulating and to get more attention than paler colours (Knapp and Hall, 2006).

Is it possible now to make a list of colours for specific schools and age levels? It is difficult to be specifically prescriptive about colours and their effects, but there appears to be advantages to the use of the colours blue, yellow, yellow-green and orange in school environments. It is most important to remember that colour is dependent on the context. You may like pink dresses, but not pink hair! It is also important to remember that we associate colours in different ways. For example, in a study undertaken by Hines in 1996, people were asked to say what the colour red meant to them. They announced that it meant warmth, danger, love, strength and safety. However, when they were asked to think of a product associated with red, they came up with Coca Cola! Hence, there is considerable variability in terms of our perceptions of the colours we use. But there are two colours worthy of specific focus – pink and black.

Pink!

In the world of colours, some stand out more than others. Certain palettes of pink seem to be important in terms of their calming effects and the suppression of aggression. Studies reported by Pelligrini and Schauss (1980) and Schauss (1985) of people exposed to environments painted in 'baker-miller' pink found that their heart rates, pulse and respiration decreased. These studies also found that pink aided the suppression of violent and aggressive behaviours in adult and juvenile correction centres, psychiatric hospitals and controlled laboratory studies. However, this is not always the case and there are some exceptions. In an amusing study undertaken in the county jail of San Jose in California, it was found that painting holding cells in the colour shocking pink did not always have this calming effect. When prisoners were placed in these cells, they were calm for about 15 minutes, but then hostility began to increase, reaching a peak after 30 minutes. After three hours, some prisoners were trying to tear the paint off the wall!

Black uniforms

Perhaps the most fascinating studies in the area of colour come from the work of Frank and Gilovich (1988) who studied colours and uniforms. In particular, they looked at the effect of wearing a black uniform. The research found that students rated black uniforms as indicating meanness and aggression by comparison to other coloured uniforms. Indeed, it may also be advisable not to tog your school hockey or football team in black. The work of Frank and Gilovich found that football teams and hockey teams who wore black were penalised the most during games. This also happened when the team who originally may have worn a different colour changed to black. Once in black, they were penalised more. In an amusing twist in this study, the researchers set up players to undertake particular playing moves and video recorded them doing these moves. In one set of moves they wore black uniforms while the exact same moves were then undertaken in a uniform of a different colour. When people were asked to act as referees, watching films of these moves, they penalised the black uniformed players more than the other players. When the researchers put black uniforms on students, they found them to become more aggressive.

So far we have covered...

Colours are often associated with emotions. Any colour that is bright is likely to be more arousing and to get more attention than paler colours. We categorise the warm end of the spectrum (red, yellow and orange) as exciting and stimulating, while the cool end (green and blue) is characterised as peaceful, cool and respectful. Red, yellow and orange are associated with excitement, stimulation and aggression. Blue and green are associated with calm, security and peace, while black, brown and grey are associated with melancholy and sadness. Yellow is connected with cheer, gaiety and fun, while purple is associated with dignity, royalty and sadness.

What about the colour of school uniforms? It has been found that students rate black uniforms as indicating meanness and aggression by comparison to other coloured uniforms. Environments that make us feel psychologically warm may also make us feel physically warmer. Some studies have found that students are perceptive of 'beautiful' and 'ugly' rooms. When in beautiful rooms, they rated teachers higher, did better on tests and solved problems more effectively than in the ugly ones. It would appear that there are advantages to the use of the colours blue, yellow, yellow-green and orange in school environments.

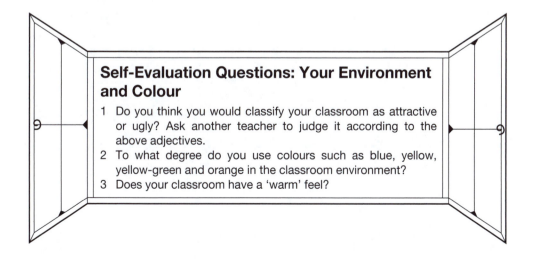

Self-Evaluation Questions: Your Environment and Colour

1 Do you think you would classify your classroom as attractive or ugly? Ask another teacher to judge it according to the above adjectives.
2 To what degree do you use colours such as blue, yellow, yellow-green and orange in the classroom environment?
3 Does your classroom have a 'warm' feel?

Part III

The X-Factor Instruments in a Classroom Symphony

This part of the book looks at some of our own classroom research on nonverbal communication. We plan to contextualise this research within the theory and various points we have discussed thus far in the book. To do this, we have decided to use fictional stories that are grounded in the key findings of this book and our own research. These stories will serve as platforms for the analysis and discussion of the various ways in which the instruments of the nonverbal communication orchestra play in symphony to achieve either a 'melodic' or 'an out of tune' learning experience for the student.

The first area to look at concerns an important and complex aspect of classroom practice: differentiated teaching and learning.

1

Your X-Factor and Differentiated Learning – The Yellow Teddy Lunchbox

The Yellow Teddy Lunchbox

Mattheus was still standing at the classroom door long after his mother's red hat had disappeared out of sight. Just six years old, and recently arrived from Brazil, the cold December wind chilled him sharply, a big change from the sunny mornings he was used to. Inside he trembled, it reminded him of the time he got lost in the mall.

FIGURE S1.1 The yellow teddy lunchbox.

Who were all these people? The sea of faces, the noise … where would he sit? **The tall lady he met at the door came towards him with a big smile and knelt down beside him.** He felt a little better inside now. Some mumbled words came out of her, but he knew she was signalling for him to do something. **Her voice is soft he thought.** She pretended to take off a coat. Ah, she wanted him to hang up his coat. Another signal? **This time she pointed at a red chair at the front of the classroom.**

Front seat! No way! Mattheus wanted a seat where he was out of sight. So he headed for the one at the corner. **Yes, he would be safer there and would be out of sight of the others.** He remembered his mother's words about minding his pencil case and eating his lunch, and so he checked they were

> Smiling and positive use of space.

> Vocal expression and soft voice intonation.

> Use of gestures.

> Territories and occupation of space.

still in his bag. Should he put them on this desk? He wanted to mark his seat in case someone else took it. **So he placed the lunchbox and his favourite pencil on the desk in front of him.** Yes, they were safe there and everyone would see his favourite 'yellow teddy lunchbox'.

Class started and the tall lady he guessed must be called Ms Mumpy (her real name was Ms Murphy) started talking. **She smiled at Mattheus and again he felt welcomed.** But all was not well for long. Suddenly the class jumped up and started singing a song he never heard before. **Ms Mumpy's face seemed to light up as the song progressed. She moved to the top of the classroom and started waving her hands and copying the pupils' actions. She was clearly excited by what was going on.** But what was this about? He knew Ms Mumpy had said something but what was it? He couldn't tell from her what she wanted ... there were no signs, no signal. **Finally, she looked at him and signalled for him to stand up with the other children.** He watched them as they touched their knees, heads and toes and tried to join in. Why was Ms Mumpy so far away? She was at the top of the room and seemed to be in another world. He could tell she had spotted something at the top of the classroom and wondered what it was. Ah, someone else had a yellow teddy lunchbox. Great! They were putting it on a table at the side of the room. Mmm.

Now Ms Mumpy came towards him. 'Great', thought Mattheus, 'she is coming to see me.' He did his best to copy the other students as he knew she was watching – heads, knees and toes – yes, he seemed to be getting it – **and Ms Mumpy was watching – fantastic – she would see how good he was**. Every now and then he would glance at her; the great strain of trying to fit in, to copy the others was telling on him.

Hands were getting mixed up, was it head and toes or head and knees? How was he doing? **Ms Mumpy was smiling, but he could see no encouragement in her face.** Was he doing it wrong? She mumbled again. **He listened keenly for the tone of her voice.** Yes, there was happiness in it ... yes, there was surprise and **he could tell from her eyes that she really was smiling like a kindred spirit ... like his Mum really ... she gave him the thumbs–up signal ... great ... he was fitting in. But then something changed in her face.** What was it? He could see a frown and look of concern. Ms Mumpy was looking at his yellow teddy lunchbox. Again she mumbled something. **She pointed towards the table at the side. In a flash he knew what she meant.** Yellow teddy would have to go to that table. With one wave

Territorial markers.

Smiling.

Expressions of emotion: movement and positive facial expressions.

Use of gesture.

Importance of being 'looked at'.

Lack of facial expressions of encouragement.

Vocal expression.

Various messages from the use of smiles, gestures and facial expression.

Positive use of gesture.

of her hand Ms Mumpy confirmed his worst suspicions ... Yellow Teddy was supposed to join the other lunchboxes on that faraway table. The stares of the other children began to burn into his consciousness.

Fear slowly began to grip him. But he was determined to keep the lunchbox beside him. He was caught. **Ms Mumpy smiled encouragingly again and pointed slowly at the dreaded table.** Did she expect him to walk all the way over there and leave his favourite teddy up there all alone? He was getting confused. Ms Mumpy mumbled again. This time, she was pointing at his school bag and seemed to be saying to put the box in there. Okay, this was better. Slowly, he put the teddy lunchbox back in the bag, but made sure to leave his face pointing outwards. Yellow teddy could still see what was going on. **Teacher nodded assuringly and gave another thumbs–up signal.** Mattheus could feel the smile stretch uncontrollably across his face. Things were looking up for him and teddy.

> Positive use of smiles and gesture.

> Positive use of gesture and back-channel responses, i.e. head-nodding.

Analysis

What did you think of Mattheus? You could probably identify with his feelings of insecurity, his need to be accepted and his dependence on the teacher for assurance and guidance. Ms Mumpy played an important role in making him feel 'at home' in the classroom. Because the little boy had difficulty in understanding her spoken English, she communicated with him largely via nonverbal means – through her X-Factor. Students with English as an additional language are dependent on the differentiated use of nonverbal signs and signals. As one of the teachers in our research noted: 'I smile more towards pupils with language difficulties to provide reassurance ... I also use gesture and hand signals more with showing a foreign language student how to hang up his coat' (White, 2008, 96). Ms Mumpy did plenty of this. She gave Mattheus the thumbs-up signal, smiled, moved in his direction and looked at him. As you will recall, these are all features of the classroom X-Factor discussed in earlier chapters of the book. If we think of Mattheus, we also get insights into the importance of where children sit, how they 'mark their territory' and of course how they read emotions on the face of the teacher. The emotional contagion effect was not lost on Mattheus. Ms Mumpy's smiling eyes and reassuring thumbs-up signal provoked an equally positive reaction from this young boy.

This story's main theme had to do with differentiated nonverbal communication in the classroom. The manner in which teachers differentiate their behaviour towards their students is one of the most fascinating fields of study. Why? Because teachers do it a lot and resemble 'the fish who doesn't know he's wet'. Teachers are often unaware of the intricate way in which they differentiate their nonverbal communication. They can do it according to their perceptions of the individual pupils' abilities, the actual class level they are teaching, the subject they are teaching and the behaviour they are trying to manage.

Back in 1968, Rosenthal and Jacobson showed how teachers communicate their expectations nonverbally through the use of eye contact. This is not always a good thing. As discussed in Chapter 12, if a teacher thinks the pupil is likely to give an incorrect answer their eye contact can be shorter. In our own work we found that teachers positively differentiated their communication towards weaker students through their use of body language and voice intonation. One of the teachers on reviewing video recordings of their teaching recognised that 'my voice is softer and more affirming when dealing with individual and weaker pupils'. We can also do it in a host of other ways such as gesturing, facial expression and occupation of space.

All of these nonverbal actions are connected into one of the central themes of this book. The expression of emotion nonverbally. Story 1 has a number of visual pictures such as children performing 'heads, knees and toes', a boy with a lunchbox, a friendly teacher and so on. But running beneath these images are currents of potentially deep emotion. In the short excerpt of this story we encounter nervousness, happiness, confusion and excitement, for example. The manner in which these emotions were communicated was both explicit and implicit. This challenges us to think about how emotion can be conveyed and how such emotion can be differentiated to better effect. In this story, the student was on a roller coaster of an emotional ride. He travelled from nervousness, to loneliness, contentment, confusion, enjoyment and finally back to contentment. When we look at the story we can see that all of these emotions have strong links with the field of nonverbal expression. This emphasises the focus on some of the big questions in this book – How do you convey emotions in the classroom? Do you smile more at some students rather than others? Do you maintain longer eye contact with students you expect will know the answer? Do you speak differently to students with special educational needs?

The answers to these questions will be rooted in perceptions of each person's students and in particular their emotional needs. We encountered this in our research. As one participant put it: 'I think it has to do with self-confidence as opposed to ability … for example sometimes you can have someone excellent who has low self-esteem … so you tailor your communication towards certain pupils' (White, 2008, 97). Such perceptions of where we see the pupil emotionally are significant. Ms Mumpy was clearly aware of Mattheus' insecurities and acted accordingly. Governing many of Mattheus' emotions was the feedback he was receiving from his teacher. Was he doing okay? Was there an assuring expression on her face? His emotional well-being was continually being nourished by the teacher's nonverbal feedback. As we mentioned earlier, the emotional contagion theory and the teacher immediacy effect are very pertinent here. Mattheus was warmed by the teacher's own expressions and indeed by the teacher's obvious immediacy in the classroom.

This story also illustrates how teachers can differentiate their communication based on student age. While we are not told directly, it is evident that we are dealing with a reception or junior class. Our own work confirmed that teachers differentiate their nonverbal communication according to student age. As one participant remarked: 'with infants their language is not as developed so they wouldn't understand as much … and it's interesting how much infants notice visually, for example my jewellery … or that you got your hair cut' (White, 2008, 98). Our work found that teachers in older classes were conscious of using nonverbal signals in a more subtle manner, such as the simple movement of an eyebrow or a quick glance.

Teacher differential behaviour does not stop here. In this story Ms Mumpy's use of space is significant. She knelt beside Mattheus and moved towards him. Being physically present and looking at the students is important. But there can often be other reasons a teacher moves into someone's area. The classic example in this case involves the teacher gravitating towards the part of the room where there may be behavioural issues. The main aim here is to redirect inappropriate behaviour. Such differentiated nonverbal communication which is grounded in the occupancy of space can often be accompanied by direct eye contact, or, as one of the teachers in our research put it, 'a withering look' (White, 2008, 98).

Finally, did you notice the manner in which Ms Mumpy was excited by the 'heads, knees and toes' exercise? Mattheus spotted the different expression on her face. Now we are not saying that all teachers should engage in 'heads, knees and toes actions' to make themselves feel better, but the point here concerns Ms Mumpy's excitement. We can all get excited by different things. As one participant viewing video recordings of their teaching remarked: 'I think my face lights up for different parts of lessons and probably different lessons too ... just the faintest of things ... like a look or a quicker movement which ... shows excitement' (White, 2008, 99). This is an important feature of what we do. Are there times in lessons or during the day when your face lights up more than others? Do you think your students can pick up on this?

2

Your X-Factor and Expressing Your Emotions – Spartacus

Spartacus

FIGURE S2.1 Spartacus.

Gonzo, as he was known to his friends, sat at the back of the class. **From there he could keep an eye on things, he could judge when and where to make his next play, where to launch his next attack, where to ambush the next teacher.**

The bell rang. 'Let the games begin', he thought. 'Maths, what a waste of time!' When he was in first grade he remembered some teacher telling him that the Greeks invented Maths. What a load of baloney. They couldn't even play football.

Mr Dingham entered the classroom. **He had a slow walk, his head slightly bowed.**

Ah, how he loved this man. He was his favourite quarry. From the first time he met him, Gonzo knew he would be easy. His finely tuned predatory instincts told him this middle-aged man was not really interested in school. **The clues were in his sneakers, his shirt, which even Gonzo could tell badly needed to be ironed, and the bag with no books in it. Mr Dingham was, in his own words, easy prey.**

And so, like Spartacus, he straightened himself for the first duel of the day.

After rummaging in his large bag for at least five minutes, Mr Dingham dragged something from its depths. 'Oh, he found a book', thought Gonzo, 'what a surprise.'

> Territorial occupation.

> Walking and conveyance of confidence.

> Attractiveness and self-presentation.

148

'I was thinking of doing data today', announced Mr Dingham, **as he rubbed his neck and stared at his book**. **He looked up at the class and darted a glance at Gonzo.**

'He knows I'm here', thought Gonzo.

'Now the first thing we need to know about data is that it represents information – take for example the World Cup soccer tournament.' **Gonzo detected a slight quiver in the voice, but for once there was enthusiasm. Now he was intrigued.**

Like a micro-surgeon, he began to scan the teacher's face. **There was a new alertness in the eyes and the head was held high. His face bore the hallmarks of enthusiasm.** Gonzo was even more intrigued.

'Did anyone watch the match last night between USA and Uruguay?' More alertness. **Mr Dingham couldn't hide his enthusiasm.** If there was one thing he loved, that was soccer. He had played for the university team as a student and was known then for his speed and passing accuracy.

Gonzo decided he would test Dingham out.

'Sir, I have a question', announced Gonzo. The class swivelled around to stare at Gonzo in expectation. He had the stage, he was about to strike his first blow.

'Sir, I did … I watched the match, but I didn't see anyone doing Maths. Are ya sure you were watching soccer?' Some muffled laughter emanated from the Gonzo fan club. Like the gladiator's first blow to a wounded opponent he moved in again for another stab.

'Data is for dodos, Sir.' He marvelled at his own brilliance. I can even alliterate, he thought.

He waited for the time old reaction of Dingbat, as he called him. **He expected a confused look. Some fear garnished with wide eyes, sideways glances, movement back behind the rostrum, scratching of the face and self-hugging. Perhaps even a stammer. Sometimes if Gonzo was lucky he would engage with him and perhaps even shout.**

Today, Mr Dingham took his time. He looked directly at Gonzo, longer than he would have liked and moved directly towards him. The silence slowly became louder. Gonzo didn't like the movement. **Someone was invading his space, his territory. Was he being circled?** A new tactic, he pondered.

'Interesting you should mention soccer and Maths – David, and I'm delighted you're interested in the topic. I love soccer. Did anyone else watch the match?' came the response from Mr Dingham. **His voice was soft and purposeful.**

Poor eye contact and displacement activities.
Conveyance of enthusiasm in voice intonation.
Facial expressions of enthusiasm. Improved eye contact.
Conveying enthusiasm.
Facial expressions of confusion, displacement activities, poor vocal expression and poor eye contact.
Occupation of space. Eye contact.
Good voice intonation.

149

The moment came and went as swiftly as it started. What? The voice seemed calm. Dingbat was looking at him directly. No fidgeting. No scratching. **His arms weren't folded in a defensive pose** and, what's more, he seemed to be giving him praise. **His face expressed encouragement and surprise. He even had the cheek to smile at him.** People were looking at him now as Spartacus the scholar.

> Positive body language, facial expressions and vocal expression.

Today, he had been ambushed by data. What's so special about data? He wondered. He was going to find out. Tomorrow, Spartacus would be better armed.

Analysis

Perhaps we can all identify with Gonzo and Mr Dingham. From time to time, teachers encounter Gonzos who lie in wait for them, who seek to disrupt their classes and even unnerve them. Of course, in this story, Mr Dingham didn't do himself any favours. He was a 'marked man', a target from the minute Gonzo spotted him; the dishevelled clothes and unconfident walk suggested easy prey as Gonzo himself commented. The other downfall for Mr Dingham lay in his body language and his voice intonation early in the lesson. His shaky voice, poor eye contact and self-touching leaked a lack of confidence and even determination in what he was about to do in the lesson. He had an underdeveloped X-Factor.

Students watch teachers carefully. In Mr Dingham's case, his clothing, voice, the way he walked, eye contact and even the manner in which he rummaged in a large bag painted a picture for the student. Throughout this book we have discussed how your X-Factor is picked up within seconds by students. It leaks how you really feel about a situation. In this case, Mr Dingham was nervous entering the class, as he probably was every time, with Gonzo at the back waiting to ambush him.

However, this story does have a twist. Mr Dingham obviously liked soccer. In this story the turning point comes when Gonzo spotted a 'slight quiver' in his voice, but this time it 'bore the hallmarks of enthusiasm'. Vocal variety is the nonverbal factor students associate most positively with learning. And monotone expression is the one most negatively associated with learning.

In our own research, we encountered a number of situations where teachers felt the 'voice can reveal annoyance, anger, surprise, confusion, amazement' (White, 2008, 108), with the pitch of voice being seen as important in scenarios where the teacher was trying to 'create suspense' or to 'convey particular meanings' (109). It is interesting that for one of the participants, there was an element of surprise with the teacher being 'shocked at how monotone my voice is … everything is clear but was all pitched at the one level' (109).

Like all aspects of nonverbal communication, Mr Dingham's change in voice, the detection of enthusiasm in his face, the 'alertness' in his eyes and the manner in which he held his head high combined like instruments in an orchestra to portray a symphony of positive intent and disposition towards the learning activity that was to follow. This resonates with the classroom 'nonverbal pzazz' which Neill and Caswell (1993) talk about. It is also closely linked to 'teacher enthusiasm' which we discussed in Chapter 4.

Enthusiastic teachers speak in a dramatic and expressive way, using varied vocal intonation, maintaining eye contact, using varied facial expression, smiling, laughing and gesturing. Now Mr Dingham didn't laugh, but he did smile, he maintained eye contact, he varied his vocal expression and there was an alertness about him.

There are other features of Mr Dingham's nonverbal communication which are worth considering. Notice how he moved into Gonzo's space as he responded to his cheekiness. Also, his use of direct eye contact, the calmness of his voice and the looks of encouragement and surprise. These nonverbal techniques seemed to have an effect on Gonzo. Like a 'lighthouse of emotion' Mr Dingham conveyed enthusiasm and interest in what was about to be learned. Our friend Gonzo was disarmed by this. What's more, he was affected by the positive teacher immediacy from Mr Dingham. His interest in data prompted Gonzo to wonder about it himself. Was there something he was missing?

3

Your X-Factor, Motivation, Nonverbal Drama and Immediacy – The Great Horse of Troy

The Great Horse of Troy

FIGURE S3.1 The great horse of Troy.

It was the first time some of the girls had ever even held a hammer. Some of them only took up the woodwork class because there were lots of boys in it and Mr Nolan was supposed to be great fun. Anyway, it was only for one semester. With all those lovely boys to look at, Sophie and Ellie both agreed it was a genius idea. But there was one thing that worried them – their nails. Messing with wood, saws, hammers and God knows what else could easily cause a girl to break a nail.

'Ellie, if I break one of these nails, we are straight outa here, babes', whispered Sophie anxiously into Ellie's ear. Ellie thought otherwise. Sophie would quickly forget about her nails when Roberto came into the room. Roberto could sing, he could play football, he had the deepest blue eyes and such sallow skin. It was no surprise he was the hottest thing in Year 10. Sophie was besotted.

For Ellie, it was a different story. She had her sights on much bigger prey. She was after a less obvious fish. Rafael. He was a year older than Roberto, shy, but liked carpentry. As far as she was concerned, the connection between her attending a woodwork class and chatting up a boy who liked carpentry could not be more obvious. As she said herself, by attending this class she would understand the boy – she would see the wood from the trees. Anyway, it would be great to use your hands and to make something.

Their teacher, Tony Nolan never entered a room. He arrived. Students never needed to scatter rose petals in his path. **He always entered with the poise and purposeful march of a leader.** Before he even got to his desk, students would be watching him. **It wasn't just the erect manner in which he held his head, nor the imposing stance he took at the window, it was those alert eyes, taking in everything and flashing confidently from his calm and relaxed face. His hands were on his hips and ready for business.**

'Hi, guys. Welcome to woodwork class for this semester. My name is Tony Nolan, your woodwork teacher. Today is your big day. I know many of you are inexperienced, but I am going to make sure no one gets knotted up. This is a joint endeavour.'

The puns were largely wasted on the class, but **his chirpy, enthusiastic voice, his lively movements and eye contact with all of them caught their attention**.

Sophie and Ellie perked up. **This guy was a bit different. Well dressed.** They studied his dark hair even more carefully. 'It's not dyed', thought Ellie, but she wasn't sure. Mmm … something to study more closely. **They liked his smile.**

'So, guys, tell me what you know about wood', chirped Mr Nolan. His hands outstretched in front of him. **He was gazing at the corner which housed Rafael and his buddies. What was he doing that for? They never answered.**

Rafael decided he would answer.

'Mr Nolan, my Dad has a carpentry business and last week we were making an oak table.'

Mr Nolan turned **deliberately to face** Rafael.

'Wonderful, yes wood is all around us. Do you know, Rafael, that right angles are very important when we make tables?' remarked Mr Nolan, **his voice much lower and softer, respectful**.

> Confident walk.

> Positive body language, eye contact and facial expressions.

> Positive voice intonation, gestures and eye contact.

> Attractiveness and smiling.

> Use of gaze towards students who tend to disengage. Open body language. Chirpy vocal expression.

> Positive body language and orientation.

> Vocal expression.

'Yes, I do', said Rafael.

'Well, let's all make some', announced Mr Nolan to the class.

The class looked at him incredulously.

'How?' came a voice from somewhere.

'Just the question! Okay, let's all stand up. **Put your left hand above your head and your right hand pointing towards the window … now that's a right angle.**'

> Use of gesture in Mathematics to illustrate and assist memory processing.

The class hesitantly undertook the exercise, it was new to them, indeed for many of them standing up doing actions in a class was 'far out'. Some of them still had their hands in a right angle pose when Mr Nolan told them they could sit down again.

'Any other ideas on wood? What about the girls? What do you know about wood?' enquired Mr Nolan, **a pleasant and curious expression crossing his face**.

> Facial expressions conveying enthusiasm and curiosity.

The girls looked at each other. No answers. Each girl thinking she would make a fool of herself talking about 'boys' stuff' yet feeling the discomfort at not being able to help this obviously nice man. Finally, Ellie decided to take the plunge.

'I don't know if this is relevant, Sir, but last term we studied Helen of Troy and the big wooden horse, and our teacher told us that it would have been a great engineering feat for its time.'

The answer seemed to seize the class with both confusion and intrigue. A wooden horse? Sure that was zillions of years ago.

'What a wonderful thought', exclaimed Mr Nolan, **bouncing off the edge of the window ledge where he had propped himself and making straight for the blackboard**.

> Changing the kite zone of participation.

'Ah the Wooden Horse of Troy, my favourite.' He sketched a poor diagram of a horse with a gigantic belly. 'Why don't we see about building one and we'll put it at the front of the school? What do you think, guys? Is it on your History course?'

The class were somewhat spellbound and yet intrigued. Yes it was on their History course. But was this guy off his rocker? A wooden horse outside the school! It would be fun though.

'Would it be hard to make, Sir?' asked Sophie.

Mr Nolan paused and nodded. He scanned the class to see if he could spot confusion, perhaps nervousness.

'I don't know; I think so, but we'll never know if we don't try', replied Mr Nolan with a big smile.

> Grounding – checking for misunderstandings. Positive use of pauses, head nods and smiling.

'Now, guys, before we build this wooden horse, we are going to have to think like the soldiers who made it. Everyone, gather in the store room', **he announced in an excited tone, his index finger tapping the rhythm of the sentence, his body moving closer towards the class**.

> Body movements convey enthusiasm. Fingers 'tap' or beat out the key words in the sentence. Positive use of space and vocal expression.

The class all moved towards the small store at the back of the room. Once inside, it was a tight squeeze for all of them, in fact very tight.

'Now, guys, this is what it must have felt like for the soldiers in the belly of the horse. We must be silent. No whispering', said Mr Nolan, exaggerating the breathlessness in his voice.

Some of the girls giggled.

'Oh that's it, we're all dead', responded Mr Nolan. 'The Trojans would have heard that. No we have to be deadly silent.'

Then to a disengaged student he enquired: 'How do you feel, Roberto?'

Question distribution.

'Nervous, Sir. I've never been squeezed into a box with 18 people before.' The class burst into laughter, a joke serving as the perfect release valve for this new and somewhat uncomfortable experience. Mr Nolan laughed loudly too.

'What about you Sophie?' he asked.

'I'm nervous. Afraid to breathe. What if I wanted to use the toilet? Or if I wanted a drink?'

Mr Nolan's face lit up. He looked at the others with wide eyes and surprise. 'Excellent answer, Sophie. They would have had to think about everything. Did anyone get a splinter in them? How do you think the Greeks would have felt with a splinter in their you know what?'

Facial expression of enthusiasm. Use of flashbulb eyes.

The students smirked again.

'They probably had to plane the inside as well as the outside', came an answer from the back of the room.

'Super. And what a wonderful word – plane. Okay, now, guys, we will return to our seats as Greeks, to build this great horse.'

The students filed back to their seats. In a way they were sorry to leave the security and intimacy of that big horse. But they felt different. Roberto was ahead of Ellie. He stopped and waved lavishly towards her and whispered: 'This way, Princess Helen.'

Ellie was thrilled and embarrassed. She glanced shyly at her nails. Things were looking good all around. Even her nails were still intact. Mmm. She wondered whether a Greek goddess would have to file her own nails. What did they use? Probably wood, she mused.

Analysis

It is probably fair to say that Mr Nolan has 'it going on' as some of the teenagers in the story would say. He has the X-Factor. There are a number of features of this X-Factor which come to the fore. His attractive sense of dress, his confident walk, openness, lively body language, chirpy voice intonation, use of eye contact, use of space and so on all combine to create a figure who is interesting and engaging. In particular we also get the sense of someone who enjoys their work and as a result infuses those around them with similar enthusiasm. There are a number of nonverbal messages at play here. First, we see the role of 'referent power' where Mr Nolan is like a role model to the students, but, more importantly, his communication style imbues the lesson with 'affective meaning'. The students like him and their affective predispositions to the subject are also affected. Of course, we can also see the emotional contagion effect, teacher immediacy and 'psychological closeness' at play here. Mr Nolan is expressive. Remember that people who are expressive are perceived as having a social advantage, being more potent in terms of influencing the moods of others.

Perhaps one of the most significant features of Mr Nolan's X-Factor revolves around a perception that he is alert. Obviously, his swift movements, lively style of interaction and use of space contribute to this, but there is also a strong sense that he is 'watching you' – that he is looking. Being 'looked at' is important in the classroom; it is a 'profound form of social acknowledgement'. We encountered this quite often in our own research. Teachers talked about using their eyes as 'tools' particularly when giving instructions, but also as one teacher put it 'I am always looking for confirmation on their faces as I speak … it's grounding' (White, 2008, 104).

There are other features of Mr Nolan's teaching style to note. In a way, you could say he is dramatic at times. This correlates with our own research. We found that teachers may use 'facial expressions which grossly exaggerate the verbal content'. Such dramatic use of the face can mirror feelings, give extra meaning to verbal content or may be a response to a pupil's input. One of our participants described the classroom as a place where 'you are on stage', while another remarked that 'it is almost like being in a play … it's not being false … I am being myself … but I know when I am overdoing it' (White, 2008, 124). The nonverbal use of drama was significant in the manner in which it helped the students understand 'how squashed it could be in the belly of the wooden horse'. Again, Mr Nolan's focus on how the students felt in the belly of the horse served to underwrite their understanding with emotional meaning.

There is also a strong visual component to the work of Mr Nolan. He drew a picture of a horse on the blackboard. He stood in central class locations. He also varied where he stood to facilitate a varied distribution of questions. He used his arms and gestures to make 'right angles'. As we mentioned in Chapter 3, gestures are closely related to cognitive processing and facilitate the recall of both visuo-spatial and verbal items.

4

Your X-Factor and Motivation – The Butterfly

The Butterfly

He was in big trouble when she got home. Of that she was sure. How dare he call her mother an interfering cow. After ten years of marriage, two children and a wedding gift of 10,000 dollars which, by the way, this interfering cow had given him, Mark Lermont was, it had to be said, an ignorant and ungrateful pig. Pigs like this deserved the spit.

But first she had to do a spelling test with second grade. She just wasn't in the mood. Quarrelling before going to work was always a bad idea. Now she felt tired and distracted. There was also something about this room which really annoyed her. **She wasn't sure, was it the lack of light or the grey walls?** Anyway, she had to get on with it. All those little faces looking up at her waiting for their first word.

She opened the book on page 14 of the level two phonics programme. Wow, she couldn't believe it. The first word in the list was pig.

'OK, children, your first word today is – pig.' **She spat the word out with as much contempt as possible**. Some of the innocent faces looked up at her in surprise. Then hands dived for the exercise books and the pupils scribbled busily.

'The next word is dig.'

Her mind trailed off. She remembered Mark's excitement the day they received the 10,000 dollars. He didn't notice any cow horns that day. Oh no. Her mum was a bovine beauty on that occasion, with not an interfering snort to be heard anywhere.

'Ms Lermont … what's the next word?' her daydreaming was interrupted.

'Twig', she responded, her voice weak, her eyes still staring at the small spellings book.

And so, Martha Lermont went through every word in the 'ig' family. But her heart wasn't in it. **Her movements felt heavy.**

FIGURE S4.1 The butterfly.

> Questionable use of colour and attractiveness of the classroom.

> Poor vocal expression.

> Weak use of voice intonation. Poor teacher immediacy and enthusiasm.

Usually she would have had the pupils up out of their seats, spelling the word pig, **making the shape of it with their hands, tracing it in the air, miming 'ig' words**, and singing the rhymes. She knew she had to get herself back in train.

Marcus put his hand up.

'Ms Lermont, my Dad said that I should bring in this fig leaf for our "ig" words table. I think we could use it for our drama too.'

Martha looked up and smiled. How clever. Marcus had this special ability to set things up. For a seven year old, he was brilliant at organising things. He had no real interest in the 'ig' table, nor was he interested in fig leaves, but boy did he love drama.

'OK, Marcus, I'm not sure about doing our *Three Little Pigs*, but we might talk about the butterfly today.'

Yesterday she had read the pupils the story of the *Hungry Caterpillar*. **Martha could feel some excitement coming back in her voice.** Like Marcus, she too enjoyed drama. What the heck, let's have a go she thought. **The pupils sensed the change.**

She moved into the centre of the room, and squiggled around pretending to eat something.

'Children, **I want you to pretend you're a little caterpillar**. Caterpillars spend their days eating. Eat, eat, eat. Oh those lovely juicy bay leaves. Be careful, remember caterpillars, you're under a leaf.' **Each time she used the word, eat, she gave it even more emphasis.** A funny word she thought.

The children immediately jumped at the challenge. They were well used to drama and quickly mirrored Martha's movements.

'Now, I want you to feel very full. Oh, your tummy is so big. You have been eating non-stop for days.'

'Pauline, how do you feel?' asked Martha

'Miss, I feel very full ... my tummy is really big.'

'Marcus, how do you feel?'

'I feel really full too', said Marcus, 'I need to sleep for a while.'

'Okay, children, you are all very full. You need to sleep for a while. But first you need to build a cocoon around you, just like the hungry caterpillar did yesterday.' Martha modelled how to build the cocoon. **She waved her hands, stood tall, bent low. She put on an excited expression. These actions seemed to lift her mood.**

Once again, the children busied themselves.

'Now we are going to go for a long sleep. Everyone, get inside your cocoon and pretend you're sleeping.' **Just before**

Use of gesture to assist memory processing.

Use of 'looking at students' and smiling.

Voice intonation conveys growing enthusiasm. Children are quick to detect happiness.

Emphasis on specific words.

Positive occupation of space. Use of nonverbal drama. Children use actions and movements to develop their understanding of the story.

Developing an emotional understanding of the content of the story.

Facial feedback theory – adopting a particular facial expression may stir the equivalent emotion within you.

Martha turned off the lights, she deliberately looked and smiled at Helena, the shy child who always gravitated to the corner of the room. Helena always needed that extra reassurance.

The class fell silent in the dimly lit room. All eyes were closed, a sense of peace reigned.

Martha's voice broke the silence. **She whispered slowly.**

'Now, children, I want you to get up out of your seats. It's a beautiful day. Esther, switch on the lights, please.'

Martha stretched her arms above her head like a butterfly emerging from the chrysalis. She wiggled. She smiled. She looked around in awe. A newborn butterfly must experience such joy and amazement she thought. **She felt it inside.**

'Now, children, pretend you are wiggling free of your chrysalis. Stretch your arms. Smile at the world. It's a bright new day. How wonderful', she exclaimed. **The excitement and enthusiasm was back in her voice. She herself began to feel better inside.**

Yes, it was nice to be a butterfly. Her thoughts about pigs and mud were slipping away. Was she like a caterpillar, feasting on too much anger? Maybe she should remodel her own cocoon. Beauty can spring from ugliness.

> Use of 'looking'. Directing gaze towards pupils in the corners of the room.

> Varied vocal expression.

> Positive use of nonverbal drama and smiling.

> Facial feedback theory – by adopting particular facial expressions we can stir their equivalent emotions.

> Positive vocal expression.

Analysis

Martha arrived at school in a red mist. She was angry. This was reflected in the silence of her thoughts, but became louder once she faced or indeed failed to face the class. Her poor use of eye contact and her snappy vocal expression leaked a lack of enthusiasm and interest in her work. Her seated position behind the chair and lacklustre efforts were in contrast to what the pupils would normally expect. There was no signing of the spelling words, no tracing, no actions. She was not in a good mood and there was a listlessness, a lack of energy about her.

In our own research we encountered the significance of 'teacher energy' and your X-Factor quite clearly. Based on the video recording of one lesson, one teacher commented: 'I did not smile enough … maybe a bit towards the end of the lesson … but on the day I was tired and I did not get a proper break.' Another teacher commented: 'I can lose my composure and teaching style depending on my energy levels' (White, 2008, 112). Nonverbal expressiveness is associated with terms such as enthusiasm, drive and energy. 'Peppy' and non-lethargic movements connote a high degree of energy for an active performance. Martha's energy levels were at a low ebb at the start of the lesson, 'her movements felt heavy'. Energy levels are important for your X-Factor.

In this story Martha's mood changed. Instrumental in this change was the direction the lesson took, moving from a spelling test to an exciting drama. The value of using your body and of using nonverbal gestures, facial expressions movements, etc., to represent and indeed instil emotions has been discussed over and over in this book. By stretching and smiling at the world, something stirred in the teacher. In this story, becoming a caterpillar, which munches bay leaves, weaves its own cocoon and stretches out as a joyous newborn butterfly, is represented powerfully nonverbally. Martha was also clever to connect such actions and her words with emotional meaning. In this story we also see that the emotional contagion effect can work both ways. The teacher was infected by the enthusiasm of the pupils, and the pupils were infected by the enthusiasm of the teacher.

This story also illustrates the multiple use of nonverbal communication, your X-Factor, as an aid or tool in lesson delivery. There is vocal variety, variations in rate of speech, changes in teacher occupancy of space, various uses of gesture, differentiated use of eye contact and varied use of facial expressions to give meaning to lesson content. In our own research, there were numerous occasions where nonverbal communication was used as a 'tool'. For example, teachers commented on voice intonation and 'fluctuations are used to express enthusiasm ... to convey particular meaning'. Gesture was used 'to provide visual expression ... to create interest in lesson content'. Eye contact was noted by one teacher as 'a centre piece of my work ... closely linked with my hand movements ... I use them as a tool together' (White, 2008, 104). Facial expressions were also used to convey enthusiasm, and interestingly for one teacher sometimes 'grossly exaggerated the verbal content'.

5

Your X-Factor, Experience and Reflection – Bushfires

Bushfires

FIGURE S5.1 The student teacher.

'Teacher, Thomas said that I took his ruler and I didn't', the announcement, which was supposed to be an answer, came from Helena and had little to do with regrouping.

'Very good, Helena, but we are doing Maths now and I will check that later', responded Ms Taylor, **concern and exasperation beginning to fill her voice as she moved towards this new bushfire**.

> Poor vocal expression – messages of exasperation.

The bushfires had been breaking out sporadically since the start of the lesson, just small ones, like Paul is making faces at Mark or Lucy took cubes from another table, but they were there and this young student teacher was at her wits' end trying to keep them under control.

Her new ploy was to head straight for the bushfire the minute it happened. Quench it in one go. However, today, this fire brigade approach was only serving to allow other 'unprotected' lands to erupt in a blaze. Why? What was she doing wrong?

She had started the lesson enthusiastically, determined to keep things going, to keep pace as she had learned at college, but there was something amiss. Of course, this wasn't the first time she had been a bushfire commando. The last lesson with this class of six year olds had also been a difficult experience. **Ms Taylor was losing confidence. She could feel it in her voice, in her movements. She knew her face was a**

> Facial expression and vocal intonation revealing weak confidence.

skyscape of storms and blustery clouds. But she had to go on, she had to try and rein in this class. She would try the bag trick. Her old teacher from first grade often used it, indeed, her mother often used it as a ploy to keep herself and her siblings 'under control' at dinner time.

'Look at this', she gushed, raising a large brown bag in her hand. The announcement was sudden and, being shrill, it captured the attention of these young minds. She eyeballed all of them, like General Custer facing a hoard of Indians crossing the horizon, but the gaze fell on one table in particular.

'Does anyone know what might be in here?' she quizzed. The children strained to make sense of the question as she spoke quickly. They pondered, but some of them were distracted with a feeling of dejection. Why did she always look towards the red table when she asked difficult questions? She even moved in their direction.

Look over here implored the children at the green table. We might know too. But alas, Ms Taylor did not. Before the question had even sunk to the deeper levels of their brains, she had asked someone from the red table. Lucy who sat at the green table was incensed, but couldn't put words on this injustice. Here it was, happening again, but she couldn't describe it. Her young brain knew little of terms such as eye contact, rate of speech, occupation of space, differentiated teaching. But she knew something was amiss.

'I think there might be cubes in it Miss ... the ones we use for addition', responded one of the children from the red table.

Ms Taylor smiled and nodded. She tried to look confident, but her darting looks and nervous body movements gave her away. She swivelled wildly from her position at the edge of the red table and headed purposefully towards the Maths resource area.

'Oh no', thought Lucy, more of those cubes. The crucifixion of tens and units continues.

Whether it was the sad look which crossed some of the faces, or the resigned stare which appeared on others, something struck Ms Taylor as she lifted the column of cubes. She paused and reflected. Was she going too fast for them? What kinds of signals was she giving? Oh to be able to see herself in action, to be a fly on the wall.

> Influence of significant others on your teaching.

> Poor vocal expression. Differentiated use of gaze.

> Rate of speech is too fast.

> Differentiated use of eye contact.

> Occupation of space revealing expectations.

> Differentiated use of gaze revealing expectations.

> Use of smiles and head nodding.

> Nervous body language and poor eye contact.

Analysis

It is clear that this young student teacher was experiencing difficulties. While Ms Taylor was aware of the necessity to keep pace, there are a number of aspects of her X-Factor which need further development. Her poor eye contact, sudden and jittery body movements, poor occupancy of space, differentiated eye contact, rate of speech and facial expressions leaked a lack of confidence in her own ability to communicate with this class and as a result bushfires ignited sporadically in this undergrowth of mixed messages.

The question must also be asked as to how often she smiled and gestured. Despite her awareness of the importance of keeping pace and appearing confident, her nonverbal communication leaked unease, exasperation and almost panic. The real emotional contagion effect may revolve around all of these emotions and perhaps could explain the sudden bushfires which erupted due to the unease and irritability pricked in her pupils.

There is also one other glaring feature of this story which stands out, and that concerns experience and reflection. Ms Taylor is a student teacher. Her teaching experience is limited. In our research we encountered the significance of experience. As one teacher remarked: 'The more experienced you are, the more you become aware of yourself in the classroom and what you are doing ... you begin to think of ways to give messages' (White, 2008, 126). Intertwined in this experiential backdrop are what could be called nonverbal traits or 'habits' which you pick up from your life experiences. In our research, this emerged clearly. These influences ranged from the influence of 'my mother' to the influence of other teachers observed during teaching practice and also to the influence of 'unknowns'. For example, one participant noted:

> I remind myself of my mother ... I use the stuff my mother used on me when I was at home ... like when myself and my cousin were causing chaos and I knew I got a look from my mother and you know it works and consciously or subconsciously you try that out with your class ... so you come around and try things from your life experience with your class (128).

A different participant made the following remark:

> I remind myself of someone who is really annoying and yet I can't think who they are ... what strikes me is that I am so teachery ... And I wouldn't mind I often say things like, she is such a teacher (128).

Gestalt psychology highlights the collective impact of experience on the behaviour and decisions of every individual. The collective impact of our own experiences as students in classrooms may result in us having deeply ingrained conceptions about teaching, which have deep experiential origins dating back to our own experiences as students in classrooms. As a teacher you might ask yourself whether there are teachers in your past experiences of schooling who have had a significant influence on you.

How do we reflect on and identify such influences? At the end of this story, Ms Taylor wondered what it would be like 'to see herself in action'. Our nonverbal communication is mostly fleeting in manner. So how aware are we of it? How do we reflect on it? In our own research, we were quite surprised by participants' lack of detailed awareness of how they communicated nonverbally. As one teacher remarked:

My first viewing of myself on video made me laugh. It was the first time I ever saw myself on video in the classroom ... it was brutal ... you're shocked at seeing yourself ... say for example the accent thing ... I knew my voice was loud, but not as loud as I thought.

In our work, we used video footage of a number of lessons and offered participants opportunities to analyse this footage using a self-evaluation questionnaire somewhat similar to the one in this book. Interestingly, one of our findings centred on teachers' enjoyment of the process of analysing themselves on video. Such an approach could be of use to Ms Taylor.

Concluding Remarks

This book has hopefully opened up opportunities for you to improve and enjoy your teaching more. We hope that you now have a bank of concrete ideas and insights into how you might develop your own X-Factor and influence your teaching for the good. Some of the key features of a teacher's X-Factor are fairly obvious (for example, confidence, poise), while others may not be so (for example, positioning in the classroom, body language). Some features of your X-Factor will come more naturally than others (e.g. smiling) but all of them can be deliberately developed to create that attractiveness and interest that appeal to students.

The various chapters in this book have shown the subtle, swift and sometimes subconscious manner in which nonverbal communication can operate. The importance of emotion in teaching and learning and the role which nonverbal communication plays in conveying this emotion has been specifically highlighted. Smiles, eye contact, gestures and body language, to mention but a few, are important 'lighthouses' for these emotions. What is most intriguing about nonverbal communication and the X-Factor is the 'magical' way in which it operates. It casts a spell, yet often leaves no tangible evidence.

To illustrate this once again, think of the story about the butterfly. Remember the part where the teacher enacts the butterfly emerging from the chrysalis. Where she 'feels' the excitement of this wondrous event, where she encourages the students to do so too, where her face, her hands and her whole body portray the cognitive and emotional power and joy of such a life-changing event. This powerful visual image serves as the key to this book.

No, we are not saying that all teachers are caterpillars! But hopefully this book has acted like a cocoon of ideas, wrapping you in the theory and practicalities of classroom nonverbal communication and preparing you to emerge from this chrysalis with a new and exciting energy.

So how do you emerge from this cocoon? How can you continue to develop your X-Factor? Well, the first step is to complete the self-evaluation framework in the Appendix. Perhaps by having the students videotape you as you teach, you could then examine footage of your teaching using the self-evaluation framework as a guide. You could also consider the value of getting critical friends to visit your class and complete the self-evaluation framework of your teaching from their perspective. You could combine such appraisal with video footage of your teaching. The value of getting students to evaluate your classroom performance has also been demonstrated in a recent BBC programme – *The Classroom Experiment*. The teachers concerned were particularly impressed by the students' insights and evaluations.

Having completed the self-evaluation framework, using any or all of the above suggestions, you could then decide to work on certain aspects of your X-Factor. Let's take the section on eye contact for example. Here are some of the questions you could ask yourself:

How can I improve my engagement in grounding?
Can I look more at students as they work?
How can I improve my use of eye contact to initiate interaction?
How can I improve my use of eye contact to regulate the flow of conversation?
How can I improve my eye contact with students for whom I have lower expectations?

There are lots more questions in the self-evaluation appendix, but you can perhaps take a few questions at a time. Reflect on them regularly. Over time, your awareness of them will grow and awareness is the first step to changing practice – of course you must want to also! Having taken eye contact as a starting point move on to another one, e.g. smiling. It is often 'fun' to undertake these endeavours with a few colleagues or perhaps even the entire school staff.

The future

The possibilities for developing your X-Factor are endless. As researchers, and writers of this book, we were greatly impressed by witnessing teachers' involvement in analysing their nonverbal communication and in learning about their X-Factors. It was a process which brought them to new discoveries about themselves. Indeed, as one of them put it: 'for the first time ever we weren't being critiqued on our results ... it had to do with my teaching style'.

So that is why we wrote this book – to focus on being a reflective and self-improving teacher and to get away from results, timetables, meetings, photocopiers, textbooks and the other plethora of items and worries which swirl around the busy teacher. Like Dorothy in *The Wizard of Oz*, we wanted to burst through the tornado to look at you, the teacher, at the epicentre. What can you do to improve your practice as a teacher? How can you develop your X-Factor? We hope you have enjoyed reading this as much as we have writing it and that in your classroom you will now have a greater understanding of the words of the bard –

Fie, fie upon her!
There's language in her eyes, her cheek, her lip.
Nay her foot speaks; her wanton spirits look out at every joint and every motive in her body.

(*Troilus and Cressida*, Act IV, Scene V)

Appendix: Self-Evaluation Framework

What kind of 'lighthouse of emotion' am I?

1   We want you to think about yourself in terms of the weather.
    How would your students describe you? Sunny? Overcast? Stormy? Calm? Drab? Dull? Drizzling?
2   When you think of yourself as a teacher, what kinds of emotions do you think you radiate?

Drama

To what extent do you use nonverbal drama such as mime, silent role-play or freeze-frame images to encourage students to interrogate, represent or empathise with the content of your lessons?

FIGURE A1.1 The face as a lighthouse of emotion.

Use of space

Territories

1   In what ways are the 'territories' in your classroom 'marked'?
2   Do you allow students to 'mark' their own territories?

Personal space

1   Would you say you are a person who needs a lot of personal space? Are you aware of the different personal space needs of your pupils?
2   Are there students you particularly like in your class? In what ways do you move towards them? Do you move more hesitantly, slowly or reservedly towards other students?

3   How close do you stand to students as you reprimand them?
4   Do you tend to stand closer to students you like?
5   When sitting next to pupils, how closely do you monitor their body language and facial expressions in order to ascertain that you are not too close to them or too distant?

Your location in the classroom

FIGURE A1.2 Zone of participation.

1   Where do you stand as you teach? Do you tend to teach from the same place?
2   Do you always stand at the front of the class-room? Are there any areas of the classroom you do not occupy regularly? Why?
3   What is the kite zone of participation like around you? Do you change where you stand in order to ensure all students are within the zone of participation?
4   How often do students participate in class? Are they within your zone of participation? How often do you question students at the periphery of the classroom?
5   When directing discussions, do you stand in different parts of the classroom?

Dominance

Do you communicate dominance by selecting where you sit and where certain other students sit? Are some students with 'higher status' or dominance allowed to sit where they want?

Conversational distances

1   Are you aware of the conversational distances students maintain with you?
2   To what degree are you aware of the cultural variances in conversational distances?

Proxemic shifts

How aware are you of proxemic shifts? (Our occupancy of space can vary according to what we are saying, giving additional meaning to parts of our sentences which we think are important.)

Who gets to go first?

1   Do the same people always get to go first?
2   Are you first to lead as you leave the classroom?

Being visually central

1   When organising discussion groups, do you ensure that quieter students are seated in more visually central positions?
2   Where is your desk? Does it act as a barrier between you and your students?

Vocal intonation

Is my voice attractive?

Record your voice during a lesson. Decide on its attractiveness by answering the following questions:

a   Does it have a pleasant quality?
b   Is it monotone?
c   Has it appropriate loudness for all students to hear?
d   Do you speak too quickly/too slowly?
e   Do you vary the intonation of your voice?
f   Are there extremes of pitch/shrillness/squeakiness?
g   Do you have clear voice projection?

Your voice and your emotions

1   What kinds of emotions do you hear in your voice? Do you think the students will be stimulated/engaged by these emotions?
2   Do you make sure your voice registers your enthusiasm?

Prosody

To what degree do you place emphasis on particular words in your sentences, e.g. Mark *is* coming with me?

Eye contact

Am I being understood?

As people talk, they tend to look for evidence that they have been misunderstood rather than understood. This searching process is an attempt by the talker to identify moments when they are misunderstood and then to 'repair the damage'. Called grounding, it involves checking for understanding. Do you actively engage in 'grounding'?

Looking/gazing

1   To what degree do you look at students as they work?
2   How often do you move around the classroom and 'look' at the work your students are doing?
3   Is there evidence that you 'look' at exercise books?
4   Do you put pupils' work on display for others to look at?

Interaction

1   Do you use eye contact to initiate interaction?
2   Do you use eye contact to regulate the flow of conversation in class discussions?
3   Do you maintain appropriate eye contact with students for whom you have lower expectations?
4   How often do you use eye contact to check whether the student has understood what has been said?
5   In group situations, do you use eye contact to ensure all students are invited to contribute?
6   Do you try to ensure you make eye contact with all students?

Blinking

Do you blink a lot? Is this a sign of anxiety?

The eye flash

The eye flash involves opening the eyelids for less than a second without involvement of the eyebrows to emphasise particular words as we speak, e.g. adjectives. Are you aware of the value and possibilities of using the eye flash?

Students' thinking

1   Do you ever think of allowing students to close their eyes as they process or interrogate ideas/comments?
2   In what ways do you interpret students who look away? Do you view this positively as 'thinking' time?

Back-channel responses

Do you make use of 'head nods' to give feedback to your students?

Smiling

When and where do you smile?

1   Try and think of the classroom instances and places where you smile. When do you smile? Why do you smile?

2   Are there occasions when you could smile more?
    a   Towards which students do you smile most?
    b   Consider the students you are least likely to smile towards. Why is this?

Smiling and emotions

1   What kinds of emotions do your smiles reveal?
2   Do you use false smiles?
3   When are your smiles 'most real'? Why?

Facial expression

Your face as a lighthouse of emotion

Do you think there are times/occasions when your facial expressions notably change? Why is this?

Syntactic display

Do you think your expressions change for important parts of the sentence?

Facial responses

1   Does your face show 'overintensification of the affect', e.g. open eyes and broad expression of enthusiasm and support for a child's answer?
2   Does your face show 'deintensified affect', e.g. underplay your emotions when perhaps annoyed or disappointed by something?

Facial feedback theory

Are you aware of the potential of creating emotions within yourself, e.g. making yourself smile to provoke that emotion within yourself?

Body language

Open and closed body language

1   Is your body language typically open or closed?
2   Is your posture and use of your arms and legs free and easy? Or sharp and sudden? Does it reveal relaxation? Are you sympathetic and warm? Nervous and anxious?
3   Do you frequently make closed body language statements by, for example, folding your arms a lot?

Body language and interaction

1. Are your actions open, conveying that you like the person to whom you are talking? Do they give messages of approachability? Of enthusiasm?
2. Do you lean forward in an enthusiastic manner as you talk to students?
3. Do you orient yourself properly when speaking/listening to students, e.g. do your head, trunk and feet face the student?
4. To what degree do you mirror students as they speak?

Walking

Examine your walk

Do you have any video footage of yourself and the manner in which you walk? Have a look at the footage and decide whether you have a confident walk.

1. Do you slouch as you walk?
2. Does your walk convey messages of confidence and 'eagerness of step'?
3. Is your posture erect?

Seated position

1. Do you have a vertical sitting posture?
2. Do you slouch? Does this convey confidence?

Movement

1. Are your movements energised, leaking enthusiasm and a high degree of actual or potential energy expenditure?
2. How would you describe your body movements? Are they smooth or sudden?
3. Are they quick or sluggish?

Gesture

Gestures and your teaching

1. To what degree do you use gesture as you teach?
2. What do your gestures reveal about your emotions as you teach?

Gestures and meaning

1. To what degree do you ask students to use gestures to help them process concepts?
2. Do you use gestures to create specific images for the pupils?

3   To what degree do you use iconic gestures?
Iconic gestures are used when the gesture bears a close resemblance to the objects or actions being described; for example, bringing your fists together to indicate 'glue together'.

4   To what degree do you use metaphoric gestures?
Metaphoric gestures are used to present abstract concepts rather than concrete objects or events; for example, moving your hand up and down when discussing the concept of gravity.

5   To what degree do you use deictic gestures?
Deictic gestures are used to indicate objects and events; for example, pointing to a red square on the wall when discussing shape.

6   To what degree do you use emblems in your teaching?
Emblems are used where the gesture is a conventional one recognised by people from the community; for example, giving the thumbs up signal to indicate approval.

How you use your hands.

Open palms

Are your palms open as you gesture? Do you think they show openness?

Using the hands to process information

Do you ask your students to use their hands to help them process information, e.g. making perpendicular lines with their hands when studying co-ordinate geometry?

Self-touching/displacement activities

1   Do you self-hug? Does this convey nervousness/anxiety?
2   Are you inclined to rub particular parts of your body when nervous?
3   Do you fidget? Why? What kinds of emotions do you think your fidgeting reveals?
4   Do you engage in self-touching? Are these touches an outlet for nervous energy? Are they a product of concentration?

Beating

To what degree do you use beats (movement of the hands or fingers at significant parts of your speech) to mark out or emphasise what you are saying?

Attractiveness

Self-presentation

1   Are you well groomed?
2   Do your clothes fit you properly?

Clothes and self-image

1   Have a look at the clothes you are wearing and try to imagine them from the perspective of your students. What kinds of messages do you think your students are picking up from these clothes?
2   What image do you seek to portray in the classroom?
3   Do your clothes reflect this image?

Clothing and the cultural milieu of your school

1   Do your clothes fit the cultural milieu of your school?
2   To what degree do you think your clothes convey messages about your expertise?

Clothing and personal confidence

1   Can you think of any particular set of clothes you wear which you think gives you confidence in the classroom?
2   Why do you think these clothes give you confidence? What are their characteristics?

Your environment and colour

1   Do you think you would classify your classroom as attractive or ugly? Ask another teacher to judge it according to the above adjectives.
2   To what degree do you use colours such as blue, yellow, yellow-green and orange in the classroom environment?
3   Does your classroom have a 'warm' feel?

References

In writing this book, we drew on a variety of sources. In particular we would like to acknowledge the valuable insights and perspectives we gained from the work of Borg (2008), Cohen (2007), Knapp and Hall (2006), Miller (2005), Hargie and Dickson (2004), Beattie (2004), Pease and Pease (2004), Ekman (2003), Neill and Caswell (1993), Neill (1991), Lyle (1990) and Argyle (1988).

Note
It is also important to point out that none of the information referenced in this book arose as a result of the work of John White in his role as a primary inspector for the Department of Education and Skills in Ireland.

Adams, R. and Biddle, B. (1970) *Realities of Teaching: Explorations with Videotape*. New York: Holt Reinhart and Winston.

Addington, D.W. (1968) The relationship of selected vocal characteristics to personality perception. *Speech Monographs*, 35, pp. 492–503.

Alder, R. and Towne, N. (1996) *Looking Out, Looking In*, 8th edn. Fort Worth, TX: Harcourt Brace.

Alibali, M.W. and Goldin-Meadow, S. (1993) Gesture–speech mismatch and mechanism of learning: What the hands reveal about a child's state of mind. *Cognitive Psychology*, 25, pp. 468–523.

Allen, V. and Feldman, R. (1978) Studies on the role of tutor. In Neill, S. (1991) *Classroom Nonverbal Communication*. London: Routledge.

Ambady, N. and Rosenthal, R. (1993) Half a minute: Predicting teacher evaluations from thin slices of behaviour and physical attractiveness. *Journal of Personality and Social Psychology*, 64, pp. 431–441.

Ambady, N., Bernieri, F.J. and Richeson, J. (2000) Toward a histology of social behaviour: Judgemental accuracy from thin slices of the behavioural stream. In Zanna, M.P. (ed.) *Advances in Experimental Social Psychology*, vol. 32. San Diego, CA: Academic Press.

Ambady, N., Koo, J., Rosenthal, R. and Winograd, C.H. (2002) Physical therapists' nonverbal communication predicts geriatric patients' health outcomes. *Psychology and Aging*, 17, pp. 443–452.

Andersen, J. (1979) Teacher immediacy as a predictor of teaching effectiveness. In Nimmo, D. (ed.) (1980) *Communication Yearbook*. New Brunswick, NJ: Transaction Books.

Andersen, P. and Andersen, J. (1982) Nonverbal immediacy in instruction. In Barker, L. (ed.) (1983) *Communication in the Classroom*. Engelwood Cliff, NJ: Prentice-Hall.

Argyle, M. (1972) *The Psychology of Interpersonal Behaviour*, 2nd edn. London: Penguin.

Argyle, M. (1988) *Bodily Communication*, 2nd edn. London: Methuen.

Aries, E.J., Gold, C. and Weigel, R. (1983) Dispositional and situational influences on dominance behaviours in small groups. *Journal of Personality and Social Psychology*, 44, pp. 779–786.

Aronoff, J., Woike, B. and Hyman, L. (1992) Which are the stimuli in facial displays of anger and happiness? Configurational bases of emotion recognition. *Journal of Personality and Social Psychology*, 62, pp. 1050–1066.

Aziz-Zadeh, L. (2007) *Discover Magazine* (January). Quoted in Iacoboni, M. (2008) *Mirroring People*. New York: Farrar, Straus and Giroux.

Babad, E. (1993) Teachers' Differential Behaviour. *Educational Psychology Review*, 5, pp. 683–690.

Babad, E. (2005) Nonverbal behaviour in education. In Harrigan, J., Rosenthal, R. and Scherer, K. (eds) *The New Handbook of Methods in Nonverbal Research*. Oxford: Oxford University Press.

Babad, E., Avni-Babad, D. and Rosenthal, R. (2003) Teachers' brief nonverbal behaviours in defined instructional situations can predict students' evaluations. *Journal of Educational Psychology*, 86, pp. 120–125.

Babad, E., Avni-Babad, D. and Rosenthal, R. (2004) Prediction of students' evaluations from professors' nonverbal behaviour in defined instructional situations can predict students' evaluations. *Social Psychology of Education*, 7, pp. 3–33.

Ball, V. (1965) The aesthetics of colour: A review of fifty years of experimentation. *Journal of Aesthetics and Art Criticisms*, 23, pp. 441–452.

Barakat, R. (1973) Arabic gestures. *Journal of Popular Culture*, 6, pp. 749–787.

Barash, D.P. (1973) Human ethology: Personal space reiterated. *Environment and Behaviour*, 5, pp. 67–73.

Barnes, D. (1975) *From Communicating to Curriculum*. Middlesex, England: Penguin.

Baum, K.M. and Nowicki, S. Jr (1998) Perception of emotion: Measuring decoding accuracy of adult prosodic cues varying in intensity. *Journal of Nonverbal Behaviour*, 22, pp. 89–107.

Beattie, G. (2004) *Visible Thought, The New Psychology of Body Language*. London, Routledge.

Beattie, G. and Shovelton, H. (1999a) Do iconic hand gestures really contribute anything to the semantic information conveyed by speech? An experimental investigation. *Semiotica*, 123, pp. 1–30.

Beattie, G. and Shovelton, H. (1999b) Mapping the range of information contained in the iconic hand gestures that accompany spontaneous speech. *Journal of Language and Social Psychology*, 18, pp. 438–462.

Bensing, J., Kerssens, J. and van der Pasch, M. (1995) Patient-directed gaze as a tool for discovering and handling psychosocial problems in general practice. *Journal of Nonverbal Behaviour*, 19, pp. 223–242.

Bernieri, F., Gillis, J., Davis, J. and Grahe, J. (1996) Dyad rapport and the accuracy of its judgement across situations: A lens model analysis. *Journal of Personality and Social Psychology*, 71, pp. 110–129.

Bickman, L. (1974) The social power of a uniform. *Journal of Applied Social Psychology*, 4, pp. 47–61.

Birdwhistle, R. (1966) Some relations between American kinesics and spoken American English. In Smith, A.G. (ed.) *Communication and Culture*. New York: Holt, Reinhart and Winston.

Birdwhistle, R. (1970) *Kinesics and Context*. Philadelphia, PA: University of Pennsylvania Press.

Blairy, S., Herrera, P. and Hess, U. (1999) Mimicry and the judgement of emotional facial expressions. *Journal of Nonverbal Behaviour*, 23, pp. 5–41.

Bloom, K., Zajac, D.J. and Titus, J. (1999) The influence of nasality of voice on sex-stereotyped perceptions. *Journal of Nonverbal Behaviour*, 23, pp. 271–281.

Blue is Beautiful (1973) *Time*, 17 September, p. 66.

Blum, D. (1998) Face it. *Psychology Today*, 31, pp. 32–40.

Borg, J. (2008) *Body Language*. London: Pearson.

Boyatzis, C.J., Chazan, E. and Ting, C.Z. (1993) Preschool children's decoding of facial emotions. *Journal of Genetic Psychology*, 154, pp. 375–382.

Breed, G. (1971) *Nonverbal Behaviour and Teaching Effectiveness: Final Report*. Vermillion, SD: South Dakota University.

Brend, R. (1975) Male–female intonation patterns in American English. In Thorne, B. and Henley, N. (eds) *Language and Sex: Differences and Dominance*. Rowley, MA: Newbury House.

Briton, N.B. and Hall, J.A. (1995) Beliefs about female and male nonverbal communication. *Sex Roles*, 32, pp. 79–80.

Brophy, J. (1983) Research on the self-fulfilling prophecy and teacher expectations. *Journal of Educational Psychology*, 75, pp. 631–661.

Brophy, J. and Good, T. (1974) *Teacher–Student Relationships*. New York: Holt, Reinhart and Winston.

Brophy, J. and Good, T. (1984) *Looking in Classrooms*, 3rd edn. New York: Harper Row.

Brunsma, D.L. and Rockquemore, K.A. (1998) Effects of student uniforms on attendance, behaviour problems, substance use and academic achievement. *Journal of Educational Research*, 92, pp. 53–62.

Buck, R., Miller, R.E. and Caul, W.F. (1974) Sex, personality and physiological variables in the communication of affect via facial expression. *Journal of Personality and Social Psychology*, 30, pp. 587–596.

Bugenthal, D., Love, L. and Gianetto, R. (1971) Perfidious feminine faces. *Journal of Personality and Social Psychology*, 17, pp. 314–318.

Bull, P. (1987) *Posture and Gesture*. Oxford: Pergamon.

Bull, P.E. and Brown, R. (1977) The role of postural change in dyadic conversation. *British Journal of Social and Clinical Psychology*, 16, pp. 29–33.

Burgoon, J.K. and Dunbar, N.E. (2006) Nonverbal expressions of dominance and power in human relationships. In Manusov, V. and Patterson, M. (eds) *The Sage Handbook of Nonverbal Communication*. London: Sage.

Burgoon, J.K. and Hobbler, G. (2002) Nonverbal signals. In Knapp, M.L. and Daly, J. (eds) *Handbook of Interpersonal Communication*. Thousand Oaks, CA: Sage.

Burgoon, J. and Saine, T. (1978) *The Unspoken Dialogue*, Boston, MA: Houghton Mifflin.

Burgoon, J., Birk, T. and Pfau, M. (1990) Nonverbal behaviours, persuasion and credibility. *Human Communication Research*, 17, pp. 140–169.

Burman, E. (2004) Language talk. In Daniels, H. and Edwards, A. (eds) *Psychology of Education*. London: RoutledgeFalmer.

Butler, E., Egloff, B., Wilhelm, F.H., Smith, N.C., Erickson, E. and Gross, J.J. (2003) The social consequences of expressive suppression. *Emotion*, 3, pp. 48–67.

Butterworth, B. and Hadar, U. (1989) Gesture, speech, and computational stages: A reply to McNeill. *Psychological Review*, 96, pp. 168–174.

Campbell, D.E. (1979) Interior office design and visitor response. *Journal of Applied Psychology*, 64, pp. 648–653.

Carney, D.R. and Harrigan, J.A. (2003) It takes one to know one: Interpersonal sensitivity is related to accurate assessment of others' sensitivity. *Emotion*, 3, pp. 194–200.

Church, R., Ayman-Nolley, S. and Mahootian, S. (2004) The role of gesture in bilingual education: Does gesture enhance learning? *International Journal of Bilingual Education and Bilingualism*, 7, pp. 303–319.

Cicero, M.T. (1942/c.55 BCE) *De oratore, book III* (Rackham, H. trans.). Cambridge, MA: Harvard University Press.

Cohen, A. (1977) The communicative functions of hand illustrators. *Journal of Communication*, 27, pp. 54–63.

Cohen, D. (2007) *Body Language, What you Need to Know*. London: Sheldon Press.

Cohen, E. (1990) Continuing to co-operate: Prerequisites for persistence. *Phi Delta Kappan*, 72, pp. 134–138.

Cohen, L., Mannion, L. and Morrison, K. (2004) *A Guide to Teaching Practice*, 5th edn. London: RoutledgeFalmer.

Condon, W.S. (1976) An analysis of behavioural organisation. *Sign Language Studies*, 13, pp. 285–318.

Condon, W.S. and Ogston, W.D. (1966) Soundfilm analysis of normal and pathological behaviour patterns. *Journal of Nervous and Mental Disease*, 143, pp. 338–347.

Cook, M. (1970) Experiments on orientation and proxemics. *Human Relations*, 23, pp. 61–76.

Cook, M. and Smith, J.M. (1975) The role of gaze in impression formation. *British Journal of Social and Clinical Psychology*, 14, pp. 19–25.

Cook, S.W. and Goldin-Meadow, S. (2006) The role of gesture in learning: Do children use their hands to change their minds? *Journal of Cognition and Development*, 7, pp. 211–232.

Cooley, E. and Triemer, D. (2002) Classroom behaviour and the ability to decode nonverbal cues in boys with severe emotional disturbance. *Journal of Social Psychology*, 142, pp. 741–751.

Cornelius, R.R. (1996) *The Science of Emotion: Research and Tradition in the Psychology of Emotion*. Upper Saddle River, NJ: Prentice Hall.

Cowie, R., Douglas-Cowie, E., Tsapatsoulis, N., Vostis, G., Kollias, S., Fellenz, W. and Taylor, J. (2001) Emotion recognition in human–computer interaction. *IEEE Signal Processing Magazine*, 18, pp. 32–80.

Curtis, V. and Biran, A. (2001) Dirt, disgust and disease. *Perspectives in Biology and Medicine*, 44, pp. 17–31.

Dahl, R. (1980) *The Twits*. London: Jonathan Cape.

Daly, J.A., Hogg, E., Sacks, D., Smith, M. and Zimring, L. (1983) Sex and relationship affect social-grooming. *Journal of Nonverbal Behaviour*, 7, pp. 183–189.

De Cecco, J. (1970) *The Psychology of Language, Thought and Instruction*. London: Holt, Reinhart and Winston.

DePaulo, B. and Rosenthal, R. (1979) Ambivalence, discrepancy and deception in non-verbal communication. In Rosenthal R. (ed.) (1980) *Skill in Nonverbal Communication*. Cambridge, MA: Oelgeschlager, Gunn and Hain.

DePaulo, B.M. (1992) Nonverbal behaviour and self-presentation. *Psychological Bulletin*, 111, pp. 203–243.

Derry, C. (2005) Drawings as a research tool for self-study. In Mitchell, C., Weber, S. and O Reilly-Scanlon, K. (eds) (2006) *Just Who Do We Think You Are?* New York: RoutledgeFalmer.

Dillon, J. (1982) The multidisciplinary study of questioning. *Journal of Educational Psychology*, 74, pp. 147–165.

Dimberg, U. and Ohman, A. (1996) Behold the wrath: Psychophysiological responses to facial stimuli. *Motivation and Emotion*, 20, pp. 149–182.

Dodge, K.A. and Newman, J.P. (1981) Biased decision-making process in aggressive boys. *Journal of Abnormal Psychology*, 60, pp. 375–379.

Donald, M. (1991) *Origins of the Modern Mind*. Cambridge, MA: Harvard University Press.

Dosey, M. and Meisels, M. (1969) Personal space and self-protection. *Journal of Personality and Social Psychology*, 11, p. 97.

Dovidio, J., Kawakami, K., Johnson, C., Johnson, B. and Howard, A. (1997) On the nature of prejudice: Automatic and controlled processes. *Journal of Experimental Psychology*, 33, pp. 510–540.

Driscoll, J. (1969) The effects of a teacher's eye contact, gestures and voice intonation on student retention of factual material. Unpublished doctoral dissertation, University of Southern Mississippi (University MICROFILMS International, Ann Arbor, MI, No. 7905119).

Duchenne de Boulogne, G. (1990/1862) *The Mechanism of Human Facial Expression* (trans. and ed. A. Cuthbertson). New York: Cambridge University Press.

Edwards, A. and Furlong, V. (1978) *The Language of Teaching*. London: Heinemann.

Edwards, A. and Westgate, D. (1994) *Investigating Classroom Talk*. London: Routledge-Falmer.

Edwards, J., Green, K., Lyons, C., Rogers, M. and Swords, M. (1998) The effects of cognitive coaching and nonverbal classroom management on teacher efficacy and perceptions of school culture. Paper presented at the Annual Meeting of the American Research Association, San Diego, CA, 13–17 April.

Efran, J.S. (1968) Looking for approval: Effect on visual behaviour of approbation from persons differing in importance. *Journal of Personality and Social Psychology*, 10, pp. 21–25.

Efran, J.S. and Boughton, A. (1966) Effect of expectancies for social approval on visual behaviour. *Journal of Personality and Social Psychology*, 4, pp. 103–107.

Eggert, M. (2010) *Brilliant Body Language*, London: Pearson.

Ekman, P. (1972) Universals and cultural differences in facial expressions of emotion. In Cole, J. (ed.) *Nebraska Symposium on Motivation*, 1971. Lincoln, NE: University of Nebraska Press.

Ekman, P. (1997) Should we call it expression or communication? *Innovation*, 10, pp. 333–344.

Ekman, P. (2003) *Emotions Revealed, Understanding Faces and Feelings*. London: Phoenix.

Ekman, P. and Davidson, R. (1994) *The Nature of Emotion: Fundamental Questions*. New York: Oxford University Press.

Ekman, P. and Friesen, W. (1969a) Nonverbal leakage and clues to deception. *Psychiatry*, 32, pp. 88–106.

Ekman, P. and Friesen, W. (1969b) The repertoire of nonverbal behaviour: Categories, origins, usage and coding. *Semiotica*, 1, pp. 49–98.

Ekman, P. and Friesen, W. (1972) Hand movements. *Journal of Communication*, 22, pp. 353–374.

Ekman, P. and Friesen, W.V. (1975) *Unmasking the Face*. Englewood Cliffs, NJ: Prentice-Hall.

Elfenbein, H.A. and Ambady, N. (2002) On the universality and cultural specificity of emotion recognition: A meta-analysis. *Psychological Bulletin*, 128, pp. 203–235.

Elfenbein, H.A. and Ambady, N. (2003) When familiarity breeds accuracy: Cultural exposure and facial emotion recognition. *Journal of Personality and Social Psychology*, 85, pp. 276–290.

Erickson, F. (1975) One function of proxemic shifts in face-to-face interaction. In Kendon, A., Harris, R.M. and Key, M.R. (eds) *Organisation of Behaviour in Face-to-Face Interaction*. Chicago, IL: Aldine.

Esteves, F. (1999) Attentional bias to emotional facial expressions. *European Review of Applied Psychology*, 49, pp. 91–97.

Exline, R.V. and Winters, L.C. (1966) Affective relations and mutual glances in dyads. In Tomkins, S. and Izard, C. (eds) *Affect, Cognition and Personality*. London: Tavistock.

Exline, R.V., Thibaut, J., Hickey, C. and Gumbert, P. (1970) Visual interaction in relation to Machiavellianism and an unethical act. In Christie, P. and Geis, F. (eds) *Studies in Machiavellianism*. New York: Academic Press.

Feldman, R. and Tyler, J. (2006) Factoring in age: Nonverbal communication across life span. In Manusov, V. and Patterson, M. (eds) *The Sage Handbook of Nonverbal Communication*. London: Sage.

Feldman, R.S., Coats, E.J. and Spielman, D.A. (1996) Television exposure and children's decoding of nonverbal behaviour. *Journal of Applied Social Psychology*, 26, pp. 1718–1733.

Field, T.M., Woodson, R., Greenberg, R. and Cohen, D. (1982) Discrimination and imitation of facial expressions by neonates. *Science*, 218, pp. 179–181.

Finando, S.J. (1973) The effects of distance norm violation on heart rate and length of verbal response. Unpublished doctoral dissertation, Florida State University, Tallahassee.

Fisher, J.D. and Byrne, D. (1975) Too close for comfort: Sex differences in response to invasions of personal space. *Journal of Personality and Social Psychology*, 32, pp. 15–21.

Flevares, L. and Perry, M. (2001) How many do you see? The use of nonspoken representations in first-grade mathematics lessons. *Journal of Educational Psychology*, 93, pp. 330–345.

Floyd, K. and Ray, G.B. (2003) Human affection exchange: VI. Vocal predictors of perceived affection in initial interactions. *Western Journal of Communication*, 67, pp. 56–73.

Foddy, M. (1978) Patterns of gaze in cooperative and competitive negotiation. *Human Relations*, 31, pp. 925–938.

Forbes, R. and Jackson, P. (1980) Nonverbal behaviour and the outcome of selection interviews. *Journal of Occupational Psychology*, 53, pp. 65–72.

Fox, L., Lester, V., Russo, R., Bowles, R., Pichler, A. and Dutton, K. (2000) Facial expressions of emotion: Are angry faces detected more efficiently? *Cognition and Emotion*, 14, pp. 61–92.

Fox, N. and Davidson, R. (1987) Electroencephalogram asymmetry in response to the approach of a stranger and maternal separation in 10-month-old children. *Developmental Psychology*, 23, pp. 233–240.

Frank, M. and Gilovich, T. (1988) The dark side of self and social perception: Black uniforms and aggression in professional sports. *Journal of Personality and Social Psychology*, 54, pp. 74–85.

Freud, S. (1905/1953) Fragments of an analysis of a case of hysteria. In *Standard Edition of the Complete Psychological Works of Sigmund Freud, Vol. 7.* London: Hogarth Press.

Fridlund, A. (1994) *Human Facial Expression: An Evolutionary View.* San Diego, CA: Academic Press.

Fridlund, A. (1997) The new ethology of human facial expressions. In Russell, J. and Fernandez-Dols, J. (eds) *The Psychology of Facial Expression.* Cambridge: Cambridge University Press.

Friedman, H. and Booth-Kewley, S. (1987) Personality, Type A behaviour, and coronary heart disease: The role of emotional expression. *Journal of Personality and Social Psychology*, 53, pp. 783–792.

Friedman, H., Prince, L., Riggio, R. and DiMatteo, M. (1980) Understanding and assessing nonverbal expressiveness: The Affective Communication Test. *Journal of Personality and Social Psychology*, 39, pp. 333–351.

Frieling, H. (1957) *Psychologische Raumgestaltung und Farhdynamik [Psychological Room Design and Color Dynamic].* Gottingen, Germany: Musterschmidt Verlag.

Funder, D.C. and Harris, M.J. (1986) On the several facets of personality assessment: The case of social acuity. *Journal of Personality*, 54, pp. 528–550.

Gallagher, P. (1992) Individual differences in nonverbal behaviour: Dimensions of style. *Journal of Personality and Social Psychology*, 63, pp. 133–145.

Gibbins, K. (1969) Communication aspects of women's clothes and their relation to fashionability. *British Journal of Social and Clinical Psychology*, 8, pp. 301–312.

Gibbins, K. and Gwynn, T.K. (1975) A new theory of fashion change: A test of some predictions. *British Journal of Social and Clinical Psychology*, 14, pp. 1–9.

Glenberg, A.M., Schroeder, J. and Robertson, D. (1998) Averting the gaze disengages the environment and facilitates remembering. *Memory and Cognition*, 26, pp. 651–658.

Goffman, E. (1956) *The Presentation of Self in Everyday Life.* Edinburgh: Edinburgh University Press.

Goldin-Meadow, S. (2004) Gesture's role in the learning process. *Theory into Practice*, 43, pp. 314–321.

Goldin-Meadow, S., Wein, D. and Chang, C. (1992) Assessing knowledge through gesture: Using children's hands to read their minds. *Cognition and Instruction*, 9, pp. 201–219.

Goldin-Meadow, S., Kim, S. and Singer, M. (1999) What the adult's hands tell the student's mind about math. *Journal of Educational Psychology*, 91, pp. 720–730.

Goldman-Eisler, F. (1968) *Psycholinguistics: Experiments in Spontaneous Speech*. London: Academic Press.

Goleman, D. (2006) *Social Intelligence: The New Science of Human Relationships*. London: Hutchinson.

Goodwin, C. (1981) *Conversational Organisation: Interaction between Speakers and Hearers*. New York: Academic Press.

Gorham, W.I., Cohen, S.H. and Morris, T.L. (1999) Fashion in the classroom III: Effects of instructor attire and immediacy in natural classroom interactions. *Communications Quarterly*, 47, pp. 281–299.

Gosselin, P., Perron, M., Legault, M. and Campanella, P. (2002) Children's and adults' knowledge of the distinction between enjoyment and nonenjoyment smiles. *Journal of Nonverbal Behaviour*, 26, pp. 83–108.

Gress, J. and Heft, H. (1998) Do territorial actions attenuate the effects of high density? A field study. In Sanford, J. and Connell, B. (eds) *People, Places and Public Policy*. Edmond, OK: Environmental Design and Research Association.

Grinder, M. (1996) ENVoY: *A Personal Guide to Classroom Management*, 3rd edn. Battleground, WA: Michael Grinder and Associates.

Haber, G. (1982) Spatial relations between dominants and marginals. *Social Psychology Quarterly*, 45, pp. 221–228.

Hadar, U., Steiner, T.J. and Rose, F.C. (1985) Head movement during listening turns in conversation. *Journal of Nonverbal Behaviour*, 9, pp. 214–228.

Hadar, U., Burstein, A., Krauss, R. and Soroker, N. (1998) Ideational gestures and speech in brain-damaged subjects. In Wagner, S., Nusbaum, H. and Goldin-Meadow, S. (2004) Probing the mental representation of gesture: Is hand waving spatial? *Journal of Memory and Language*, 50, pp. 395–407.

Halberstadt, A.G. (1985) Race, socioeconomic status and nonverbal behaviour. In Siegman, A.W. and Feldstein, S. (eds) *Multichannel Integrations of Nonverbal Behaviour*. Hillsdale, NJ: Erlbaum.

Halberstadt, A.G. and Hall, J.A. (1980) Who's getting the message? Children's nonverbal skill and their evaluation by teachers. *Developmental Psychology*, 16, pp. 564–573.

Hall, E. (1966) *The Hidden Dimension*. Garden City, NY: Doubleday.

Hall, J.A., Friedman, H.S. and Harris, M.J. (1984) Nonverbal cues, the Type A behaviour pattern and coronary heart disease. In Blanck, P.D., Buck, R. and Rosenthal, R. (eds) *Nonverbal Communication in the Clinical Context*. University Park, PA: Pennsylvania State University Press.

Hamilton, J. and Warden, J. (1966) Student's role in a high school community and his clothing behaviour. *Journal of Home Economics*, 58, pp. 789–791.

Hargie, O. and Dickson, D. (2004) *Skilled Interpersonal Communication: Research, Theory and Practice*. London: Routledge.

Hargreaves, A. (1998) The emotional practice of teaching. *Teaching and Teacher Education*, 14, pp. 835–854.

Hargreaves, A. (2001) The emotional geographies of teaching. *Teachers College Record*, 103, pp. 1056–1080.

Harker, L. and Keltner, D. (2001) Expressions of positive emotion in women's college yearbook pictures and their relationship to personality and life outcome across adulthood. *Journal of Personality and Social Psychology*, 80, pp. 112–124.

Harkins, S. and Szymanski, K. (1987) Social facilitation and social loafing: New wine in old bottles. In Hendrick, C. (ed.) *Review of Personality and Social Psychology*, Vol. 9. Beverly Hills, CA: Sage.

Harp, S.S., Stretch, S.M. and Harp, D.A. (1985) The influence of apparel on responses to television news anchormen. In Solomon, M.R. (ed.) *The Psychology of Fashion*. Lexington, KY: Heath.

Harrigan, J. and O Connell, D. (1996) How do you look when feeling anxious? Facial displays of anxiety. *Personality and Individual Differences*, 21, pp. 205–212.

Harris, M. and Rosenthal, R. (1985) Mediation of interpersonal expectancy effects: 31 meta-analyses. *Psychological Bulletin*, 97, pp. 363–386.

Harris, M.B., James, J., Chavez, J., Fuller, M.L., Kent, S., Massanari, C., Moore, C. and Walsh, F. (1983) Clothing: Communication, compliance and choice. *Journal of Applied Social Psychology*, 13, pp. 88–97.

Hart, A.J. (1995) Naturally occurring expectation effects. *Journal of Personality and Social Psychology*, 68, pp. 109–115.

Hatfield, E. and Sprecher, S. (1986) *Mirror, Mirror, On the Wall*. Albany, NY: State University of New York Press.

Hatfield, E., Cacioppo, J.T. and Rapson, R.L. (1992) Primitive emotional contagion. *Review of Personality and Social Psychology*, 14, pp.151–177. Newbury Park, CA: Sage.

Hatfield, E., Cacioppo, J.T. and Rapson R.L. (1994) *Emotional Contagion*. New York: Cambridge University Press.

Hatfield, E., Rapson, R. and Yen-Chi, L. Le (2009) Emotional contagion and empathy. In Decety, J. and Ickes, W. (eds) *The Social Neuroscience of Empathy*. Bradford, MA: Massachusetts Institute of Technology.

Hayduk, L.A. (1981) The permeability of personal space. *Canadian Journal of Behavioural Science*, 13, pp. 274–287.

Hayduk, L.A. (1983) Personal space: Where we stand now. *Psychological Bulletin*, 94, pp. 293–335.

Heaven, L. and McBrayer, D. (2000) External motivators of self-touching behaviour. *Perceptual and Motor Skills*, 90, pp. 338–342.

Hines, T. (1996) *The Total Package*. New York: Little Brown.

Hodgins, H.S. and Belch, C. (2000) Interparental violence and nonverbal abilities. *Journal of Nonverbal Behaviour*, 24, pp. 3–24.

Hollien, H. (1990) *The Acoustics of Crime: The New Science of Forensic Phonetics*. New York: Plenum.

Hoult, R. (1954) Experimental measurement of clothing as a factor in some social ratings of selected American men. *American Sociological Review*, 19, pp. 324–328.

Iacoboni, M. (2008) *Mirroring People: The New Science of How We Connect with Others*. New York: Farrar, Straus and Giroux.

Ikeda, T. and Beebe, S. (1992) A review of teacher nonverbal immediacy: Implications for intercultural research. Paper presented at the Annual Meeting of the International Communication Association, Miami, May.

Iverson, J. and Goldin-Meadow, S. (1998) Why people gesture when they speak. *Nature*, 396, pp. 297–298.

Izard, C.E., Fine, S., Schultz, D., Mostow, A., Ackerman, B. and Youngstrom, E. (2001) Emotion knowledge as a predictor of social behaviour and academic competence in children at risk. *Psychological Science*, 12, pp. 18–23.

Johnson, D.W. and Johnson, R. (1989) *Cooperation and Competition: Theory and Research*. Edina, MN: Interaction Book Co.

Johnson, D.W., Johnson, R.T. and Holubec, E.J. (1998) *Cooperation in the Classroom*. Edina, MN: Interaction Book Co.

Johnson, M.H., Dziuraweic, S., Ellis, H. and Morton, J. (1991) Newborns' preferential tracking of face-like stimuli and its subsequent decline. *Cognition*, 40, pp. 1–19.

Kaiser, S. (1985) *The Social Psychology of Clothing and Body Adornment*. London: Collier Macmillan.

Keith, L., Tornatzky, L. and Pettogrew, L. (1974) An analysis of verbal and nonverbal classroom teaching behaviours. *Journal of Experimental Education*, 42, pp. 30–38.

Keltner, D. (1997) Signs of appeasement: Evidence for the distinct displays of embarrassment, amusement and shame. In Ekman, P. and Rosenberg, E. (eds) *What the Face Reveals: Basic and Applied Studies of Spontaneous Expression using the Facial Action Coding System (FACS)*. Oxford: Oxford University Press.

Keltner, D. and Bonanno, G.A. (1997) A study of laughter and dissociation: Distinct correlates of laughter and smiling during bereavement. *Journal of Personality and Social Psychology*, 4, pp. 687–702.

King, M.J. (1966) Interpersonal relations in preschool children and average approach distance. *Journal of Genetic Psychology*, 109, pp. 109–116.

Kirk, T. (2005) Enhancing teaching and learning through co-operative learning. *Oideas*, 51, Government Publications, Ireland, pp. 6–54.

Kleck, R.E. and Nuessle, W. (1968) Congruence between the indicative and communicative functions of eye-contact in interpersonal relations. *British Journal of Social and Clinical Psychology*, 7, pp. 241–246.

Kleinke, C.L. (1986) Gaze and eye contact: A research review. *Psychological Bulletin*, 100, pp. 78–100.

Klinzing, H. and Aloisio, B. (2004) Intensity, variety and accuracy in nonverbal cues and decoding: Two experimental investigations. Paper presented at the annual meeting of the American Educational Research Association, San Diego, CA, April.

Knapp, M. and Hall, J. (2002) *Nonverbal Communication in Human Interaction*, 5th edn. Belmont, CA: Wadsworth/Thompson Learning Inc.

Knapp, M. and Hall, J. (2006) *Nonverbal Communication in Human Interaction*, 6th edn. Belmont, CA: Wadsworth/Thompson Learning Inc.

Koneya, M. (1973) The relationship between verbal interaction and seat location of members of large groups. Unpublished doctoral dissertation, Denver University, Denver, CO.

Krauss, R., Dushay, R., Chen, Y. and Rauscher, F. (1995) The communicative value of conversational hand gestures. *Journal of Experimental Social Psychology*, 31, pp. 533–552.

Kuehne, S.H. and Creekmore, A.M. (1971) Relationships among social class, school position and clothing of adolescents. *Journal of Home Economics*, 63, pp. 555–556.

LaFrance, M. (1985) Postural mirroring and intergroup relations. *Personality and Social Psychology Bulletin*, 11, pp. 207–217.

LaFrance, M. and Mayo, C. (1978) *Moving Bodies: Nonverbal Communication in Social Relationships*. Monterey, CA: Brooks/Cole.

Lakoff, R. (1973) Language and woman's place. *Language in Society*, 2, pp. 45–80.

Lalljee, M.G. (1971) Disfluencies in normal English speech, DPhil. thesis, University of Oxford.

Lalljee, M.G. and Cook, M. (1973) Uncertainty in first encounters. *Journal of Personality and Social Psychology*, 26, pp. 59–67.

Lapitsky, M. and Smith, C.M. (1981) Impact of clothing on impressions of personal characteristics and writing ability. *Home Economics Research Journal*, 9, pp. 327–335.

LaPlante, D. and Ambady, N. (2003) On how things are said: Voice tone, voice intensity, verbal content and perceptions of politeness. *Journal of Language and Social Psychology*, 22, pp. 434–441.

Larsen-Helweg, M., Cunningham, S., Carrico, A. and Pergram, A. (2004) To nod or not to nod: An observational study of nonverbal communication and status in female and male college students. *Psychology of Women Quarterly*, 28, pp. 358–361.

Laver, J. (1949) *Style in Costume*. Oxford: Oxford University Press.

Lawrence, S.G. and Watson, M. (1991) Getting others to help: The effectiveness of professional uniforms in charitable fund-raising. *Journal of Applied Communication Research*, 19, pp. 170–185.

Leathers, D.G. (1992) *Successful Nonverbal Communication*. New York: Macmillan.

Lefkowitz, M., Blake, R. and Mouton, J. (1955) Status factors in pedestrian violation of traffic signals. *Journal of Abnormal and Social Psychology*, 51, pp. 704–706.

Leipold, W.E. (1963) Psychological distance in a dyadic interview. Unpublished doctoral dissertation, University of North Dakota, Grand Forks, ND.

Lennon, S.J. and Miller, F.G. (1984) Salience of physical appearance in impression formation. *Home Economics Research Journal*, 13, pp. 95–104.

Lippa, R. (1998) The nonverbal display and judgement of extraversion, masculinity, femininity and gender diagnosticity: A lens model analysis. *Journal of Research in Personality*, 32, pp. 80–107.

Lott, D.F. and Sommer, R. (1967) Seating arrangements and status. *Journal of Personality and Social Psychology*, 7, pp. 90–95.

Lyle, J. (1990) *Body Language*. London: Reed.

McBride, G., King, M.G. and James, J.W. (1965) Social proximity effects on galvanic skin responses in adult humans. *Journal of Psychology*, 61, pp. 153–157.

McClure, E.B. and Nowicki, S. Jr (2001) Associations between social anxiety and nonverbal processing skill in preadolescent boys and girls. *Journal of Nonverbal Behaviour*, 25, pp. 3–19.

McCroskey, J., Richmond, V. and McCroskey, L. (2006) Nonverbal communication in instructional contexts. In Manusov, V. and Patterson, M. (eds) *The Sage Handbook of Nonverbal Communication*. London: Sage.

McCroskey, J.C., Hamilton, P.R. and Weiner, A.H. (1974) The effect of interaction behaviour on source credibility, homophily and interpersonal attraction. *Human Communication Research*, 1, pp. 42–52.

McCroskey, J.V. (1998) *An Introduction to Communication in the Classroom*, 2nd edn. Acton, MA: Tapestry Press.

McCuller, C. (1983) Perceptions of videotaped classroom simulations by disruptive and non-disruptive students. Paper presented at the Annual Meeting of the American Educational Research Association, Montreal, April.

McGilchrist, I. (2010) *The Master and his Emissary*. London: Yale University Press.

McNeill, D. (1992) *Hand and Mind: What Gestures Reveal about Thought*. Chicago, IL: University of Chicago Press.

McNeill, D. (2000) *Language and Gesture*. Cambridge: Cambridge University Press.

Mahnke, F. (1996) *Colour, Environment and Human Response*. New York: John Wiley and Sons.

Major, B., Carrington, P.I. and Carnevale, P.J.D. (1984) Physical attractiveness and self-esteem: Attributes for praise from an other-sex evaluator. *Personality and Social Psychology Bulletin*, 10, pp. 43–50.

Malatesta, C.Z., Jonas, R. and Izard, C.E. (1987) The relation between low facial expressibility during emotional arousal and somatic symptoms. *British Journal of Medical Psychology*, 60, pp. 169–180.

Marsh, P., Rosser, E. and Harré, R. (1978) *The Rules of Disorder*. London: Routledge and Kegan Paul.

Maslow, A. and Mintz, N. (1956) Effects of esthetic surroundings: I. Initial effects of three esthetic conditions upon perceiving 'energy' and 'well-being' in faces. *Journal of Psychology*, 41, pp. 247–254.

Matarazzo, J., Saslow, G., Wiens, A., Weitman, M. and Allen, B. (1964) Interviewer head nodding and interviewee speech durations. *Psychotherapy: Theory, Research and Practice*, 1, pp. 54–63.

Mathes, E.W. and Kahn, A. (1975) Physical attractiveness, neuroticism, and self-esteem. *Journal of Personality*, 90, pp. 27–30.

Matthews, A., Fox, E., Yield, J. and Calder, A. (2003) The face of fear: Effects of eye gaze and emotion on visual attention. *Visual Cognition*, 10, pp. 823–835.

Mayer, R. and Andersen, R. (1991) Animations need narrations: An experimental test of dual-coding hypothesis. *Journal of Educational Psychology*, 83, pp. 484–490.

Mehrabian, A. (1968) Inference of attitudes from the posture, orientation and distance of a communicator. *Journal of Consulting and Clinical Psychology*, 32, pp. 296–308.

Mehrabian, A. (1969) Significance of posture and position in the communication of attitude and status relationships. *Psychological Bulletin*, 71, pp. 359–372.

Mehrabian, A. (1972) *Nonverbal Communication*. Chicago, IL: Aldine-Atherton.

Mehrabian, A. (1981) *Silent Messages: Implicit Communication of Emotions and Attitudes*, 2nd edn. Belmont, CA: Wadsworth.

Mehrabian, A. and Blum, J. (1997) Physical appearance, attraction and the mediating role of emotions. *Current Psychology: Developmental, Learning, Personality, Social*, 16, pp. 20–42.

Mehrabian, A. and Friedman, S.L. (1986) An analysis of fidgeting and associated individual differences. *Journal of Personality*, 54, pp. 406–429.

Mehrabian, A. and Williams, M. (1969) Nonverbal concomitants of perceived and intended persuasiveness. *Journal of Personality and Social Psychology*, 13, pp. 37–58.

Millenson, J. (1985) Psychosocial strategies for fashion advertising. In Solomon, M.R. (ed.) *The Psychology of Fashion*. Lexington, KY: Heath.

Miller, F.G. and Rowold, K.I. (1980) Attire, sex-roles and responses to requests for directions. *Psychological Reports*, 47, pp. 661–662.

Miller, J. (1979) Proxemics: A hidden dimension in the classroom. *International Journal of Instructional Media*, 7, pp. 55–58.

Miller, P. (2005) *Body Language: An Illustrated Introduction for Teachers*. Evansville, IN: Miller and Associates.

Mintz, N. (1956) Effects of esthetic surroundings: II. Prolonged and repeated experience in a 'beautiful' and 'ugly' room. *Journal of Psychology*, 41, pp. 459–466.

Mithen, S. (2006) *The Singing Neanderthals: The Origins of Music, Language, Mind and Body*. London: Phoenix.

Modigliani, A. (1971) Embarrassment, face-work and eye-contact: Testing a theory of embarrassment. *Journal of Personality and Social Psychology*, 17, pp. 15–24.

Morris, D. (1971) *Intimate Behaviour*. New York: Random House.

Morris, T.L., Gorham, J., Cohen, S.H. and Huffman, D. (1996) Fashion in the classroom: Effects of attire on student perceptions of instructors in college classes. *Communication Education*, 45, pp. 135–148.

Mottet, T. and Beebe, S. (2000) Emotional contagion in the classroom: An examination of how teacher and student emotions are related. Paper presented at the 86th Annual Meeting of the National Communications Association, Seattle, Washington, 9–12 November.

Mullen, B. (1986) Newscasters' facial expressions and voting behavior of viewers: Can a smile elect a president? *Journal of Personality and Psychology*, 51, pp. 291–295.

Murphy, N.A., Hall, J. and Colvin, C.R. (2003) Accurate intelligence assessments in social interaction: Mediators and gender effects. *Journal of Personality*, 71, pp. 465–493.

Murphy, S.T. and Zajonc, R.B. (1993) Affect, cognition and awareness: Affective priming with optimal and suboptimal stimulus exposures. *Journal of Personality and Social Psychology*, 64, pp. 723–739.

Murray, H. (1983) Low-inference classroom teaching behaviours and students ratings of college teaching effectiveness. *Journal of Educational Psychology*, 48, pp. 630–635.

Murray, I.R. and Arnott, J.L. (1993) Toward the simulation of emotion in synthetic speech: A review of the literature on human vocal emotion. *Journal of the Acoustical Society of America*, 93, pp. 1097–1108.

Natfulin, D., Ware, J. and Donnelly, F. (1973) The Doctor Fox lecture: A paradigm of educational seduction. *Journal of Medical Education*, 48, pp. 630–635.

Navarro, J. (2008) *What Everybody is Saying*. New York: Collins.

Neill, S. (1989) The effects of facial expression and posture on children's reported responses to teacher nonverbal communication. *British Educational Research Journal*, 15, pp. 195–204.

Neill, S. (1991) *Classroom Nonverbal Communication*. London: Routledge.

Neill, S. and Caswell, C. (1993) *Body Language for Competent Teachers*. London: Routledge and Keegan Paul.

Nichol, J. and Watson, K. (2000) Video tutoring, nonverbal communication and initial teacher training. *British Journal of Educational Technology*, 31, pp. 135–144.

Omata, K. (1996) Territoriality in the house and its relationship to the use of rooms and the psychological well-being of Japanese married women. *Journal of Environmental Psychology*, 15, pp. 147–154.

Otterson, J. and Otterson, C. (1980) Effects of teacher gaze on children's story recall. *Perceptual and Motor Skills*, 50, pp. 35–42.

Paek, S.J. (1986) Effects of garment style on the perception of personal traits. *Clothing and Textiles Research Journal*, 5, pp. 10–16.

Patterson, M.L. (1968) Spatial factors in social interaction. *Human Relations*, 21, pp. 351–361.

Patterson, M.L. and Sechrest, L.B. (1970) Interpersonal distance and impression formation. *Journal of Personality*, 38, pp. 161–166.

Pease, A. and Pease, B. (2004) *The Definitive Book of Body Language*. London: Orion Books.

Pelligrini, R. and Schauss, A. (1980) Muscle strength as a function of exposure to hue differences in visual stimuli: An experiential test of Kinesoid theory. *Journal of Orthomolecular Psychiatry*, 2, pp. 144–147.

Perry, M., Berch, D. and Singleton, J. (1995) Constructing shared understanding: The role of nonverbal input in learning contexts. *Journal of Contemporary Legal Issues*, 6, pp. 213–235.

Pfeifer, J. and Dapretto, M. (2009) 'Mirror, mirror in my mind': Empathy, interpersonal competence and the mirror neuron system. In Decety, J. and Ickes, W. (eds) *The Social Neuroscience of Empathy*. Bradford, MA: Massachusetts Institute of Technology.

Poe, E.A. (1844) The Purloined Letter. *The Gift for 1845*.

Pollak, S.D. and Sinha, P. (2002) Effects of early experience on children's recognition of facial displays of emotion. *Developmental Psychology*, 38, pp. 784–791.

Putnam, J. (1997) *Co-operative Learning in Diverse Classrooms*. Englewood Cliffs, NJ: Prentice Hall.

Puttallaz, M. and Gottman, J. (1981) Social skills and group acceptance. In Asher, S. and Gottman, J. (eds) *The Development of Children's Friendships*. Cambridge: Cambridge University Press.

Reeder, E.N. and King, A.C. (1984) Are teachers dressing for success? *Illinois Teacher*, May/June, pp. 212–213.

Rees, D.W., Williams, L. and Giles, H. (1974) Dress style and symbolic meaning. *International Journal of Symbology*, 5, pp. 1–8.

Reid, A., Lancuba, V. and Morrow, B. (1997) Clothing style and formation of first impressions. *Perceptual and Motor Skills*, 84, pp. 237–238.

Reid, D. (1980) Spatial involvement and teacher–pupil interaction in school biology laboratories. *Educational Studies*, 6, pp. 31–40.

Reis, H.T., Wheeler, L., Spiegel, N., Kernis, M.H., Nezlek, K.J. and Perri, M. (1982) Physical attractiveness in social interaction: II. Why does appearance affect social experience? *Journal of Personality and Social Psychology*, 43, pp. 979–996.

Reiss, M. and Rosenfeld, P. (1980) Seating preferences as nonverbal communication: A self-presentational analysis. *Journal of Applied Communication Research*, 8, pp. 22–30.

Richards, J.M. and Gross, J.J. (1999) Composure at any cost? The cognitive consequences of emotional suppression. *Personality and Social Psychology Bulletin*, 25, pp. 1033–1044.

Richmond, V., Graham, J. and McCroskey, J. (1987) The relationship between selected immediacy behaviours and cognitive learning. *Communication Yearbook*, 10, pp. 574–590.

Rimé, B. (1982) The elimination of visible behaviour from social interactions: Effects on verbal, nonverbal and interpersonal variables. *European Journal of Social Psychology*, 12, pp. 113–129.

Roach, K.D. (1997) Effects of graduate teaching assistant attire on student learning, misbehaviours and ratings of instruction. *Communication Quarterly*, 45, pp. 125–141.

Rohles, F.H. Jr (1980) Temperature or temperament: A psychologist looks at thermal comfort. *ASHRAE Transactions*, 86, pp. 541–551.

Rollman, S.A. (1980) Some effects of teachers' styles of dress. Paper presented at the annual meeting of the Southern Speech Communication Association, Birmingham, AL, April.

Rosenshine, B. (1970) Enthusiastic teaching: A research review. *School Review*, 78, pp. 499–514.

Rosenthal, R. and Jacobson, L. (1968) *Pygmalion in the Classroom*. New York: Holt, Reinhart and Winston.

Rosenthal, R., Hall, J.A., Di Matteo, M.R., Rogers, P.L. and Archer, D. (1979) *Sensitivity to Non-verbal Communication: The PONS Test*. Baltimore, MD: Johns Hopkins University Press.

Russell, J., Firestone, L.J. and Baron, R.M. (1980) Seating arrangement and social influence: Moderated by reinforcement meaning and internal–external control. *Social Psychology Quarterly*, 43, pp. 103–109.

Russell, J., Bachorowski, J. and Fernandez-Dols, J. (2003) Facial and vocal expression of emotion. *Annual Review of Psychology*, 54, pp. 329–349.

Russo, N. (1967) Connotation of seating arrangements. *Cornell Journal of Social Relations*, 2, pp. 37–44.

Rutherford, M.D., Baron-Cohen, S. and Wheelwright, S. (2002) Reading the mind in the voice: A study with normal adults and adults with Asperger syndrome and high functioning autism. *Journal of Autism and Developmental Disorders*, 23, pp. 189–194.

Sacks, O. (1993, 27 December) An anthropologist on Mars. *New Yorker*, pp. 106–125. In Knapp, M. and Hall, J. (2006) (eds) *Nonverbal Communication in Human Interaction*, 6th edn. Belmont, CA: Wadsworth/Thompson Learning Inc.

Schauss, A. (1985) The physiological effect of colour on the suppression of human aggression: Research on Baker-Miller pink. *International Journal of Biosocial Research*, 7, pp. 55–64.

Scherer, K. (1979) Acoustic concomitants of emotional dimensions: Judging affect from synthesised tone sequences. In Weitz, S. (ed.) *Nonverbal Communication: Readings with Commentary*, 2nd edn. New York: Oxford University Press.

Scherer, K.R. (1986) Vocal affect expression: A review and model for further research. *Psychological Bulletin*, 99, pp. 143–165.

Scherer, S.E. (1974) Proxemic behaviour of primary school children as a function of their socioeconomic class and subculture. *Journal of Personality and Social Psychology*, 29, pp. 800–805.

Schmid Mast, M. (2002) Dominance as expressed and inferred through speaking time: A meta-analysis. *Human Communication Research*, 28, pp. 420–450.

Schooler, J.W., Ohlsson, S. and Brooks, K. (1993) Thoughts beyond words: When language overshadows insight. *Journal of Experimental Psychology: General*, 122, pp. 166–183.

Schwartz, B., Tesser, A. and Powell, E. (1982) Dominance cues in nonverbal behaviour. *Social Psychology Quarterly*, 45, pp. 114–120.

Scott, M., McCroskey, J. and Sheahan, M. (1978) The development of a self-report measure of communication apprehension in organisational settings. *Journal of Communication*, 28, pp. 104–111.

Segerstrale, U. and Molnar, P. (1997) *Nonverbal Communication: Where Nature meets Culture*. Hillsdale, NJ: Lawrence Erlbaum Associates.

Sharpe, D. (1975) *The Psychology of Colour and Design*. Totowa, NJ: Littlefield, Adams.

Shavelson, R., Webb, N., Stasz, C. and McArthur, D. (1988) Teaching mathematical problem solving: Insights from teachers and tutors. In Charles, R. and Silver, E. (eds) *The Teaching and Assessing of Mathematical Problem Solving*. Reston, VA: NCTM.

Siegman, A.W. (1987) The telltale voice: Nonverbal messages of verbal communication. In Siegman, A.W. and Feldstein, S. (eds) *Nonverbal Behaviour and Communication*, 2nd edn. Hillsdale, NJ: Erlbaum.

Simon, A. and Boyer, G. (eds) (1970) *Mirrors for Behaviour: An Anthology of Classroom Observation Instruments*. Philadelphia, PA: Research for Better Schools.

Singer, M.A. and Goldin-Meadow, S. (2005) Children learn when their teacher's gestures and speech differ. *Psychological Science*, 16, pp. 85–89.

Sinha, S. and Mukherjee, N. (1996) The effect of perceived cooperation on personal space requirements. *Journal of Social Psychology*, 136, pp. 108–111.

Sinha, S., Alka, R. and Parul, V. (1999) Selective attention under conditions of varied demands, personal space and social density. *Journal of the Indian Academy of Applied Psychology*, 24, pp. 105–108.

Sissons, M. (1971) The psychology of social class. In Tunstall, F.S., Sissons, J. and Brooman, M. (eds) *Money, Wealth and Class*. Milton Keynes: Open University Press.

Skinner, M. and Mullen, B. (1991) Facial asymmetry in emotional expression: A meta-analysis of research. *British Journal of Social Psychology*, 30, pp. 113–124.

Slavin, R. (1985) An introduction to cooperative learning research. In Slavin, R., Sharan, S., Kagan, S., Hertz-Lazarowitz, R., Webb, C. and Schmuck, R. (eds) *Learning to Cooperate, Cooperating to Learn*. New York: Longman.

Slavin, R. (1989) *Co-operative Learning: Theory, Research and Practice*, 1st edn. New York: Prentice Hall.

Smithers, A. and Robinson, P. (2001) *Teachers Leaving*. London: National Union of Teachers and University of Liverpool, Centre for Education and Unemployment Research.

Solomon, M.R. and Schopler, J. (1982) Self-consciousness and clothing. *Personality and Social Psychology Bulletin*, 8, pp. 508–514.

Sorce, J.F., Emde, R.N., Campos, J.J. and Klinnert, M.D. (1985) Maternal emotional signaling: Its effect on visual cliff behaviour in 1-year olds. *Developmental Psychology*, 21, pp. 195–200.

Stein, S. (1976) Selected teacher verbal and nonverbal behaviours as related to grade level and student classroom behaviours. Unpublished PhD dissertation, Northwestern University, Evanston, IL.

Stevanoni, E. and Salmon, K. (2005) Giving memory a hand: Instructing children to gesture enhances their event recall. *Journal of Nonverbal Behaviour*, 29, pp. 217–233.

Strack, F. and Neumann, R. (2000) Furrowing the brow may undermine perceived fame: The role of facial feedback in judgments of celebrity. *Personality and Social Psychology Bulletin*, 26, pp. 762–768.

Strack, F., Martin, L.L. and Strepper, S. (1988) Inhibiting and facilitating conditions of the human smile: A nonobtrusive test of the facial feedback hypothesis. *Journal of Personality and Social Psychology*, 54, pp. 768–777.

Tharin, L. (1981) Dress codes, observed attire and behaviour in recreational settings. Unpublished ms, University of California, Davis, CA.

Thompson, T. (1982) Gaze toward and avoidance of the handicapped: A field experiment. *Journal of Nonverbal Behaviour*, 6, pp. 188–196.

Titsworth, B. (2001) The effects of teacher immediacy, use of organisational lecture cues and students' note taking on cognitive learning. *Communication Education*, 50, pp. 283–297.

Tizard, B., Hughes, M., Carmichael, H. and Pinkerton, G. (1983) Children's questions and adult answers. *Journal of Child Psychology and Psychiatry*, 24, pp. 269–281.

Triplett, N. (1898) The dynamogenic factors in pacemaking and competition. *American Journal of Psychology*, 9, pp. 507–533.

Trout, D.L. and Rosenfeld, H. (1980) The effect of postural lean and body congruence on the judgement of psychotherapeutic rapport. *Journal of Nonverbal Behaviour*, 4, pp. 176–190.

Tusing, K. and Dillard, J. (2000) The sounds of dominance: Vocal precursors of perceived dominance during interpersonal influence. *Human Communication Research*, 26, pp. 148–171.

Valenzo, L., Alibali, M. and Klatzky, R. (2003) Teachers' gestures facilitate students' learning: A lesson in symmetry. *Contemporary Educational Psychology*, 28, pp. 187–204.

Van Houten, R., Nau, P., MacKenzie-Keating, S., Sameoto, D. and Colavecchia, B. (1982) An analysis of some variables influencing the effectiveness of reprimands. *Journal of Applied Behaviour Analysis*, 15, pp. 65–83.

Wagner, S., Nusbaum, H. and Goldin-Meadow, S. (2004) Probing the mental representation of gesture: Is handwaving spatial? *Journal of Memory and Language*, 50, pp. 395–407.

Walker, W. and Trimboli, C. (1983) The expressive function of the eye flash. *Journal of Nonverbal Behaviour*, 8, pp. 3–13.

Ware, J. and Williams, R. (1975) The Dr. Fox effect: A study of lecturer effectiveness and ratings of instruction. *Journal of Medical Education*, 50, pp. 149–156.

Ware J. and Williams, R. (1977) An extended visit with Dr. Fox: Validity of student satisfaction with instruction ratings after repeated exposures to a lecture. *American Educational Research Journal*, 14, pp. 449–457.

Weare, K. (2004) *Developing the Emotionally Literate School*. London: Paul Chapman Publishing.

Weaver, J.C. and Anderson, R.J. (1973) Voice and personality interrelationships. *Southern Speech Communication Journal*, 38, pp. 262–278.

Weinstein, R. (2002) *Reaching Higher: The Power of Expectations in Schooling*. Cambridge, MA: Harvard University Press.

White, J. (2008) Nonverbal communication in the primary classroom. Doctoral dissertation, Queen's University, Belfast.

Willemyns, M., Gallois, C., Callan, V. and Pittman, J. (1997) Accent accommodation in the job interview: Impact of interviewer accent and gender. *Journal of Language and Social Psychology*, 16, pp. 3–22.

Wilson, G. and Nias, D. (1999) Beauty can't be beat. In Guerrero, L. and De Vito, J. (eds) *The Nonverbal Communication Reader: Classic and Contemporary Readings*. Prospect Heights, IL: Waveland Press.

Woolfolk, A. (2001) *Educational Psychology*. Boston, MA: Allyn and Bacon.

Woolin, D. and Montagre, M. (1981) College classroom environment: Effects of sterility versus amiability on student and teacher performance. *Environment and Behaviour*, 13, pp. 707–716.

Wundt, W. (1921/1973) *The Language of Gestures*. The Hague: Mouton.

Yarbus, A.L. (1967) *Eye Movement and Vision* (trans. B. Haigh). New York: Plenum Press.

Zuckerman, M. and Driver, R.E. (1989) What sounds beautiful is good: The vocal attractiveness stereotype. *Journal of Nonverbal Behaviour*, 13, pp. 67–82.

Zuckerman, M. and Miyake, K. (1993) The attractive voice: What makes it so? *Journal of Nonverbal Behaviour*, 17, pp. 119–135.

Zweigenhaft, R. (1976) Personal space in the faculty office: Desk placement and the student–faculty interaction. *Journal of Applied Psychology*, 61, pp. 529–532.

Index

Page numbers in *italics* denote tables, those in **bold** denote figures.